GREENWOOD G

SOUTH AFRICAN HIGHLIGHTS

hand-picked things to do
and places to eat

the team

Jamie Crawford

Pom Jenkins

Adam Barnes

Simon Greenwood

Jamie Crawford
Jamie really puts the career into career path. When I first heard of him a year ago he was a Reuters journalist. Since then he has done a full stint as a Greenwood Guides accommodation inspector in South Africa, he has delivered beer to prize-winners in the North of England in a white van, he has done three trips as a kids' wildlife programme TV presenter (Michaela's Wild Challenge) (!)... oh yes, and he has researched and written this guide.

Even as I write he is diving with sharks in Hawaii.

This book was a huge trial of perseverance and patience, as he battled to get all the necessary information off busy restaurateurs and the like. The frustrations were weathered throughout with a brave little smile. Not only did he write the book, but he also took most of the photos.

Pom Jenkins
Pom came into the project at a needful hour and injected a much-needed boost in the arm, which kept us on course for our deadlines. (Which we then missed anyway once she had gone back to her real career....)

Adam Barnes
Adam, an old GG faithful, was cajoled out of retirement for one last case. As always he was a model of thoroughness and good-naturedly ploughed into the data chase without complaint.

Simon Greenwood
A colourless, myopic, office-bound figure, sensitive to sunlight and fresh air, at his happiest tapping addresses into a database in some forgotten back room ...

ACKNOWLEDGEMENTS

We reckon that we know South Africa pretty well. However, writing this book would have been impossible without the recommendations of the hundreds of owners from our accommodation guides and others who have furtively been tipping us off for more than a year about the best their country has to offer. So, a big thank-you to all of you. We'd also like to thank especially a few whose enthusiasm and response to our constant badgering has gone beyond the call of duty. They are, in no particular order:

Patrick Cardwell (for his excellent birding bits), Urs Huber (for Cape Town walks) Deborah and Richard Johnson, Lucille Byrnes, Nicki and Tim Scarborough, Chantelle Cook, Karen and Paul Davies, Mariette van Wyk, Tom and Lucinda Bate, Steve and Kathy Bergs, Liz Delmont, Ingrid Wessolowski, Libby Goodall, Jackie Solomon, Jôke Glauser, Gail Voigt, James Irving, Niki Neumann, Nick Garsten, Judy Badenhorst, Pam Mills, Tim and Caroline Holdcroft, Sue McNaughton, Arthur McWilliam Smith, Nini Bairnsfather Cloete, Judi Rebstein, Dora Hattingh, Philda Benkenstein, David and Fiona Ramsay, Dee and Robin Pelham-Reid, Caroline Jankovich, Peta Parker, Ted and Bits Quin, Ryk and Bea Becker, Sue Truter, Chris Harvie, Phil Harvey.

Many apologies if I have forgotten anyone.

Series Editor Simon Greenwood
Written by Jamie Crawford
Maps, pictorial icons and book design Tory Gordon-Harris
Printing Printed in China through Colorcraft Ltd., Hong Kong
UK Distribution Portfolio, London
SA Distribution Quartet Sales and Marketing, Johannesburg

Photo credits at the back of the book.

introduction

We've been driving about in South Africa for some seven years now, truffling for the best (by which we mean friendly and fun) lodges, B&Bs, farm stays, guest-houses and self-catering cottages for our accommodation guide. In the course of these years I have been buttonholed many a time by our travellers (not least my own mother) who complained that if we could provide them with the most interesting places to stay, what was stopping us from stumping up the Greenwood take on where to eat and what to do? What was holding us back? For goodness sake?! Come on!!

Eventually I felt that we had a wide enough experience in South Africa to produce a new guide-book, the likes of which you are now holding in your sophisticated, expensively manicured and well-travelled hands.

What we wanted from the outset was a new kind of guide-book that showcased genuinely exciting things to do and places to eat, rather than exhaustively listing a bewildering series of possibilities accounting for all ages and tastes... and leaving you to take pot luck.

Thus the common denominator for all entries has been the positive attitude of the owners or staff. We are looking at all times for people who enjoy what they do, but who also take genuine pleasure in looking after their customers. This is our approach with the accommodation guides, and we have applied exactly the same philosophy (a grand word I know) to restaurants, cafés, wineries, tour guides, bird-watching enthusiasts etc. The lists of Things we Like and Things we Don't Like on the back cover sums up our prejudices as neatly as we know how.

WHAT DOES THE BOOK CONTAIN?

We have researched and divided the book up into the following rough categories:

Restaurants, cafés, bars, delis and wineries:
All are atmospheric, with genuinely friendly waiting staff. We have leant towards small, family-run places in interesting or sensational settings... but always making sure that good food is a given. If you are ever disappointed we would like to be told.

Nature:
This includes walking and hiking, bird-watching, whale-watching, nature reserves etc.

Tour Guides and Experts:
There are also many guides throughout the book who can take you on tours, treks or excursions. They are usually very small outfits, often just

one-man bands. They are all people who mix high levels of expertise in their various fields (birds, walks, flora and fauna, golf, abseiling, surfing, wine, you name it...) with great charisma. They appear at the start of each area, but there is also a listing for all tour guides on pages xviii and xix so you can see where they go and what they do.

Cultural activities:
These include battlefields tours, tours into townships, the odd museum, theatres... and many miscellaneous others. 'Miscellaneous others' are everywhere in this book in fact.

Outdoor activities:
These include many fun things to do with the kids, and exciting things to do for the young at heart, such as micro-lighting, helicopter and small aircraft trips, bungy jumps, horse-riding, quad-biking, river trips, diving and surfing... the list goes on and on. The key to successfully enjoying these activities are the people that organise them for you. We have only included highly recommended outfits, which have been tried and tested many times with reliably good reports.

WHO IS THE GUIDE AIMED AT?

Anyone looking for a unique personal experience from their holiday, who is prepared to leave the beaten track every now and again... but would rather not at the same time sacrifice too much on creature comfort. We put a great deal of emphasis on the charm of the people that are behind each entry, whether it be a restaurant or a walking guide. You can find both cheap and expensive restaurants run by relaxed and amusing people. So long as a place sees hospitality as its real goal then our radar starts to bleep.

If this approach appeals then the book is for you. The guide is not really aimed at backpackers for whom cheapness is paramount... or at 'high-rollers' for whom expensiveness is paramount!

HOW DID WE PUT THE GUIDE TOGETHER?

In researching our accommodation guide (5 times now and counting) we have doggedly driven up virtually every dirt road in the country, visiting farms and out-of-the-way places. Both Jamie and I have been to every corner of the country and have plundered our own experiences and that of other GG inspectors for much of our material. In the end I doubt whether there are many - or even any - South Africans who have seen as much of the country as our faithful inspectors. But to get beneath the surface in a more extensive way we have called upon our accommodation owners....

... of whom there are some 300 resident across the whole of South Africa. We had already whittled these 300 places down from a gigantic list of possible places to stay, finally selecting those that fulfil our requirements for genuine, friendly hospitality. (Their lodges, B&Bs and guest-houses can be found in the Greenwood Guide to South Africa, Hand-picked Accommodation. This book is an annual edition and can also be viewed online at **www.greenwoodguides.com**. We recommend, as of course we would, that you consult both guides when making your plans. There is an order form at the back of this book if you would like to order a copy direct from us.)

Who better, then, than these enthusiastic few to guide us to the best places to eat and things to do that each area has to offer? This is after all their unofficial job!

We interviewed everyone who is featured in the accommodation guide over a four-month period and collected together their top recommendations. We then scoured through these lists of recommendations, removing any that seemed to have missed the point or were not quite interesting enough. We then produced new more concentrated lists and these we passed by a handful of particularly trusted Greenwood Guides owners for a final sieve. Anything that got the thumbs down at this stage we also removed.

The final residue, therefore, consists only of highly recommended restaurants, tour guides (in many different fields), wineries, nature reserves, walks, etc.

Comments in quote marks in the entries themselves have come on the whole from our accommodation owners. To save space we haven't credited each comment to a particular person... except sometimes.

Finally, we have taken the view that you are better served by a limited number of great options, than by an exhaustive list of ALL the options. We have done the hard work for you, and as with our accommodation guide, pared down the range of possibilities to just those that you can rely on.

WALKING OR HIKING

South Africa is riddled with fantastic walking, so we have included only the most regularly and highly recommended. On the whole these are included where they crop up in any specific area, but in Cape Town and in the Garden Route we have created special walking sections at the end of each chapter.

When walking or hiking in SA you should carry the following checklist of items about your person. Any walker or hiker worthy of the name will, of course, already be only too aware of what to take, but here you go anyway...

A day rucksack, sun protection cream, a hat (more sun protection - let's hope it's sunny), a lightweight raincoat, a map of the area, good walking boots, swimming things (unless you know you won't be passing a water-hole, a river or a sea), a large bottle of water, something to eat. And take your mobile phone, although you may not get coverage all the time.

It is unfortunately recommended that you hike in groups for safety.

See the index at the back of the book for page numbers of walks.

We have given the BOOT symbol for walks.

KIDS

Any activity that we feel is particularly suited to taking your kids to we have given the following symbol .

You will see from the index at the back of the book that children are pretty well catered for in the guide, although we have tried to include only activities and restaurants that will appeal to both parents and their offspring. I would welcome any reports on this issue from parents (or kids I suppose!).

The index lists all the entries suitable for children under their relevant area.

HOW TO USE THE BOOK

The best thing you can do is to read the whole book through before making any decisions. This will throw up all sorts of ideas for things to do before it is too late.

You will not find much accommodation in this guide as our recommendations for places to stay are found in our companion guide, the Greenwood Guide to South Africa, Hand-Picked Accommodation. Those places that wear more than one hat and therefore appear in both books have been given the G symbol. You will particularly need the accommodation guide for the game-viewing options available in South Africa. There are many reserves and game parks, but the best way to experience the big game animals and wild areas of the country is by staying in a lodge in one of the private game reserves. It is by its nature an expensive option (running luxury in the wild always is), but definitely the best and we have only included the friendliest places, offering the most genuine wilderness experience whatever their price level.

Much of the accommodation has been chosen because it is far more than just that. Many places offer so much more than a bed and a breakfast. The other activities on offer take place on their private property and are only available to their staying guests, so we have not included them in this guide. If you get your hands on both books, your options will increase greatly.

DRIVING

There is nowhere in South Africa that would make a 4-wheel drive a necessity.

CAR HIRE

Make sure that you have considered the amount of daily mileage your car hire company gives you. 100km or even 200km a day is virtually nothing and the final cost can be far higher than you estimated. Try and work out roughly what distances you will be covering and ask for the correct daily allowance.

As for who to hire cars from you will find all the usual suspects at the airports, but in Cape Town we have always successfully used Vineyard Car Hire, 298 Main Rd, Kenilworth, 7708, tel: 021-761-06711, fax: 021-761-7136, email info@vineyardcarhire.co.za. Their cars are in good condition and they will come and meet you from the airport. You will need to be 23 years old (or older, obviously...).

MOBILE/CELL PHONES

Airports have shops that provide mobile phones. They are invaluable and we recommend that you get one. You can buy a cheap handset or just rent one for the duration of your stay and then pay for calls as you go with recharge cards.

TELEPHONE NUMBERS

To call South Africa from the UK dial 0027 then drop the 0 from the local code.

To call the UK from South Africa dial 0944 then drop the 0 from the local code.

The numbers printed in this book are all from within South Africa.

TIPPING

- In restaurants we tend to give 15%.
- At a petrol station my policy is to give no tip for just filling up, 3 rand for cleaning the windows, and 5 rand for cleaning the windows and checking oil and water. If you really don't want the attendant to clean your windows you need to make this a statement when you ask for the petrol… or he will often do it anyway.

TIME OF YEAR

I will limit myself to one observation. It seems to me that most Europeans come to South Africa in January, February and March to avoid their own miserable weather and write taunting postcards home from a sunny Cape. I've been doing this myself for the last few years.

However, the very best time of year to visit the Northern Cape, Mpumalanga, Limpopo, North-West Province, KwaZulu Natal and the Karoo, i.e. the whole country except the southern Cape, is from May to October. The air is dry and warm, game viewing is at its best and there are fewer tourists keeping the prices higher.

DISCLAIMER

We make no claims to god-like objectivity in assessing what is or is not special about the restaurants and other establishments that we feature. They are there because we like them. Our opinions and tastes are mortal and ours alone. We have done our utmost to get the facts right, but apologize for any mistakes that may have slipped through the net. Some things change which are outside our control: people sell up, prices increase, exchange rates fluctuate, marriages break up and even acts of God can rain down destruction. And clearly we cannot make provision for personality clashes between guests and owners! It does happen. We would be grateful to be told about any factual errors or changes. Emails to **simon@greenwoodguides.com**.

DON'T TRY AND DO TOO MUCH. PLEASE.

It is the most common way to spoil your own holiday. South Africa is a huge country and you cannot expect to see too much of it on one trip. Don't over-extend yourself. Stay everywhere for at least two nights and make sure that you aren't spending your hard-earned holiday fiddling with the radio and admiring the dashboard of your hire car.

PLEASE WRITE TO US

Our email address is **simon@greenwoodguides.com** for all comments. This is the first edition of this guide and as such we are under no illusions that there won't be ways we can improve it. If there is some area in which you feel this guide is lacking then do please let us know. Bear in mind that we are not trying to plug every gap in the country with places to eat and things to do. We are trying to find only those restaurants and organisations that will provide the kind of happy experience that we - and I hope you - are looking for. So if you come across anything that you feel we have missed out on let us know on the above email address. Equally if an entry has disappointed we would be grateful to hear your story. We are always most concerned to hear that the hosting has been inattentive.

SECOND EDITION

A note to owners of prospective entries.

All the entries in this guide-book have been recommended by trusted friends of the firm who have tried and tested their suggestions many times. This means that inclusion is by invitation only. We must stick to this editorial approach to retain the integrity of the guide and thus its usefulness to those who use it.

OUR OTHER GUIDES

These can be ordered directly from us, either via the above email address or by sending in the coupon at the back of this book, or via our web site at **www.greenwoodguides.com**. Or by telephone on **+44 207-731-8953**.

We also have accommodation guides to Australia, New Zealand and Canada. These books are available by emailing us direct or, again, by mailing us the order form at the back of this book.

Simon.

SOME AFRIKAANS WORDS TRANSLATED FOR YOU BY ME IN NO PARTICULAR ORDER AND PROBABLY OF LITTLE PRACTICAL VALUE:

Bakkie = small pick-up truck or van, **lekker** = niiiice!, **lanie** = posh, **dagga** = pot (not the ornamental or water-carrying type), **dorp** = village, **klein** = small, **groot** = big, **kop** = head, **kloof** = ravine or valley, **vlei** = a snappy translation is "hollow in which rain collects during the rainy season", **weg** = way, **straat** = street, **kerk** = church, **krans** = cliff, **kruis** = circle, **baai** = bay, **oos** = east, **noord** = north, **suid** = south, **hoek** = corner, **poort** = pass through a mountain range, **rivier** = steak-knife (not really, it means 'river' really), **stein** = stone, **fontein** = spring (as in river), **berg** = mountain, **burg** = town, **gat** = hole, **gans** = goose, **klip** = stone, **koppie** = small rocky hill, **veld** = uncultivated land or The Bush, as in "it's out there somewhere in the bush", **laager** = a temporary camp formed by a circle of wagons used by the Voortrekkers (but not just by the Voortrekkers... I imagine you could create one yourself without needing a licence) to protect themselves from attack, **-tjie**. Anything ending in -tjie is smaller than it would be if -tjie had not been thusly suffixed. -tjie is pronounced '-key' so that Annetjie (little Anna) is pronounced 'annekey'.

I don't know much more (oh yes "gans" means goose as in Gansbaai) but I hope that this small offering (offer-tjie?) helps at some point on your travels. If not, as Boris Becker once said on losing Wimbledon, nobody died.

For my last linguistic trick, I am now going to demonstrate how to do the clicks that characterize Xhosa and Zulu. Put your tongue onto your palette… there… that's it, and now make a clicking sound in the back of your throat… no that's not quite right… anyway have a practice at home and you'll soon get the hang of it… as I did.

contents

WESTERN CAPE:

contents

KLEIN KAROO AND KAROO:

EASTERN CAPE:

contents

NORTHERN CAPE:

FREE STATE:

GAUTENG:

NORTH WEST PROVINCE:

LIMPOPO:

MPUMALANGA:

guides and experts

WHERE THEY GO AND WHAT THEY DO

OPERATOR	ACTIVITY	WHERE THEY GO	PAGE
Ordo Tours	Everything	Everywhere	234
Andrew Wilson Tours	Culture & History	CT, GR	7
Calabash Tours	Culture & History	EC	161
Campaign Trails	Culture & History	KZN	176
Cottonwood Tours	Culture & History	M	270
Dance For All	Culture & History	CT	6
DTours	Culture & History	EC	154
eZethu Cultural Tours	Culture & History	EC	154
Footsteps to Freedom	Culture & History	CT	6
Intibazwe Township Tours	Culture & History	KZN	197
Origins From Africa	Culture & History	GR	114
Paul Le Roux	Culture & History	CT	7
Pure Afrikan Tours	Culture & History	EC	158
Raymond Heron	Culture & History	KZN	177
Spirits of the Past	Culture & History	EC	154
Stonehaven Tours	Culture & History	KZN	176
Township History Tour	Culture & History	CT	6
Zululand Eco-Adventures	Culture & History	KZN	176
Andulela	Cult & Hist + more	Everywhere	7
Earth Africa Tours	Cult & Hist, Nature	M, L	270
Mountain Lake Adventures	Cult & Hist, Nature	KZN	177
Travel Africa Trails	Cult & Hist, Nature	L, M	256
Amber Tours	Wine, Cult & Hist	CT, CW, O, WC, K, EC	64
Happy Holidays	Wine, Cult &Hist	CW, CT, O, GR, WC, K	65
La Rochelle Tours	Wine, Cult &Hist	CT, CW, O, GR, K	64
Telescope S.A.	Astronomy	NC	219
Nini Bairnsfather Cloete	Wine, Cult &Hist	CW	64
Ann Williams	Birding	EC	169

Note: Cape Town = CT, Cape Winelands = CW, Overberg = O, West Coast and Cederberg = WC, Karoo = K, Garden Route = GR, Eastern Cape = EC,

OPERATOR	ACTIVITY	WHERE THEY GO	PAGE
Avian Leisure	Birding	Everywhere	10
Brian's Birding	Birding	CT, CW, WC, GR, O, K	10
Cape Town Pelagics	Birding	CT	10
Lawson's Birding	Birding	Everywhere	270
New Holme Karoo Birding	Birding	FS	224
West Coast Bird Club	Birding	WC	50
Elsa Pooley	Nature	KZN	177
Ex Libris	Nature	NC	218
Hamish Rogers	Nature	L	257
Kalahari Safaris	Nature	NC	216
Kalahari Tours and Travel	Nature	NC	217
Shakabarker Tours	Nature, Cult & Hist	KZN	176
Turaco Tours	Nature, Cult & Hist	EC	155
Blyde River Tours	Adventure activites	M	277
Townsend Adventure	Adventure activities	L, M	257
Unbottled African Adventure	Adventure activities	Everywhere	7
Airborne Adventures Africa	Ballooning	KZN, M, G	258
Bushwhacked Outdoor Adventures	Canoeing	NC	213
Gravity Adventures	Canoeing	CW, O, WC, NC	9
Daytrippers	Cycling + more	CT, CW, O	9
Outeniqua Tours	Cycling + more	GR, K	114
Boma Helicopter Tours	Everything	EC	155
African Ramble	Flights safaris	GR, EC	114
Winelands Golf Tours	Golf + more	CT, CW, O, GR, WC, EC	65
Active Africa	Hiking	CT, CW, GR, WC, KZN	8
Peninsula Ramblers	Hiking	CT	8
Winescape Tours	Hiking	CW	65
Para-Pax	Paragliding	CT, CW, O, GR, WC	8

KwaZulu Natal = KZN, Northern Cape = NC, North-West Province = NWP, Gauteng = G, Mpumalanga = M, Limpopo = L, Free State = FS

distance chart

Distances in South Africa are vast and to give you an idea of just how vast, here is a distance chart in kilometres that we hope will be useful when planning your trip.

	BL	CT	D
Beaufort West	**544**	**460**	**1178**
Bloemfontein (BL)	-	1004	634
Britstown	**398**	**710**	**1032**
Cape Town (CT)	1004	-	1753
Colesberg	**226**	**778**	**860**
De Aar	346	762	980
Durban (D)	**634**	**1753**	**-**
East London (EL)	584	1079	674
George	**773**	**438**	**1319**
Graaff-Reinet	424	787	942
Grahamstown (G)	**601**	**899**	**854**
Harrismith	328	1331	306
Jo'burg (JHB)	**398**	**1402**	**588**
Kimberley (K)	177	962	811
Klerksdorp	**288**	**1271**	**645**
Kroonstad	211	1214	537
Ladysmith	**410**	**1413**	**236**
Mafikeng	464	1343	821
Musina	**928**	**1932**	**118**
Nelspruit	757	1762	707
Oudtshoorn	**743**	**506**	**1294**
Pietermaritzburg	555	1674	79
Polokwane	**717**	**1721**	**907**
Port Elizabeth (PE)	677	769	984
Pretoria (P)	**456**	**1460**	**646**
Queenstown	377	1069	676
Umtata	**570**	**1314**	**439**
Upington	588	894	1222
Welkom	**153**	**1156**	**564**

EL	G	JHB	K	PE	P
605	**492**	**942**	**504**	**501**	**1000**
584	601	398	177	677	456
609	**496**	**725**	**253**	**572**	**783**
1099	899	1402	962	769	1460
488	**375**	**624**	**292**	**451**	**682**
557	444	744	305	520	802
674	**854**	**588**	**811**	**984**	**646**
-	180	982	780	310	1040
645	**465**	**1171**	**762**	**335**	**1229**
395	282	822	490	291	880
180	**-**	**999**	**667**	**130**	**1057**
822	929	282	505	1068	332
982	**999**	**-**	**472**	**1075**	**58**
280	667	472	-	743	530
872	**889**	**64**	**308**	**1009**	**222**
795	812	87	339	888	245
752	**932**	**364**	**587**	**1062**	**422**
1048	1065	287	380	1141	294
1512	**1529**	**530**	**1071**	**1605**	**472**
1226	1358	335	827	1434	322
704	**532**	**141**	**703**	**394**	**1199**
595	775	509	732	905	567
1301	**1318**	**319**	**791**	**1394**	**261**
310	130	075	743	-	1133
1040	**1057**	**58**	**530**	**1133**	**-**
207	269	775	554	399	833
235	**415**	**869**	**747**	**545**	**928**
982	851	796	411	945	854
737	**754**	**258**	**294**	**830**	**316**

Cape Town

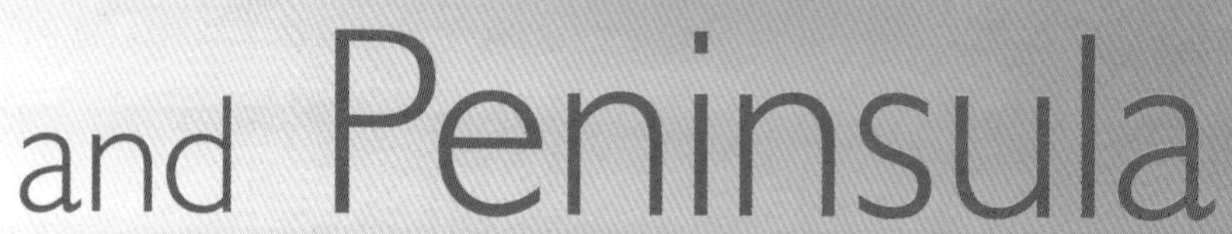

and Peninsula

3

MAKING SENSE OF CAPE TOWN

Like any big city Cape Town is made up of many constituent parts. We've tried to bring some order to this by starting with the city centre and City Bowl, anything between the top of Table Mountain and the waterfront, then working south down the western side of the peninsula and back up the eastern side, along the back of the mountain.

And so the order goes:

Get your bearings

If you have a day to spare and a car to drive, a loop of the mountain and city is a great way to get your bearings and an overview of Cape Town.

The M3 is a surprisingly pleasant drive for a main road and will take you from the city centre around the back of Table Mountain through the rich greenery and smart suburbs of Bishopscourt and Constantia. Where the road stops turn left to Muizenberg, then right at the lights and follow Main Rd beside the train tracks and beaches to Kalk Bay. There's a string of intriguing antique and furniture shops here to investigate, a great daily fish market in the harbour and plenty of good eateries to stop at for lunch.

From here continue on to Fish Hoek (with an optional detour on to Simon's Town) and cross the peninsula to Noordhoek where the hair-raising corniche of Chapman's Peak leads you around to Hout Bay. Then it's just a short hop over to the coast road, running below the imposing Twelve Apostles to the white sands of Camps Bay (in time for sunset drinks) and back past Lion's Head to the City Bowl.

GUIDES & EXPERTS

Tour guides usually roam wherever you want to go, so instead of slotting them into specific areas they're divided up and listed in alphabetical order at the beginning of the province section.

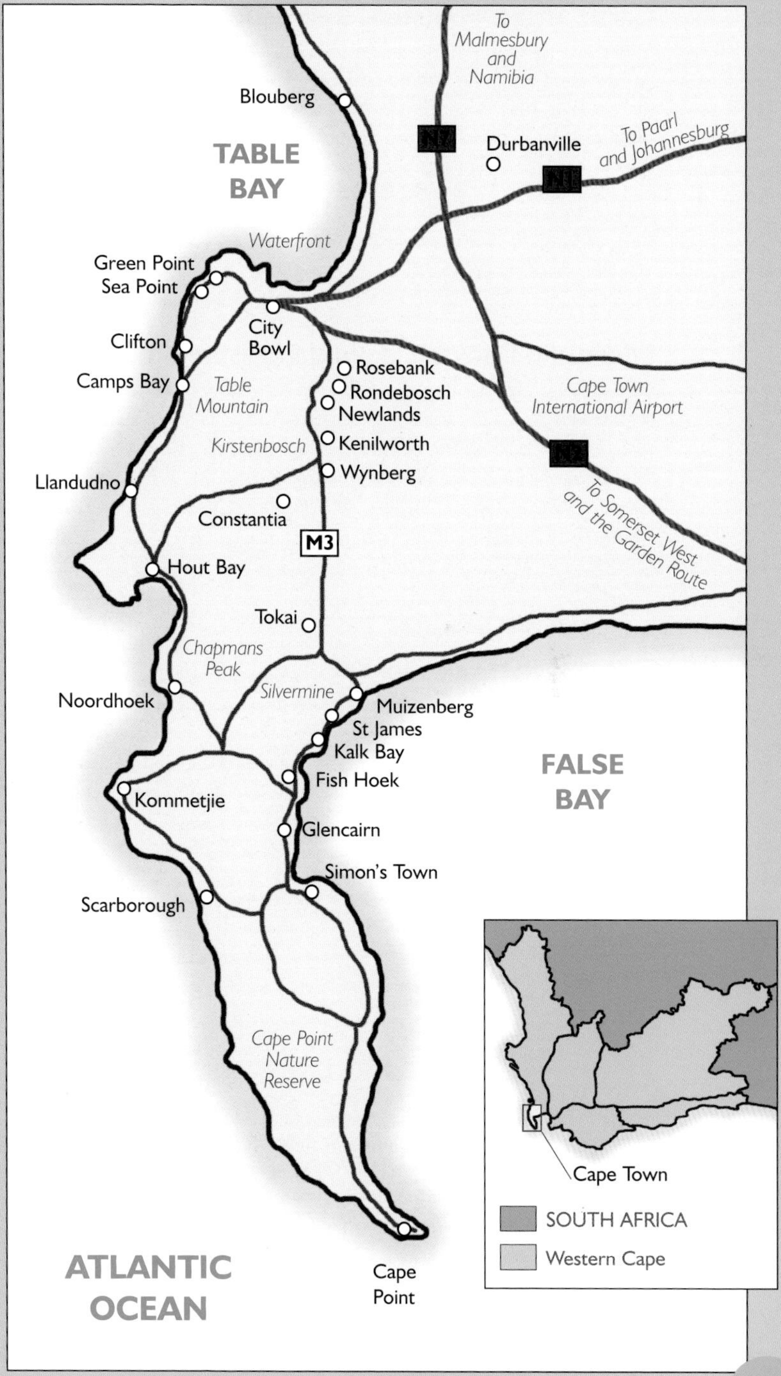

To Malmesbury and Namibia
Blouberg
Durbanville
To Paarl and Johannesburg
TABLE BAY
Waterfront
Green Point
Sea Point
City Bowl
Clifton
Camps Bay
Table Mountain
Rosebank
Rondebosch
Newlands
Cape Town International Airport
Kirstenbosch
Kenilworth
Wynberg
Llandudno
Constantia
To Somerset West and the Garden Route
M3
Hout Bay
Tokai
Chapmans Peak
Silvermine
Noordhoek
Muizenberg
St James
Kalk Bay
FALSE BAY
Fish Hoek
Kommetjie
Glencairn
Simon's Town
Scarborough
Cape Point Nature Reserve
Cape Town
SOUTH AFRICA
Western Cape
ATLANTIC OCEAN
Cape Point

GUIDES AND EXPERTS
CULTURE and HISTORY

Garth Angus, Footsteps to Freedom

This is a small group of tour guides who truly love their city and its story (an excellent start). Be it climbing Table Mountain, meandering through the Bo-Kaap Malay quarter or visiting a township, you will come away enlightened and having felt the beat of Cape Town's pulse.

Prices: *R100 pp for 3-hr walking tour of historic Cape Town. Small group private tours including District Six museum visit R150 pp (minimum R450).*
Tel: *021-465-2032*
Cell: *083-452-1112 or try Henry on 021-426-4260*
info@footstepstofreedom.co.za
www.footstepstofreedom.co.za

Nkululeko Booysen, Township History Tour

Nkululeko is a former member of the military wing of the ANC who shares with guests the history of his country and his struggle. Not only the struggle to overcome the Apartheid system, but also to acclimatise to the new South Africa. This is first-hand experience of South Africa's turbulent recent history - utterly fascinating and very personal.

Prices: *R240 - R260 pp.*
Tel: *021-705-7048*
Cell: *082-721-9447*
welcome@lezardbleu.co.za

Philip Boyd, Dance for All

A dance school launched in 1991 to help keep underprivileged kids off the streets. The school visits poorer areas of Cape Town and teaches some 400 young people everything from ballet to tap and jazz. Visitors are taken to watch classes in action at the township teaching centres and you may also be treated to an impromptu performance.

Prices: *Tours leave at 2.45pm, Mon - Thurs, R100 pp. Book ahead and see website for upcoming performance details.*
Contact: *Joseph Stone Theatre, Klipfontein Rd, Athlone.*
Tel: *021-633-4363*
admin@danceforall.co.za
www.danceforall.co.za

Blame it on Napoleon

The British might never have been involved in South Africa had it not been for Napoleon. Cape Town was originally the product of Dutch expansion when Jan van Riebeeck founded a colony in 1652 as a staging post en route to the East Indies. But when Napoleon occupied the Netherlands in 1795 during the Napoleonic Wars, the British retaliated and took the Cape. Four years later they (very sportingly) handed it back before snatching it again in 1806 to control the Far East trade routes and prevent the diminutive French emperor from getting there first. The colony remained in British hands for more than a century until the formation of the Union of South Africa in 1910.

Monique Le Roux, Andulela Experience

You'll eat such good Malay curry in Cape Town that you will undoubtedly want to learn how to cook it. Now you can with this excellent tour in the Bo-Kaap Malay quarter. Take a guided stroll through the streets, buying the necessary ingredients at the market, then visit a family home for a curry-cooking workshop before sharing the table with your hosts and instructor.

Prices: *From R295 pp for half-day cooking tour (every Sat 10am - 2pm or private tours for bookings of more than 4). All sorts of other adventures also arranged (meerkats, biplane flights, African cooking, jazz...). Check website for details.*

Tel: *021-790-2592*

info@andulela.com

www.andulela.com

Paul Le Roux, The Bishops' Court

"Real, personal and informative tours". Paul is a great man and runs The Bishops' Court to perfection. But as a qualified guide (... and ex-accountant as it goes), he also offers great township trips, including visits to housekeeper Connie's home.

Prices: *Township tours for R250 - R350 pp.*

Contacts: *The Bishops' Court, 18 Hillwood Ave, Bishopscourt.*

Tel: *021-797-6710*

info@thebishopscourt.com

www.thebishopscourt.com

Andrew Wilson Tours

"My rates are negotiable, but my quality of service and attention isn't," Andrew tells me. A Brit long-ensconced in S.A., he'll be your host away from home who can take up to six passengers for private tours of Cape Town and the Garden Route in his own licensed van.

Prices: *R2,000 - R3,000 per day for Andrew plus his combi van, depending on hours spent touring and distances covered.*

Tel: 021-762-2464

anorbury@iafrica.com

ACTIVITIES

Lance Blaine, Unbottled African Adventures

Lance gave me a list of the activities he can organise. I lost count after about 30. For adrenaline junkies there is literally every imaginable adventure sport on offer from scuba and shark diving to jet fighter flights and quad biking. Whatever your passion, whatever your skill level, there's something for you.

Prices: *So many different prices, so best to call them or check the website for specific details.*

Contact: *91 Kloofnek Rd, Tamboerskloof.*

Tel: *021-422-0192*

lance@unbottledafrica.co.za

www.unbottledafrica.co.za

Chris Goodwin, Active Africa

These guys are trekking specialists based in Cape Town, but ready to take you almost anywhere (including the top of Kilimanjaro). They have fully-escorted walks all over S.A. (i.e. they do all the hard work for you). Some are for leisurely-paced explorers while other porter-assisted treks are designed for adventurous spirits who want to delve deeper. First-class accommodation and food all the way and they are great (and knowledgeable) company too.

Prices: *4 - 8 day itineraries from R4,800 for walking tours and R3,800 for adventure trekking. Itineraries include an 8-day Cape Peninsula walk, 4-day High Cape route, 7-day Wild Coast trek, 8-day country walks and wine farms and 7-day Kilimanjaro expedition (Tanzania).*

Tel: *021-788-5396/8750.*

Cell: *083-310-1747*

chris@activeafrica.co.za

www.activeafrica.co.za

Urs Huber, Peninsula Ramblers

There are dozens and dozens of great walks around the Cape, but it's not always easy to find them. So for simple navigation (you just follow the group) and interesting local company join the Peninsula Ramblers. They head out every weekend for full- and half-day hikes around the Cape and visitors are welcome to team up with them.

Prices: *Visitors are asked to make a R5 donation.*

Contact: *Urs Huber (chairman) 021-559-7947 or 084-713-5545, uhh@nettex.co.za. Barbara Hughes (secretary) 021-790-4743 or 072-368-2747. Luciana Degiovanni (treasurer) 021-558-4623*

www.ramblers.org.za

Stef Juncker, Para-pax tandem paragliding

Take to the air with Stef and his pilots in a customised tandem glider for an amazing bird's-eye view of Cape Town, or Franschhoek... or wherever you choose to fly. They've done it more than 3,600 times so you're in very safe hands. All kit supplied, you just need a warm jacket, lace-up shoes and a passion for adventure.

Prices: *Flights (incl transport, snacks, lunch and drinks) R750 in and around Cape Town, additional R100 for flights or half-day tours out of town. Usually last about 20mins. In-flight photos R100 pp per flight.*

Tel: *021-461-7070*

Cell: *082-881-4724.*

parapax@absamail.co.za

www.parapax.com

Mark Loftus and Andrew Kellett, Gravity Adventures

In Mark and Andrew's eyes adventure is the essence of Africa and they serve it up by the bucket-load in a wide range of activities of which kayak trips are a favourite. Whether you're bobbing along the Breede or racing down the Orange River, tours are tailored to small groups and, being paddle-powered, are designed to have a minimal impact on the environment.

Prices: *Palmiet River from R295 pp for half-day, Breede River from R395 pp for the day, Orange River from R1,995 pp for 4-night trip, Langebaan sea kayak hire from R195 per day.*
Contact: *21 Selous Rd, Claremont.*
Tel: *021-683-3698*
adventure@gravity.co.za
www.gravity.co.za

Steve Thomas, Daytrippers

Steve is a great bloke who loves his biking and hiking. He offers relaxed and informative half- and full-day Cape tours (with and without bikes/boots) that take in the peninsula, the townships, the ups and downs of Table Mountain; almost anything really. Once you're done there, he can take you whale-watching, kloofing and on expeditions right across S.A... so prepare for action!

Prices: *Day-tour R350, 1/2 day R250, kloofing R475.*
Tel: *021-511-4766*
Cell: *082-808-2212*
steve@daytrippers.co.za
www.daytrippers.co.za

NATURE GUIDES

Patrick Cardwell, Avian Leisure

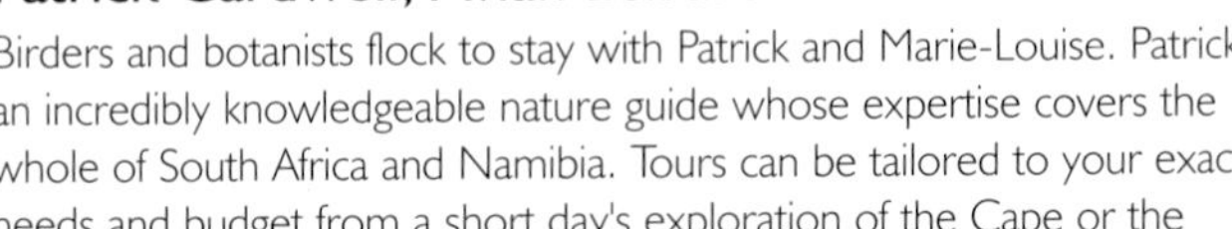

Birders and botanists flock to stay with Patrick and Marie-Louise. Patrick is an incredibly knowledgeable nature guide whose expertise covers the whole of South Africa and Namibia. Tours can be tailored to your exact needs and budget from a short day's exploration of the Cape or the Winelands "Vine Bird" tour to a 21-day pan-South African adventure.

Prices: *Cape day-tour from R600 pp for 4 people including guide, vehicle, park entry fees and picnic lunch. Ideal group max 6.*
Contact: *88 Dorries Drive, Simon's Town.*
Tel: *021-786-1414*
Cell: *083-272-2455*
enquiries@avianleisure.com
www.avianleisure.com

Callan Cohen, Cape Town Pelagics

Here's one for general nature-lovers and serious birders alike. Cape Town Pelagics run specialist seabird-watching day-tours. You'll see masses of birds (up to 4,000 at once behind a single fishing boat), including albatrosses, often from just 2m away. All guides are ornithologists, and impart plenty of info about birds and their environment. Furthermore, it's a non-profit organisation, donating all the proceeds to seabird conservation - more than R50,000 so far!

Prices: *Seabird tours R950 pp currently, unlikely to increase beyond R1,200 by end of 2007. Trips leave from Simon's Town Pier at 7am and last all day.*
Tel: *021-685-4081*
Cell: *083-256-0491 or Ross Wanless 073-675-3267*
info@capetownpelagics.com
www.capetownpelagics.com

Brian Vanderwalt, Brian's Birding

There are more than 900 bird species in South Africa, so best to have someone on hand to put a name to a face. Brian leads birding trips from Cape Town to as far as the Kalahari National Park, the Karoo and Garden Route. Trips can be geared for everyone and anyone, using his own vehicle for up to three clients, and a hired one thereafter.

Prices: *Rates depend on the trip. Cape Peninsula day trip for min 2 people from R550 pp.*
Tel: *021-010-2192*
Cell: *082-999-9333*
info@brians-birding.co.za
www.brians-birding.co.za

CITY BOWL
EATING and DRINKING

Aubergine

Harald Bresselschmidt spoils you for choice in fabulous five-star Aubergine. Not only does he offer sumptuous set menus of three to five courses, which are constantly updated with seasonal variations, but there are more than 350 wines to go with them. A great bistro menu is also available May - Sept. Open for dinner Mon - Sat, lunch on Thurs.

Prices: *3-course menu R230, R330 with wine, 4-course menu R280, R390 with wine, 5-course menu R320, R440 with wine. A la carte menu is similarly priced.*
Contact: *39 Barnet Street, Gardens.*
Tel: *021-465-4909*
aubergin@mweb.co.za (note no 'e')
www.aubergine.co.za

Bascule Bar at Cape Grace

A taste of Scotland in the southern hemisphere, Bascule has more than 420 whiskies including single malts and blends as well as bourbons from around the world. Evening tastings of six whiskies need to be pre-booked, while there's also a light South African menu for you to attack, either outside at the water's edge or in the lounge (available from 11am).

Prices: *Tasting presentations, from R130 pp, take place in Bascule at 6pm on various evenings through the week.*
Contact: *Cape Grace Hotel, West Quay, V&A Waterfront.*
Tel: *021-410-7100*
bascule@capegrace.com
www.basculebar.com

Biesmiellah Restaurant

Hailed from far and wide as serving the best Cape Malay curry around, Biesmiellah is a truly authentic restaurant where, in keeping with Muslim tradition, no alcohol is served. Run by the Osman family for some 23 years it's in the Bo-Kaap Malay quarter and open from midday onwards Mon - Sat. Take-away available.

Prices: *Mains usually R40 - R55. Tomato breedie, Pienang curry, denning vleis (a lamb stew) R57, crayfish and prawn curry R70, and much more....*
Contact: *2 Upper Wale St, cnr Pentz and Wale St, Bo Kaap.*
Tel: *021-423-0850*
osman7278@yahoo.com

Carlucci's (Café and Deli)

The perfect way to start the day in Cape Town or, indeed, finish it. Fantastic coffee and fresh pastries, countless croissants, myriad muffins and stacks of good sandwiches to take away, or better still, sit and enjoy, looking out towards the bay far below. Open 8am - 8pm every day so you can spend all day there.

Prices: *About R35 for snacks with coffee or juice.*
Contact: *22 Upper Orange St, Oranjezicht.*
Tel: *021-465-0795*

Carlyle's on Derry

Italian is the name of the game (if not the venue) at this bar and restaurant run by brothers Rob and Murray. It's super-relaxed, pizzas are cooked in a wood-burning oven, there are pastas and salads aplenty alongside a good wine list and prices are pitched for the regular local crowd rather than the tourists.

Prices: *Mains R30 - R70, pizza R35 - R45, wines R45 - R190 (R12 per glass), beer and cider around R10, corkage R20.*
Contact: *17 Derry St, Vredehoek.*
Tel: *021-461-8787*
carlylesonderry@absamail.co.za

Caroline's Fine Wine Cellar Kitchen

Wine buffs take note: though not underground, Caroline's is a cellar in every other sense, its walls lined floor to ceiling with more than 1,000 different wines. It's open all day as a shop and serves modern Cape food from 12pm - 2.30pm. For those born indecisive, handy wine-tastings with Caroline are available if you book ahead.

Prices: *Starters R30, mains average R59. Shop open 9am - 5.30pm Mon - Fri, Sat 9am - 1pm.*
Contact: *15 Long St.*
Tel: *021-419-8984*
carowine@mweb.co.za

Caveau Wine Bar and Deli

Your chance for a world-wine tour. Caveau, next to the city centre's Cape Heritage Hotel (see GG accommodation guide), specialises in tapas-style meals and superb wines which you may not find anywhere else. They come by the glass or bottle depending on your thirst.

Prices: *Breakfast about R35, lunch about R55, supper about R80, wines from R90. Open Mon - Sat, 7am - 10.30pm.*
Contact: *Heritage Square, 92 Bree St.*
Tel: *021-422-1367*
info@caveau.co.za
www.caveau.co.za

Col'Cacchio Pizzeria

An Italian pizzeria that cuts no corners (pizzas are round anyway) and has been serving fresh, made-to-order, crisp-base, gourmet pizzas and pasta for more than 12 years with an accent on healthy grub and a "vibey" atmosphere.

Prices: *Average spend is R75 incl all food and drinks. Open Mon - Sat, midday - 11pm, Sun 6.30pm - 11pm.*

Contact: *Shop 2, The Spearhead, 42 Hans Strijdon Avenue, Foreshore.*

Tel: *021-419-4848*

michael@colcacchio.co.za

www.colcacchio.co.za

Daily Deli

Tucked away in Tamboerskloof, the diminutive and super-friendly Daily Deli is a great pavement café favoured by the locals who meet there for coffee and chit-chat, casseroles, cheesecakes, lasagne, four-cheese pasta, lentil bobotie, focaccia, muffins, baguettes, pastries, croissant-based bread and butter pudding, mocca pecan pie… if they're feeling hungry.

Prices: *Mains R37 all served with salad, cakes R13-R18. Open 8am -10pm every day.*

Contact: *13 Brownlow Rd, Tamboerskloof.*

Tel: *021-426-0250*

Five Flies Restaurant and Bars

Come here for the buzzy atmosphere (and I am not talking about flies). Set in a Cape Dutch house there's a courtyard, inter-leading dining rooms hung with enviable art and an upstairs cigar lounge and bar. The menu is revamped seasonally and Irish chef Gerard Reidy is particularly proud of his grilled kingklip with prawn tail, sautéed spinach and langoustine sauce.

Prices: *Salads and starters R35, mains R80, cheese platter R42, desserts R35. 2-course meal R115, 3 courses R145, 4 courses R165. Open for lunch Mon - Fri, dinner every day.*

Contact: *14 - 16 Keerom St.*

Tel: *021-424-4442*

info@fiveflies.co.za

www.fiveflies.co.za

Limoncello Ristorante

Endless praise for Luca Castiglione, the owner and chef of Limoncello. He's from Naples (the true home of the Italian pizza) and here you'll eat authentic southern Italian cuisine rarely found outside its borders. There's a wood-burning pizza oven and great seafood too.

Prices: *Starters R34 - R38, pizza R42 - R55, pasta R44 - R48, mains R60 - R68.*

Contact: *8 Breda St, Gardens.*

Tel: *021-461-5100*

wapa@intekom.co.za

www.limoncello.co.za

Miller's Thumb

"A place where everyone knows your name." David and Jane's family-run bistro bustles and buzzes with conviviality, and bursts at the seams with locals feasting on a fishy menu that includes specialities such as Jambalaya, chicken prawn and cashew curry, and fisherman's chilli. Also caters for meat-eaters and vegetarians.

Prices: *Starters and salads R35 - R40, grilled fish, calamari or rump R75 - R95, Jambalaya, chilli, stir-fries and curries R70 - R85, desserts R20 - R25. Open for lunch Tues - Fri, dinner Mon - Fri.*

Contact: *10b Kloofnek Rd, Tamboerskloof.*

Tel: *021-424-3838*

thethumb@mweb.co.za

Royale Eatery

If you're going to eat a burger in Cape Town, the always-busy, 70s-feel Royale is the place to do it. They have 30 burgers, from 6 different cheese-burgers and 10 vegetarian ones to Thai fish and tofu. All come with a choice of fries, potato wedges and sweet potato fries, and I found them best washed down with a Royale shake.

Prices: *Burgers for R45 - R65. Open 12pm - late, Mon - Sat.*

Contact: *279 Long St.*

Tel: *021-422-4536*

Rozenhof Restaurant

Refined and inviting, Rozenhof is set in a 150-year-old house with magnificent chandeliers, polished wood floors and richly-painted walls - enough to woo you even before you try the food. Speaking of which, how does smoked marlin on sushi rice sound? Or perhaps you'd opt for braised guinea fowl in a wild mushroom sauce?

Prices: *Starters R20 - R40, mains R60 - R120, desserts R25 - R45, house wines R60 - R65. Lunch Mon - Fri, dinner Mon - Sat.*

Contact: *18 Kloof St, Gardens.*

Tel: *021-424-1968*

rozenhofrestaurant@mweb.co.za

Savoy Cabbage

Literally dozens of recommendations for Caroline Bagley's restaurant in the heart of the city. She describes her food as "un-messed-about-with" and changes her menu of fresh, seasonal and often organic ingredients daily to keep a step ahead of those making return visits in the same stay... of which you may well be one.

Prices: *Starters R45 - R70, mains R60 - R110 (excluding shellfish), desserts and cheese around R35. Kitchen serves from 12pm - 2pm Mon - Fri and from 7pm Mon - Sat.*

Contact: *101 Hout St.*

Tel: *021-424-2626*

savoycab@iafrica.com

Vida e Caffè

"A shrine for the wonderful bean and the drinking of it in its purest form; the espresso," says owner Brad. Inspired by the cafés of Rome, Lisbon, Paris and Barcelona, he aims to offer the very best coffee flattered by the best pastries and snacks... so what's your verdict?

Prices: *Espresso-based coffees R7 - R15, pastries R6 - R12.50, rolls R16 - R22.*
Contact: *Shop 1 Mooikloof, 34 Kloof St, Gardens.*
Tel: *021-426-0627*
www.caffe.co.za
Other branches on Thibault Sq and V&A Waterfront.

Pretty interesting fact

Table Mountain and the Cape Peninsula, which cover some 470 km2, are home to 2,256 different plant species - that's more than the whole of Great Britain, an area 5,000 times bigger.

CITY BOWL
NATURE and ACTIVITIES

The Blue Train

A five-star hotel on wheels. For those ready to splash out the Blue Train is the ultimate way to get across this vast country. Routes from Cape Town to Pretoria and Port Elizabeth cross some fantastic landscapes. Personal butlers make life just about bearable, the food and wine are first class and journeys include en-route stop-offs.

Prices: *Cape Town/Pretoria (1 day, 1 night) from R7,860 pp; Cape Town/P.E. (2 days, 1 night) from R8,910.*
Spoornet's Premiere Classe offers a similar experience, if slightly less luxurious, that leaves Pretoria for Cape Town on a Thursday and returns on a Tuesday. The leisurely 28hr journey costs from R2,050 pp.
Tel: *012-334-8459 (blue train) 8039 (premier classe)*
bluetrain@spoornet.co.za
www.bluetrain.co.za
info@premierclasse.co.za
www.premierclasse.co.za

Dragon Boat Racing

This ancient Chinese sport made its way to Cape Town in the '90s when a Taiwanese sister city donated two boats. These days there are a number of clubs operating and you're welcome to join them for practice sessions and monthly races. There are 22 people per boat (including one to steer and one to beat the drum!) and the more in time you are, the faster you go.

Prices: *R10 per session on weekday afternoons and Sat mornings. You do get wet so wear appropriate shoes, shorts and t-shirt and bring spare clothes and water.*
Contact: *Meet at the Marina Basin, near Cape Grace hotel, V&A Waterfront.*
Call Pam to check details on 021-447-2820 or 082-564-6257
pam@dragonboat.org.za
www.dragonboat.org.za

CITY BOWL
CULTURE and HISTORY

Aqua Opera

Water-borne opera at the V&A Waterfront that runs for a few days towards the end of Feb each year. The stage is set on a barge and allows the audience a great view from the pier with a stunning backdrop of the mountains and ocean.

Prices: *Tickets R100 - R350.*
Contact: *Cape Town Tourist Offices, cnr Berg and Castle Sts or at V&A Waterfront.*
Tel: *021-408-7600 or 021-426-4260*
Or buy tickets from Computicket on 021-418-7134
www.aquaopera.co.za

Cape Town Holocaust Centre

With discrimination and racism such a scar on South Africa's own recent history, this is a poignant place of remembrance for the six million Jews and all other victims of the Holocaust, with real insight into the tragic consequences of unchecked prejudice. The permanent exhibition features multi-media displays, artefacts and archival documents as well as video testimonials by survivors who made their home in Cape Town.

Prices: *Free entry.*
Contact: *88 Hatfield St, Gardens.*
Tel: *021-462-5553*
admin@ctholocaust.co.za
www.museums.org.za/ctholocaust

District Six Museum

Until the 1970s, District Six was home to almost a tenth of Cape Town's population. In 1965, the apartheid government declared the area "white" and over 50,000 people were forcibly uprooted and relocated to the plains of the Cape Flats. This museum tells the stories of those removals and helps in the reconstitution of the community of District Six. That 60,000 people visit every year shows just how well that story is told.

Prices: *Adults R10, kids R5, site tour R50 (bookings one week in advance for this). Open 9am - 4pm, Mon - Sat.*
Contact: *25a Buitenkant St.*
Tel: *021-466-7200*
info@districtsix.co.za
www.d6.co.za

Jazzathon

If you're in Cape Town in early January, don't miss this four-day jazz and music festival at the V&A Waterfront. It's free to the public and features some of South Africa's best-known names and brightest new talent.

Contact: *Takes place at the amphitheatre, V&A Waterfront.*
Call the tourist office on 021-426-4260
www.jazzathon.co.za

MCQP - Mother City Queer Project

See the fantastic costumes at Cape Town's annual gay festival, a riot of music and a huge, 24-hour fancy-dress party aimed at bringing homo- and heterosexuals together. Held over a weekend in the run-up to Christmas with dozens of DJs playing to thousands of party-goers. Tickets usually go on sale in November.

Contact: *postbox@mcqp.co.za*
www.mcqp.co.za

Robben Island and Nelson Mandela

For almost 400 years Robben Island, a small barren patch of land 12km out from Cape Town's harbour, was a place of exile and punishment. During the apartheid years it became renowned for the institutional brutality inflicted on its inmates, including one Nelson Mandela.

Born in a tiny village in the Eastern Cape's Transkei on July 18th 1918, Nelson Mandela is today a living icon, the ultimate symbol of South Africa's oppressed black majority during the apartheid years. He trained originally as a lawyer. Helping found the African National Congress Youth League in the 1940s, he later became the ANC's deputy president, advocating non-violent resistance to apartheid. The party was banned following the massacre in 1960 of a group of peaceful black demonstrators in Sharpeville and Mandela went underground to form a new convention.

The MK military wing of the ANC was born and under Mandela's leadership made armed attacks on the government. Mandela was eventually jailed for life for sabotage. He was released on February 11th 1990 after almost two decades imprisoned in a small cell on Robben Island.

In the multiracial elections of 1994, Mandela became the first democratically elected president of South Africa, and served until 1999. He was awarded the Nobel Peace Prize alongside F.W. De Klerk. Today he lives in his birthplace in the Transkei.

Trips to the Robben Island museum give a taste of this remarkable history. They last 3.5hrs including the transfer to the island, a visit to the maximum-security prison and guided tour of the island by an ex-political prisoner.

Prices: *Tickets cost R150 for adults and R75 for children (4 - 17 year-olds) and can be bought at the tourist information offices or from the Nelson Mandela Gateway at the V&A Waterfront.*
Tel: *021-409-5100 or 021-413-4200*
ebookings@robben-island.org.za
www.robben-island.org.za

GREEN POINT
EATING and DRINKING

Giovanni's Deliworld

These guys work really hard (open 7.30am - 8.30pm every day) and foodie fans can't get enough of it. It's a truly international deli that sells selected groceries from across the world (the jam's from Tiptree, Essex, the hams from Italy and Spain...) as well as turning out fantastic coffee and a menu of more than 40 meals. Always busy.

Prices: *Ciabatta with a cappuccino R32, hot main meals R35, cappuccino R9.95.*
Contact: *103 Main Rd, Green Point.*
Tel: *021-4346893*
giodeli@iafrica.com

The Nose Restaurant and Wine Bar

British expats Kevin and Cathy Marston serve 35 South African wines by the glass with healthy and hefty portions of home-cooked comfort food (deep-fried camembert, smoked fish pie, beef braised in red wine...). Eat inside or out and book a tasting too. "Snob-free and welcoming with really nice, chatty waiters!"

Prices: *Glasses of wine from R15, all a quarter of a bottle in size and price. Starters from R30, mains from R45, desserts from R30. Open all day every day.*
Contact: *72 Waterkant St, Green Point.*
Tel: *021-425-2200*
info@thenose.co.za
www.thenose.co.za

GREEN POINT
CULTURE and HISTORY

Green Point Flea Market

Cape Town's largest flea market and the best place to pick up bargain souvenirs (much better than the very expensive shops at the V&A Waterfront). This happens every Sunday morning beside the stadium. It is massive! Be prepared to come away with far more than you planned to buy - soap stone figures, jewellery, pictures, African drums, wooden carvings and much, much more.

SEA POINT
EATING and DRINKING

0932 Restaurant

0932, not only the dialling code for Belgium, but also a great restaurant specialising in Belgian beers, 24 of them in fact. Try one upstairs in the "Monk" bar then devour beautifully presented food at rows of wooden tables looking on to the kitchen. The only restaurant in the country to serve Leffe, Hoegaarden and Stella Artois on tap.

Prices: *Starters R30 - R45, mains R49 - R275 for shellfish, mussel platters R49, wines R70 - R248. Open all day every day.*
Contact: *79 Main Road, Green Point.*
Tel: *021-439-6306*
zero932@iafrica.com

Beluga

A big and busy eatery and bar in the Foundry, a century-old, red-brick building which was once home to the city metal works and is now a hang-out for the movies and modelling set. The food is feisty and contemporary and cooked in front of you in an open kitchen. Plenty of wines and exciting cocktails to choose from.

Prices: *Starter R40 - R60, mains R80 - R120, desserts R45. Open all day Mon - Fri and for dinner only at weekends.*
Contact: *The Foundry, Prestwich St, Green Point.*
Tel: *021-418-2948*
info@beluga.co.za
www.beluga.co.za

CLIFTON
EATING and DRINKING

La Med

A beach bar with a Mediterranean feel. Drink down cocktails, soak up great mountain and ocean views then move on to some food and dance the night away.

Prices: *Prawn, calamari and mussels combo R98, gourmet pizzas R32 - R69, burgers R35 - R45, bacon, brie and avocado salad R46. Open until late every night.*
Contact: *Victoria Rd, Clifton.*
Tel: *021-438-5600*
lamed@kristensen.co.za
www.lamed.co.za

CAMPS BAY
EATING and DRINKING

The Codfather
Definitely on the beaten track this one, and for good reason. It's one of Cape Town's best-loved seafood and sushi restaurants just off one of its best-loved beaches. There are no menus and you can just choose food randomly according to your budget and waistline. Large sliding windows and a big, open fireplace make it equally pleasant in summer as in winter.

Prices: *From R150 for a meal with wine. Open 12pm onwards every day.*
Contact: *37 The Drive, Camps Bay.*
Tel: *021-438-0782*
codfather@mweb.co.za

Theo's Grill and Butcher
Directly opposite the beach this is a casual but cool grill house that also does a great line in seafood (lobster in particular) and plenty of Mediterranean vegetables. Top people-watching spot and great for dinner before sampling the Camps Bay nightlife.

Prices: *Average R80 for 3 courses without wine. Open 11am onwards every day.*
Contact: *Shop 2, The Promenade, Victoria Rd, Camps Bay.*
Tel: *021-438-0410*
kmoss@fqv.com

LLANDUDNO

Llandudno Beach
Before heading over the hill to Hout Bay on the coast road, turn right down to Llandudno. The beach is a good alternative to Camps Bay beach. It's usually quieter, it's more sheltered (there are huge climbable boulders at either end) and the surf is great too.

HOUT BAY
EATING and DRINKING

Chapmans Peak Hotel

"The best calamari and Stifado (little bits of spicy Portuguese steak) in town, all served in the little pans they cook them in." Chapmans Peak Hotel is the grand old lady of Hout Bay and has been here since the 1880's. A huge, sun-drenched verandah and dining area looks over the bay, beach and valley and the cigar bar is a great place to rub shoulders with characters out of a Wilbur Smith novel.

Prices: *Starters from R25, mains (seafood, calamari and meats) from R60, desserts from R25, wine from R50, cocktails from R25.*
Contact: *Foot of Chapmans Peak Drive, Hout Bay.*
Tel: *021-790-1036*
info@chapmanspeakhotel.co.za
www.chapmanspeakhotel.co.za

Comida

Snuggled up next to the hotel (above), a great spot for thin-crust pizza and a menu that spans from the Med to the Pacific Rim. Eat on the outdoor deck and watch the sailors of Hout Bay Yacht Club battle it out in an evening regatta or the whales (in season) taking life somewhat more easily.

Prices: *Starters R25 - R45, mains, wok, noodles etc R45 - R80, pizza R40 - R60, desserts R25 - R40, wine R45+, cocktails R25+. Lunch and dinner every day.*
Contact: *Foot of Chapmans Peak Drive, Hout Bay.*
Tel: *021-791-1166*
info@comida.co.za

The Butcher's Grill House

As you might imagine, this is a meat-eater's paradise of grain-fed beef where you can choose your meat from the fridge and your wine from the walk-in cellar. The three McKechnie's who run it (Rob, Lyn and Mike) also turn out great seafood, salads and other dishes. Eat outside under the 100-year-old milkwood tree in summer.

Prices: *Average meal from R120. Open from 5pm every day for dinner.*
Contact: *33 Victoria Avenue, Hout Bay.*
Tel: *021-790-7760*
mckechr@iafrica.com

HOUT BAY
NATURE and ACTIVITIES

Hout Bay Yacht Club

If you're keen for some sailing the members here are often on the lookout for crew for their weekly races (Weds in summer, Sun in winter). Even if you're not a yachtsperson this is a great place to come and socialise and enjoy the view across the water from the centre of Hout Bay's bowl of mountains. Mooring facilities, maintenance support and boatyard all available.

Prices: *Participation in races is free, but call the club to check availability.*
Contact: *Hout Bay Harbour, Victoria Rd, Hout Bay.*
Tel: *021-790-3630*
hbyc@iafrica.com
www.hbyc.co.za

Tigger 2 Charters

Cruise the Cape shores on a super sleek 53ft catamaran cruiser. There's space for dining, a bar and fore and aft sundecks (that's front and back to many of us). Cruises can be tailor-made for full-day charters, crayfish cruises, casual braai or dinner cruises, Champagne sunset cruises… and even clay-pigeon shooting cruises.

Prices: *Start at R200 pp for a 1.5 hr sunset cruise to about R800 for a full-day cruise incl 3-course lunch. Minimum of 6 required for a non-private cruise. Cruises leave from Hout Bay marina.*
Contact: *Philippe and Michelle Parmentier.*
Tel: *021-790-5256*
Cell: *082-852-4383*
tigger@netactive.co.za
www.tiggertoo.co.za

Chapman's Peak

Chapman's Peak is the most thrilling drive in Cape Town bar none - when it's open. It's an astonishing piece of engineering that cost millions of rand to construct and millions more to maintain so that it is safe. The authorities close the road whenever it rains, or the wind blows hard as there was a fatal accident involving falling rocks 6 years ago. Following this accident the road was closed until late 2003 for major fortification work to ensure that it was safe. Carved into fynbos-cloaked mountainside, the single track coast road links Hout Bay to Noordhoek via a sinuous route that clings to the contours and in places burrows through the sheer cliff face. It's best driven from Noordhoek over to Hout Bay, simply because that way around you'll be on the seaward side of the road and can easily pull in to the various view points - make sure you do this. The views are spectacular and during the whale season (Jun - Dec, as you'll read about a million times in this book) you can look straight down on to the black-brown backs of bobbing southern rights. Make sure you take your binoculars. These also make great picnic spots. The toll (they have to pay for it somehow) costs R22 for a car.

NOORDHOEK
NATURE and ACTIVITIES

Solole Game Reserve

As close as you'll get to the Kruger in Cape Town. Solole is an urban conservation reserve in the Noordhoek Valley where on a game drive or guided walk you'll see buffalo, black rhino and antelope (as well as the magnificent Cape views). There's also a restaurant, a wellness centre for pampering and shop from which all funds go back into the reserve. A great one for the kids.

Prices: *Free entry. Guided walks R90 pp, game drives R20 - R95 pp.*
Contact: *6 Wood Rd, Sunnydale, Noordhoek.*
Tel: *021-785-3248*
info@solole.co.za
www.solole.co.za

SIMON'S TOWN
EATING and DRINKING

Black Marlin Seafood Restaurant

Not only is the Black Marlin renowned for its fabulous seafood but it has an amazing view and a cracking wine list to help wash it all down. Looking out from the restaurant garden across False Bay you're very likely to see wallowing whales in season (best from Aug - Oct).

Prices: *Salads R25 - R45, prawn tempura R50, grilled sardine R45, fish carpaccio R45, line fish R70, kingklip spit R87, grilled prawns R120, fillet beef R89, fisherman's platter R95....*
Contact: *Miller's Point, Simon's Town.*
Tel: *021-786-1621*
blackmarlin@kristensen.co.za
www.blackmarlin.co.za

Penguin Point Restaurant

Penguin Point is the heart of Boulders Beach Lodge, its wide terrace the perfect look-out point for whales and the resident African penguins that regularly waddle past. Seafood is great (I had the king prawns) but there are plenty of other offerings to suit all appetites.

Prices: *Breakfast R45, light lunches (salads, wraps etc) R35 - R50, seafood specials R140 - R450, other mains R60 - R90, desserts R20 - R30. Open 8am - 9pm every day.*
Contact: *4 Boulders Place, Boulders Beach, Simon's Town.*
Tel: *021-786-1758*
boulders@iafrica.com
www.bouldersbeach.co.za

The African penguin

The African penguin is one of South Africa's most unexpected wildlife attractions. There are now about 120,000 of these squid-munching flightless birds left following a massive population decline caused unequivocally by human intervention. Numbers have fallen 90% over the last century due to increased commercial fishing, penguin egg harvesting and oil spills.

Today the best (and most easily accessible) place to see them is Boulders Beach in Simon's Town (and Stony Point at Betty's Bay in the Overberg). Here boardwalks wind through the penguin colony, where a noisy and smelly mass of little black and white penguins are usually seen snoozing or waddling down the sand to the water's edge.

Vital statistics

- *They are also called the jackass penguin because of their donkey-like braying.*
- *They are great navigators; one oiled penguin which was rescued and released from Robben Island in 1971 travelled 800km to Port Elizabeth in a month.*
- *Their predators include sharks, Cape fur seals and killer whales.*
- *They are endemic to the Southern African coastline.*
- *Their colouring is an essential camouflage - a white belly for predators looking up from below and black for those looking down from above.*
- *Though they breed throughout the year they are monogamous.*

Most of the penguins are in the Boulders Beach park itself (entry R15) but you can also see them sitting on the boulders and bobbing about in the water in the neighbouring inlets. Park your car just beyond the golf course and walk back along the coastal path which, even if you don't see penguins, makes for a pleasant stroll.

Contact: Boulders Beach park is off Seaforth road, beyond Simon's Town harbour as you drive towards Cape Point. It's open 8am - 5pm every day.
Tel: 021-786-2329
www.cpnp.co.za

Salty Sea Dog Restaurant

Head here for fish 'n' chips at their greatest. The building is the old fish market on the wharf and you can eat in or take away freshly grilled or fried fish, calamari, squid, prawns and all sorts of other marine delights. Friendly service and packed with locals - just what we like.

Prices: *Fresh line fish and chips/rice R54. Open every day.*
Contact: *Wharf St, Waterfront, Simon's Town.*
Tel: *021-786-1918*
saltydog@mweb.co.za

The Meeting Place

The Meeting Place is just that, a restaurant made for slurping coffee and nattering, looking out over bobbing yachts in the harbour in summer or sinking into a fireside sofa and eating cake in winter (though you may have to move a large snoring dog from it first). "A favourite of ours, they also sell deli products like great coffee, wrapped sweets and muffins," says GG's Jôke of Frogg's Leap, Hout Bay.

Prices: *R40 - R50 daily menu, R65 - R75 in the evening, fully licensed.*
Contact: *Above Standard Bank, Main Road, Simon's Town.*
Tel: *021-786-1986*

SIMON'S TOWN
NATURE and ACTIVITIES

Apex Shark Expeditions

False Bay is famous for its breaching great white sharks, as photographed by Chris and Monique Fallows (you'll see his photos in Cape Town's aquarium). They have worked with sharks for the past 14 years and lead small groups on shark viewing and diving eco-tours as well as pelagic shark diving with mako and blue sharks.

Prices: *Great white shark (Apr - Sept) or pelagic shark trips (Oct - May) for R1,500 pp incl dive gear.*
Contact: *Trips leave from Simon's Town harbour.*
Tel: *021-788-1863*
sharky1@mweb.co.za
www.apexpredators.com

Fisherman's Cove

Gavin offers trips to snorkel with yellowfin tuna 20 miles off Cape Point. You'll need to be an experienced swimmer and bring or hire your own wetsuit, mask and snorkel. Bring an underwater camera too as these huge fish, which can grow up to 2m, will swim around within metres of you.

Prices: *R1,000 pp, minimum of 4. Available Nov - May.*
Contact: *Trips leave from Simon's Town harbour.*
Tel: *Gavin Hau on 021-794-4133 or 083-628-8133.*
gavinh@jacqueshau.co.za

Scratch Patch

Mining for the kids. Here they can rustle around among the thousands of tumble-polished gemstones that - quite literally - cover the floor and fill a small bag with stones to take away with them. Watch gemstones being tumble-polished and crafted into a wide variety of products at the Topstones factory (Simon's Town only).

Prices: *Entry and factory visit free, bags from R10 - R65. Open every day.*
Contact: *Simon's Town - Dido Valley Rd, Simon's Town.*
Tel: *021-786-2020*
topstones@topstones.co.za
V&A Waterfront - Dock Rd, Tel: 021-419-9429.

Scuba Shack

Learning to dive is a fantastic experience and the Cape is a great place to do it. Scuba Shack offer introductory and open-water PADI courses for beginners, while for experienced divers there's everything from wrecks to reefs and kelp forests to seal dives.

Prices: *PADI discover scuba R695, PADI open-water dive course from R1,995, boat dives R120, shore dives R90.*
Contact: *Shop 2, Glencairn Shopping Centre, Glencairn (next to Simon's Town).*
Tel: *021-782-7358*
Cell: *083-277-1843*
info@scubashack.co.za
www.scubashack.co.za

Able Seaman Just Nuisance R.N.

Just Nuisance is a great dane firmly ensconced in Simon's Town history. Born in 1937 this dog grew up among the Royal Navy sailors stationed in Simon's Town (still the base of the South African Navy today). Utterly spoilt by beer-swilling seamen he grew into a gigantic hound that became accustomed to following them onto ships and on the train into town.

Persistent train travel almost led to his being put down but the naval commander-in-chief enlisted him in the navy, securing his rescue and permitting him free train travel. Official papers read: christian name "Just", trade "bone-crusher", religious denomination "Canine Divinity League". As a member of the R.N. he was duly given a medical examination and his own billet.

The dog served until his death in 1944 and, as well as a statue looking over the harbour, his collar, papers and photographs are on display in the Simon's Town Museum (The Residency, Court Rd, Simon's Town, tel 021-786-3046, open 9am - 4pm Mon - Fri, 10am - 1pm Sat, 11am - 3pm Sun).

Sea Kayak Simon's Town

Undoubtedly one of the best ways to see the area's marine mammals, particularly the Boulders Beach penguins. Double kayaks are stable and easy to paddle - if you're fit enough to hike a few miles you're fit enough for this. Head out in search of the penguins, seals, sea-birds and whales (in season), then stop on a quiet beach for refreshments, swimming and snorkelling. Longer trips to Cape Point also available.

Prices: *R200 pp for the penguin trips and R700 pp to Cape Point.*
Contact: *Call Derek Goldman on 082-501-8930*
derek@webworkers.co.za
www.kayakcapetown.co.za

CAPE POINT

Cape Point marks the southern tip of the Table Mountain National Park, which stretches for 60km from Signal Hill in the north encompassing Table Mountain and the spiny finger of peaks that stretch south into the Atlantic. Cape Point itself is a wild and windy spot where a footpath leads to its needle-sharp southern tip. It's well worth a visit for hiking and mountain biking and some vigorous fresh air away from the city. To get there drive right through Simon's Town and just keep going. You will pay R35 to enter.

Monkey business

Visit Cape Point and, aside from antelope and ostriches, you may cross paths with a chacma baboon, or more likely an entire flange of them. Also called the dog-faced monkey, the olive-grey chacma has beady (disturbingly human) eyes and a bare dog-like muzzle housing sharp canines. You'll often see them crossing the road or marching along in a column and they will generally move out of your way. They are fun to watch and photograph, but DO NOT feed them.

The Cape baboons have been around for a long time and know every trick in the book when it comes to an easy lunch. When I visited the park a family left their car doors wide open and their shopping on display. Three or four baboons sidled over, hopped into the back of the car and noisily laid waste to the groceries. One of them ended up sitting on the roof eating a packet of crisps, and was not going to be moved.

Should you find yourself in a similar situation with an inclination to try and shoo them away, here are a few points to be aware of:

- Baboons live in troops, ruled by dominant males, that number 50 to 100 strong.
- They can be extremely aggressive and would viciously counter-attack their predators (leopard and cheetah) when threatened.
- They are the largest members of the monkey family with a mature male measuring 1.5 m from head to tail and weighing in at up to 33kg.
- They can run up to 35 - 40 miles per hour.

Bear this in mind.

KALK BAY
EATING and DRINKING

Olympia Café and Deli

Probably one of the best-known cafés in Cape Town. Olympia is great for breakfast, lunch and supper. A ramshackle café/deli/bakery it's always busy and they take no bookings. Service is fast though and you won't wait long for piles of wonderfully fresh and filling grub. Living just down the road, we ate here all the time and were never disappointed.

Prices: *Breakfast about R50, lunch about R60, supper about R100. Serving 7am - 9pm-ish every day.*
Contact: *134 Main Rd, Kalk Bay.*
Tel: *021-788-6396*
olympia@my.co.za

The Brass Bell

A very popular waterside pub with four eateries and three bars built practically in the water (the sea spray splashes against the windows). A particularly good stop-off in summer when you can dive for your own crayfish in summer and attack an appropriately seafood-based menu. Try the shared seafood platter, it will keep you going for weeks. Downstairs can be pretty rowdy so make sure you book a table upstairs looking onto the sea.

Prices: *Meals R30 - R200, beers R9 - R15. Lunch and dinner every day.*
Contact: *Next to Kalk Bay Station, Main Road, Kalk Bay.*
Tel: *021-788-5456*
thebrassbell@mweb.co.za

Theresa's

Candle-lit and cosy, this is one of our favourites. Theresa Lewis is owner and chef and you'll see her hard at work in her open-fronted kitchen turning out great traditional Cape food of which the meat dishes are particularly good (the lamb curry is a must). Line fish comes fresh every day from the harbour and make sure you save space for excellent malva (sticky-toffee) pudding. Be sure to book ahead, as it's often busy.

Prices: *R45 - R75 for mains served with a selection of vegetables and salads. R15 corkage. Open every night except Mon, open for Sun lunch in winter.*
Contact: *Cnr Harbour and Clarivaux Rd, Kalk Bay.*
Tel: *021-788-8051*

KALK BAY
CULTURE and HISTORY

Kalk Bay Theatre

An ideal combination of food and intimate theatre productions. Built in a renovated Dutch Reform church, the restaurant is upstairs in a gallery overlooking the 72-seat theatre. Eat starters and mains up there before the show then return upstairs for dessert, coffee and a mingle with the actors afterwards. The food is great and the set menu changes with each show (and is loosely linked to it).

Prices: *Dinner and theatre R175 pp, show only R75. Specials often apply in first week of a show (e.g. two for one). Performances Tues - Sat nights.*
Contact: *52 Main Rd, Kalk Bay.*
Tel: *021-788-7257*
bluebottle@iafrica.com
www.kbt.co.za

MUIZENBERG
EATING and DRINKING

The Olive Station

This is a chilled-out restaurant with a well-stocked deli and an olive-curing cellar. Regulars love the courtyard and sea views and the piles of authentic mezze-style grub. Get stuck into some pitta pockets with hot veg and lamb before great coffees, cakes and pastries.

Prices: *Breakfasts R25 - R40, light meals R20 - R40, main meals R60 - R80. Open Mon - Sat, 8am - 5pm though open till 9pm on Thurs. Sunday 9am - 5pm.*
Contact: *165 Main Rd, Muizenberg.*
Tel: *021-788-3264*
theolivestation@icon.co.za

MUIZENBERG
NATURE and ACTIVITIES

Gary's Surf School

Gary and his surf team have been riding the waves of Muizenberg for years and can teach everyone and anyone from 6 years old upwards. Lessons last around two hours and are one-on-one or one-on-two. Once you've got it licked you have use of the board and wetsuit for the rest of the day. Sandboarding also available.

Prices: *R380 for adults, R280 for kids, prices incl board and wetsuit.*
Contact: *Shop 34 Beach Road, Muizenberg.*
Tel: *021-788-9839*
Cell: *083-324-5110*
garysurf@intekom.co.za
www.garysurf.co.za

TOKAI
NATURE and ACTIVITIES

Action Paintball

Take the opportunity to zap and splat your friends and family in a paintball clash. Games are usually played twice a day at the base in Tokai, but are transferable to any suitable venue. They run other activities too and can organise everything from African drumming to microlight flights.

Prices: *R95 per adult, R85 for under-15s includes kit and 100 paintballs.*
Tel: *Craig Killops on 021-790-7603 or 083-454-9090.*
craig@actionpursuit.co.za
www.actionpaintball.co.za

Joseph Lister Arboretum

On hot summer days this is a great place to enjoy some shade alongside the dog-walkers and joggers. Botanists, horitculturalists, silviculturalists and pretty much any nature-loving "-ist" will enjoy it. Tokai and much of Constantia has been thickly forested for hundreds of years. As the influx of early settlers expanded the Cape Colony timber stocks dwindled and forest conservator Joseph Storr Lister received permission in the 1880's to use Tokai as a plantation ground. The enormity and diversity of today's 610ha forest and the exotic arboretum (situated at the very top of Tokai road) are therefore thanks to him - though the tea garden is a more recent addition.

CONSTANTIA
EATING and DRINKING

Buitenverwachting Winery and Restaurant

Buitenverwachting Restaurant is consistently rated amongst the best in the country, serving classical European cuisine and overlooking a cracking panorama of vines and hillside. Fans rate the winery's day-time picnics the best bar none. Those are available Mon - Sat, Nov - Apr and must be booked.

Prices: *Restaurant starters R50 - R70, mains R110 - R160, desserts R50 - R70. Picnics R75 pp.*
Contact: *Klein Constantia Rd, Constantia.*
Tel: *021-794-5190*
Restaurant tel: *021-794-3522*
restaurant@buitenverwachting.com
www.buitenverwachting.com

Constantia Uitsig

Frank Swainston is chef and host at the magnificent Constantia Uitsig. Set at the heart of this 300-year-old wine farm, the restaurant occupies the old manor house and is a grand affair with a convivial atmosphere and first-class service. Robust flavours herald mostly from Italy with forays into Asia.

Prices: *About R300 for a 3-course meal with Constantia wine. Booking is essential.*
Contact: *Constantia Uitsig, Spaanschemat River Rd, Constantia.*
Tel: *021-794-4480*
frank@uitsig.co.za
www.constantiauitsig.co.za

La Colombe

Undoubtedly one of the most popular eateries in Cape Town, La Colombe, also on the Constantia Uitsig wine estate, is sophisticated but casual and serves (as some South Africans would put it) "simply divine" food based around the recipes of southern France. The restaurant itself overlooks a cricket pitch.

Prices: *About R300 for a 3-course meal with Constantia wine. Booking is essential.*
Contact: *Constantia Uitsig, Spaanschemat River Rd, Constantia.*
Tel: *021-794-2390*
lc@uitsig.co.za
www.lacolombe.co.za

The River Café

This is informal day-time dining at its best in the old schoolhouse, this time at the entrance to Constantia Uitsig. Sumptuous breakfasts, lunches and teas are best eaten in the sunny outside seating area, surrounded by a riot of bright blooms, herbs, rhubarb and beets. Hefty portions and primarily organic ingredients.

Prices: *About R100 for a 3-course meal with Constantia wine. Booking is essential.*
Contact: *Constantia Uitsig, Spaanschemat River Rd, Constantia.*
Tel: *021-794-3010*
therivercafe@uitsig.co.za
www.constantiauitsig.co.za

Pastis

A country restaurant in the heart of Constantia that matches a robust French menu with wines from the surrounding wine fields. Ideal for breakfast, brunch, a languid lunch or balmy evenings on the terrace. Great fireplace for cold winter days too. Open pretty much all day, every day.

Prices: *Starters R30 - R45, mains R60 - R90, desserts R35, breakfasts R20 - R60.*
Contact: *High Constantia Centre, Constantia Main Rd, Constantia.*
Tel: *021-794-8334*
pastis@mweb.co.za

WYNBERG
EATING and DRINKING

High Tea

Eclectic décor and the perfect setting for breakfast, lunch and, of course, tea. High Tea is in a beautiful garden, its tables shaded by umbrellas and surrounded by herb beds and water features. Space only for 20 or so inside and 6 - 8 outside, so do book your place. Irma's incredible cakes stand out on a pleasantly simple but scrumptious menu.

Prices: *Breakfast from R25, lunch R30, coffees and teas around R10 and individual cakes around R20.*
Contact: *Farriers, 53 Constantia Rd, Plumstead.*
Tel: *021-797-1421*
celebrationcakes@absamail.co.za

Lupos Restaurant

Warm and relaxed, Lupos serves cracking Italian food with an always-popular buffet of freshly-prepared antipasti and a great à la carte menu. Coenie and Johan are excellent hosts and as well as making food for you they'll teach you to cook at their fun and relaxed winter cookery school.

Prices: *Buffet R99, mains R75, pasta R65, desserts R30. Open for dinner Mon - Sat. Cookery school winter only Mon, R300 per lesson include all ingredients recipes to take home.*
Contact: *19 Wolfe St, Chelsea, Wynberg.*
Tel: *021-762-3855*
lupos@telkomsa.net

NEWLANDS
EATING AND DRINKING

Barristers Grill, Café and Fish Restaurant

"Down-to-earth and good value." Barristers has been filling guests with fantastic steaks for nearly a quarter of a century and today offers various menus including great fresh fish and healthy salads. Bang in Newlands village it has a pretty fountain courtyard that's ideal for breakfasting by and it's in easy driving/taxi distance of both sides of the mountain.

Prices: *From R30 for a salad with orange juice to around R115 for a 3-course meal with coffee. Wines from R50. Open for breakfast, lunch and dinner Mon - Sat, dinner only Sun.*

Contact: *Kildaire Rd and Main St, Newlands.*

Tel: *021-671-7907 / 674-1792*

barrister@iafrica.com

NEWLANDS
NATURE and ACTIVITIES

Kirstenbosch Botanical Gardens

This is one of the musts of South Africa, a tidal wave of fabulous greenery that flows off the back of Table Mountain from indigenous woodland down into lush gardens, perfect beds and kempt lawns. And if you visit on a summer Sunday evening you'll have the added bonus of the extremely popular open-air concerts. Though the concerts themselves usually last around an hour it's as much a social as a musical event and whole gangs of Capetonians come armed with picnics, rugs and drinks - as should you.

Prices: *Concerts start at 5.30pm and cost R35, including the entry fee. Come early to ensure you get a good pitch on the sloping lawn that provides the auditorium. Music varies from week to week. There are also Jun - Aug winter concerts held in the Kirstenbosch Silvertree Restaurant (tickets cost R80 incl welcome drink and a starter).*

Contact: *Rhodes Drive, Newlands (off M3).*

Tel: *021-799-8783 / 8620 weekdays, 021-761-4916 weekends.*

Tel: *021-762-9585 for winter concert inquiries.*

www.kirstenbosch.co.za

KENILWORTH
EATING and DRINKING

Jakes on Summerley

The perfect antidote to a day's hectic holidaying, this Jakes (there's another not far away) is a beautifully restored family home turned into a welcoming restaurant. Flavours from all over the world are translated into hot soups and warming mains for winters by the fire and salads and seafood for summer meals in the shade of the pepper tree. Set menus and a lighter, café menu available.

Prices: *Starters about R30, mains about R65, desserts about R30.*
Contact: *5 Summerley Rd, Kenilworth.*
Tel: *021-797-0366*
www.jakes.co.za

KENILWORTH
NATURE and ACTIVITIES

Kenilworth Karting

For budding Michael Schumachers (young and old) Kenilworth Karting has a 220m track to zoom around in 160cc karts (only 140 cc for kids!). They'll arrange everything from kids' parties to endurance races and grand prix clashes. Try racing model cars on their Scalextric track first if you need to get the hang of it!

Prices: *10 lap races from R35 for adults and R25 for under 16s. Special bookings for groups of 12 or more from R50 pp.*
Contact: *10 Myhof Rd, Claremont.*
Tel: *021-683-2670/6174*
kenilworthkarting@karting.co.za
www.karting.co.za

RONDEBOSCH
EATING and DRINKING

Cargill's

Tiny and romantic, there's only space for 28 at Cargill's, where tables are candle-lit and laid with fresh roses, music is classical and a diminutive, French-driven menu comes accompanied by South African wines from smaller, less well-known wineries. Joszka greets you, talks you through the food, cooks it and often serves it too.

Prices: *Starters R35 - R40, mains R75 - R95, shellfish R140+.*
Contact: *20 Station Rd, Rondebosch.*
Tel: *021-689-2666*

Rhodes Memorial Restaurant

Reward/prepare yourself for a Table Mountain walk with breakfast, lunch or tea at this restaurant which, as the name would suggest, is on the lower slopes next to the Rhodes memorial and has a great view over the city. The menu caters for all tastes and remember to save space for the cakes, which are home-made and delicious.

Prices: *Average breakfast R20 - R40, average lunch R30 - R70. Open 9am - 5pm every day.*

Contact: *Groote Schuur Estate, Rondebosch.*

Tel: *021-689-9151*

roy@global.co.za

Who was this Rhodes character?

You can't travel far in South Africa without coming across the name Cecil Rhodes, so here is a little information about him to arm yourself with.

A key player in South Africa's colonial history, Cecil John Rhodes was an Englishman who made his fortune in diamond mining and fought for the expansion of the British Empire at all costs with visions of British colonies stretching from the Cape to Cairo.

R = Rhodesia. *Modern-day Zimbabwe and Zambia were former colonies developed by Rhodes and the British South Africa Company for their mining potential and named Southern and Northern Rhodesia in his honour.*
H = Hertfordshire. *Where he was born, in England in 1853. A sickly child, he was sent to South Africa in 1870 to farm cotton with his brother in Natal, before later moving into diamond mining and politics. Not necessarily the obvious remedy for a sickly child!*
O = Oxford. *He returned home in 1873 to attend Oxford University but took some years to complete his education there, so busy was he with his South African exploits. Today, money from his will funds the Rhodes scholarships for students from former British colonies, Germany and the U.S. (of which Bill Clinton was one).*
D = Diamonds. *Prospecting around Kimberley made him financially independent by 19. By 35 he controlled 90% of the world's production of diamonds through the De Beers mining company.*
E = Elections. *Rhodes was Prime Minister of the Cape Colony from 1890 to 1895 when he resigned after implication in the Jameson Raid (1895-96) which aimed to overthrow Paul Kruger's government in the Boer Republic of Transvaal.*
S = Siege. *During the South African/Anglo-Boer War, Boer troops besieged Kimberley for 124 days, with Rhodes in it. Towards the end, with the expectation that bombardments would worsen, Rhodes ordered the townsfolk into the diamond mine shafts for protection. Rhodes never saw the end of the war, dying in Cape Town in 1902.*

For more information on Rhodes visit the Rhodes Cottage museum at 246 Main Rd, Muizenberg. It's the humble home where he died and is free to visit Tues - Sun, 10am - 1pm and 2pm - 5pm.

ROSEBANK
CULTURE and HISTORY

University of Cape Town Irma Stern Museum

Irma Stern was a well-known South African painter who lived here from 1927 until her death in 1966. Her collections (in particular her famous collection of Congolese art), add to the impact of her bold expressionist paintings. Subject matter included exotic figures, portraits and lush landscapes and the media everything from oils and water colours to gouache and charcoal.

Prices: *Entrance is R8 and R4 for concessions. Books and reproductions and postcards are for sale. Special tours cost R15 pp.*
Contact: *UCT, Cecil Rd, Rosebank.*
Tel: *021-685-5686*
mvblom@protem.uct.ac.za
www.irmastern.co.za

DURBANVILLE
EATING and DRINKING

The Mount Restaurant

A treasure for good-food junkies, hidden among the Durbanville winefields. The Mount is home to The Mount School of Cookery where top chef Peter Ahern runs the kitchen and guests feast on combined international flavours and local ingredients and panoramic views of farmlands, vineyards and mountains.

Prices: *Average 3-course meal R90 - R140 excluding wines (many of them local). Open for lunch and dinner Tues - Sat, lunch on Sun.*
Contact: *40 Ibis St, Sonstraai, Durbanville.*
Tel: *021-975-0103*
info@themount.co.za
www.themount.co.za

DURBANVILLE
CULTURE and HISTORY

Rust-en-Vrede Gallery

A listed Cape Dutch monument in the heart of Durbanville with art galleries and a much-praised ceramics museum showing monthly exhibitions of S.A. artists. The Gallery Café serves light Mediterranean meals best eaten in the courtyard in summer or scoffed around the log fire in winter.

Prices: *Free entry to the galleries and clay museum. About R100 for a 2-course meal and glass of wine in the Gallery Café.*
Contact: *10 Wellington Rd, Durbanville.*
Tel: *021-976-4691*
rustenvrede@telkomsa.net

Climbing Table Mountain

You cannot come to Cape Town and not visit Table Mountain, but there are zillions of different ways to do it and so to make it simple we've focused on just one. It's quite a tough climb though easy to follow (even without a map) and it's our favourite. Starting in Kirstenbosch botanical gardens the path leads you up the back of the mountain via Skeleton Gorge (not as terrifying as it sounds) and across the top to the cable car, which makes for an easier way down into town than the zig-zagging, knee-nailing Platteklip path. So:

Going up...

The Skeleton Gorge path is signed within Kirstenbosch gardens and starts on its upper boundary with a steady but steep ascent alongside a stream that in winter cascades down the mountainside. It's definitely a path to take at your own pace as it's fairly strenuous going but even in the height of summer it remains cool thanks to the constant shade from thick indigenous forest. The vegetation becomes steadily more sparse as you climb and once at the top of the gorge you'll soon realise that Table Mountain's tabletop is anything but flat.

Follow signs to Maclear's Beacon along a path that winds its way around and over hillocks and hummocks to the highest point on the mountain at 1,086m (3,563ft), named after Sir Thomas Maclear who built the cairn in 1865 as a trigonometry point.

Pat yourself on the back, stop for snacks and photos and general view appreciation - from up here you can see down the Cape Peninsula, east across to the Winelands and Hottentots Holland mountains and north to the pointed Devil's Peak. From the beacon, follow the easy path across the top to the cable car station. More likely than not there will be a great many people here (looking somewhat fresher than you - if less satisfied with the whole experience) but it's well worth a wander around the fantastic lookout points built into the cliff top. The views down over the city bowl and out to Robben Island really are breathtaking.

Jamie Crawford proving he's been there.

Coming down...

If you're still bursting with energy and yearning for the satisfaction of having walked the whole thing the Platteklip path is the most direct route down. Beginning beside the cable car it's a steep zig-zagging descent, often via steps, to the car-park below. It's probably the most used route and you'll see a lot of dassies nibbling the grass. This descent will turn your legs to jelly and the path is very exposed to the sun in summer and the wet in winter, so be warned.

Alternatively, you can take the cable car. The cars themselves rotate as they move so even if it is full you're assured great views of the bay and the mountainside. There are plenty of taxis in the car park to take you down into town or over to Camps Bay; alternatively they can run you back round to Kirstenbosch to collect your car.

Or follow signs to Nursery Gorge which returns you to Kirstenbosch via a parallel gorge to Skeleton.

Practicalities

Clearly the timing depends very much on how fit you are and how long you want to spend taking pictures and picnicking, but do allow at least five hours to climb Skeleton Gorge, cross the mountain, take in the view and walk down. It can be very hot and dry in summer so take sun-cream, sun hats and water and wear stout walking shoes or boots. Avoid climbing the mountain when covered by its "cloth" of thick cloud as the view is terrible (often just a few metres) and it is easy to lose your way.

Entry into Kirstenbosch (see separate entry) costs R22 and it's open every day from 8am - 6pm (Apr - Aug) and 8am - 7pm (Sept - Mar), parking is free.

The cable car costs R57 one way or R110 return. It opens at 8.30am, with the last car going up at 5pm and down at 6pm. It sometimes closes if it is too windy.

A taxi from the cableway car park back to Kirstenbosch cost us around R150.

There are dozens of other paths on and around the mountain and walking maps are available from the two Cape Town tourist offices for R50 and also from the Kirstenbosch bookshop.

Contact: *Cape Town tourist offices.*
Tel: *021-426-4260 Cnr Berg and Castle St,*
Tel: *021-405-4500 V&A Waterfront*
info@cape-town.org
www.cape-town.org

Kirstenbosch Botanical Gardens

Rhodes Drive, Newlands (off M3).
Tel: 021-799-8783 / 8620 weekdays, 021-761-4916 weekends.
www.kirstenbosch.co.za

Silvermine

The Silvermine Reserve covers a large area of hillside behind Kalk Bay and, littered with caves, is well worth investigating. To do just that, try this walk which is popular with the locals and will give you great views across to Simon's Town and towards Cape Point.

Starting beside Kalk Bay harbour, take any of the steep alleys and stairways that lead from Main Road up to Boyes Drive, the high road that runs above Kalk Bay and St. James. Walk along this until you are roughly in line with the lighthouse and harbour entrance below you. Here take a flight of stairs where a signpost marks an entrance to the Silvermine Reserve. A clear path heads off right through the brush, across wooden footbridges and up towards two resting points. You should reach the first, known as Weary Willy's for its convenient sit-on-me boulder, after about 25 minutes. Here, another path comes in from the right across a stream. This is the way you will return later.

Another half hour or so uphill and you'll reach Hungry Harry's, a collection of boulders just made for snacking on and the approximate half-way point to the top. This marks the entrance to Echo Valley, which bisects two rocky peaks that tower above you; Cave Peak on the left and Ridge Peak on the right. A rough path off to the left leads to the front of Cave Peak. We went off-road here and - armed only with candles and an adventurous spirit - ventured into the various caves, crawling through one almost half-way into the mountain before it became too narrow (and us a little too nervous) to proceed.

GG accommodation inspector Ed Chivers "a little too nervous to proceed".

Anyway, continue uphill from Hungry Harry's between the peaks and the path flattens out, leading you through beautiful brush bristling with proteas and onto a boardwalk that delves into a fantastically tangled milkwood grove. Once out of the other side follow the path as it veers uphill to the right, past turnings to other caves. A few minutes on, at the fork, turn right to the amphitheatre itself, a rough scattering of boulders in the bowl of the surrounding hills. Eat more snacks, rest and ponder the mysteries of the universe. Take a look in Robin Hood's cave before leaving (just next to the amphitheatre).

We took a slight detour from the path here (which leaves the amphitheatre from the far left corner seen from where you came in) and scrambled to the top of Ridge Peak to make the most of the views. Soak it up, then return the same way but cut down to your right into the next-door kloof (small valley), rejoining the path as it heads downhill towards the Spes Bona forest and Kalk Bay. Once again you're plunged into mysterious woods of low, contorted yellowwood and milkwood, whose branches often intertwine with the boardwalk built through it. Emerging from the other side continue downhill until you hit a gravel track and head right towards Simon's Town. This winds down the hill and, narrowing to a path, leads you back down into the kloof you originally walked up and brings you back across the stream to Weary Willy's. From here you complete this P-shaped circuit with the easy skip down the hill the same way you came up, back to Boyes Drive, Kalk Bay and civilisation.

Practicalities

Allow about three hours to complete the circuit plus any extra you want for cave investigation, picnics and universal ponderings. Wear stout walking shoes or boots (especially in winter) and suntan cream in summer. Don't forget the binoculars... and perhaps a candle or torch for cave exploration....

What is a dassie?

A dassie, or rock hyrax, looks rather like a cross between a guinea pig and a rabbit but its closest relative is, actually, the elephant. You may well find this hard to believe since the dassie is the very incarnation of the opposite of an elephant: small, furry and no trunk at all. They do share similarities of the feet and teeth apparently... though, again, it is hard to see what these might be. Dassies feed on vegetation and, quite accustomed to onlookers, you'll see them nonchalantly munching the grass all over Table Mountain and the Cape Peninsula.

Urs Huber, chairman of the Peninsula Ramblers, suggests this walk:

Lion's Head

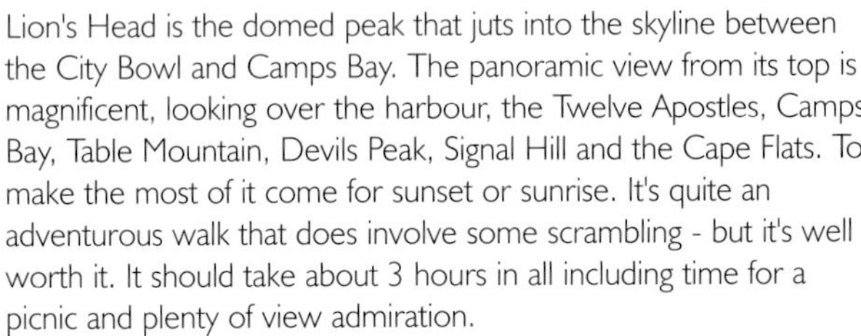

Lion's Head is the domed peak that juts into the skyline between the City Bowl and Camps Bay. The panoramic view from its top is magnificent, looking over the harbour, the Twelve Apostles, Camps Bay, Table Mountain, Devils Peak, Signal Hill and the Cape Flats. To make the most of it come for sunset or sunrise. It's quite an adventurous walk that does involve some scrambling - but it's well worth it. It should take about 3 hours in all including time for a picnic and plenty of view admiration.

To get to the start of the climb, drive up to Kloof Nek Rd and turn right onto the road to Signal Hill. Drive along for about 500m on the Signal Hill road, where you will see a parking area on the left side. Leave your car here and start walking!

From the parking area start climbing up the jeep track on the opposite side of the road. The track goes up fairly steeply, then does a right turn and begins to level out after about 200 metres. You will then encounter a fork; take the right-hand path, which continues to ascend and encircles the mountain. Just before you turn the corner to the right, the path splits again into a lower and upper contour. At this point (A) you can see the parking area below where you parked your car.

The upper path is the easier one and ascends 50 metres towards the summit cliff onto a contour path. Follow the path along the eastern flank until you turn the corner. Then climb up the last 120 metres along the ridge to the top. You will encounter some easy rock scrambling and a short steel ladder on the way up.

There is another more adventurous way up, which involves more rock scrambling and chains. It starts from point A. Take the lower contour until you find an open crack with a chain hanging in it. This provides an easy scramble up with another short length of chain just above the first one. Go straight up until you cross the higher contour path. Above is a more difficult rock section (about 10 metres), which is also secured by a long chain. After that scramble you continue the ascent on a well-known path until the southern ridge is reached, 60 metres below the top. Follow the ridge until you reach the summit.

Elsie's Peak 

Elsie's Peak Walk is an easy half-day walk requiring minimal fitness and, on a clear day, offers stunning views across False Bay as far as Hangklip. During the whale season you may see southern right whales with their calves in the bay below.

Drive along Fish Hoek Main Road towards Simon's Town and when you reach the traffic circle at the end of the road, turn right into Kommetjie Road. A few metres along to your left you will see a large parking area (diagonally opposite the Outspan pub) where you can leave your vehicle.

The walk starts by going up some steepish stairs in-between the houses; the first flight takes you to a road; cross this and continue up the next flight. When you reach the bench in front of you, take the right-hand path and follow it. It will take you through some fine fynbos (there are plenty of erica species and the metalasia muricata or blomb has a wonderful herbal pungency). You will walk along some stony gabions (rocks that have been placed in wire cages to stabilise the area) and the path will begin to rise and double back. Watch out for stone signs marking the route (the first one will point you to Elsie's Peak) and stay on the left side of the "Circular Route" marker. Soon after this you will notice two rocky koppies towards your right; continue walking so that you pass between them and then behind the right-hand one.

Presently you will see the mast attached to a small building at the base of Elsie's Peak, and a few more metres will take you to the beacon on the top of the peak. It can be very windy there, and you may prefer to stop for tea next to the telecommunications building, where it is usually quite sheltered.

From the top of the Peak you will see Glencairn to your right and Fish Hoek and Muizenburg to your left. If you look behind you, you will see the beaches of Noordhoek, and the Atlantic Ocean.

Your return is initially the same as the path you came up on, but take the left-hand fork at the cairn so that you complete the circle. Back at the Circular Route beacon, you will rejoin your original path and descend towards the car park again.

The route will take approximately 2 hours and it is wise to take an extra jersey even on the hottest day, as the wind can become very cold. Take water with you, as there is no water on the route. Dogs, on leads, are permitted.

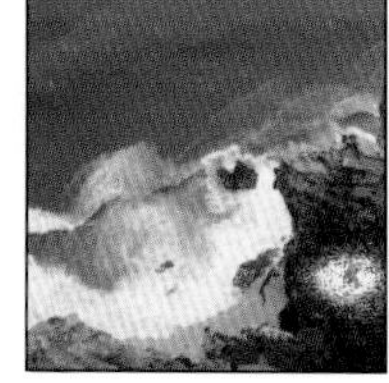

AND FINALLY A COUPLE OF OTHERS TO KEEP YOU OUT OF MISCHIEF...

Constantia Nek

This is probably the easiest route to climb to the top of the Back Table of Table Mountain and sets out from the car park at the top of the Constantia Nek pass along a smooth and step-less jeep track through the magnificent (and shady!) Cecilia Forest. From here you can see east to the Hottentots Hollands and south towards False Bay and Cape Point. You're also not far from the spectacular Disa Gorge and Woodhead Dam if your legs are up to it. Allow about 3 to 4 hours.

Camps Bay Contouring

This walk gives you remarkably good views in return for surprisingly little effort. It's a contour route that follows a pipe and track along the mountainside above Camps Bay and Bakoven and begins where Kloof Nek Rd meets Tafelberg Rd before it climbs towards the Table Mtn. cable car. Park your car/bike/helicopter in the parking lot here, cross the road and climb a few steps. At the top you'll spot the beginning of the pipe and track you are to follow. Head off along this and keep going for as long as you like. There are a number of paths that branch off up the mountain, but ignore these and enjoy the stroll and views up to the towering Twelve Apostles above and down to the brave swimmers below. The water off Camps Bay beach looks so inviting but it is utterly Antarctic.

Contact: *For more details and maps contact the Cape Town tourist offices.*
Tel: *021-426-4260 - cnr Berg and Castle St*
Tel: *021-405-4500 - V&A Waterfront.*
info@cape-town.org
www.cape-town.org

BIRDING BITS

You will see:
Cape Sugarbird
Cape Bulbul

You'll be very lucky to see:
Knysna Scrub Warbler, Forest Canary

You might see:
Orange-breasted Sunbird, Malachite Sunbird

Eyes peeled around Kirstenbosch.

West Coast

and

Cederberg

For a relatively small city, Cape Town spreads out a long way, but I always find it remarkable how easily you can escape the urban sprawl and find yourself in wild country if you travel along the west coast. The West Coast and Cederberg make for low-stress, high-reward travel, all within just an hour or two of the so-called Mother City.

I 'd advise a route up the coast and back through the mountains (or of course the other way around). Heading through Darling (hotspot for wine-makers and desert flowers which bloom at the end of August and early September) you'll quickly reach Langebaan and the coastal villages typified by Paternoster and its bright white, low-roofed fishermen's cottages. Beaches are equally white and there are plenty of water sports on offer in the area. More leisurely pursuits include superb birding and whale- and dolphin-watching plus some great seafood restaurants right on the beach. Many people regularly drive from Cape Town just for lunch.

Looping east you reach the N7 and it's a very easy drive south through the rooibos tea farms of the Cederberg. Do your best though to get off the main road and take the back route through the mountains (though make sure you have a full tank of petrol). Walking boots and a bird book are an essential in this small but special part of the world that stretches around 50km north to south by 20km east to west. The buckled sweeps of reddish sandstone make for dramatic scenery and plenty of scope for leg-stretching before you head back south, or, for the adventurous, set out on an exciting circuit of the Northern Cape.

west coast and cederberg

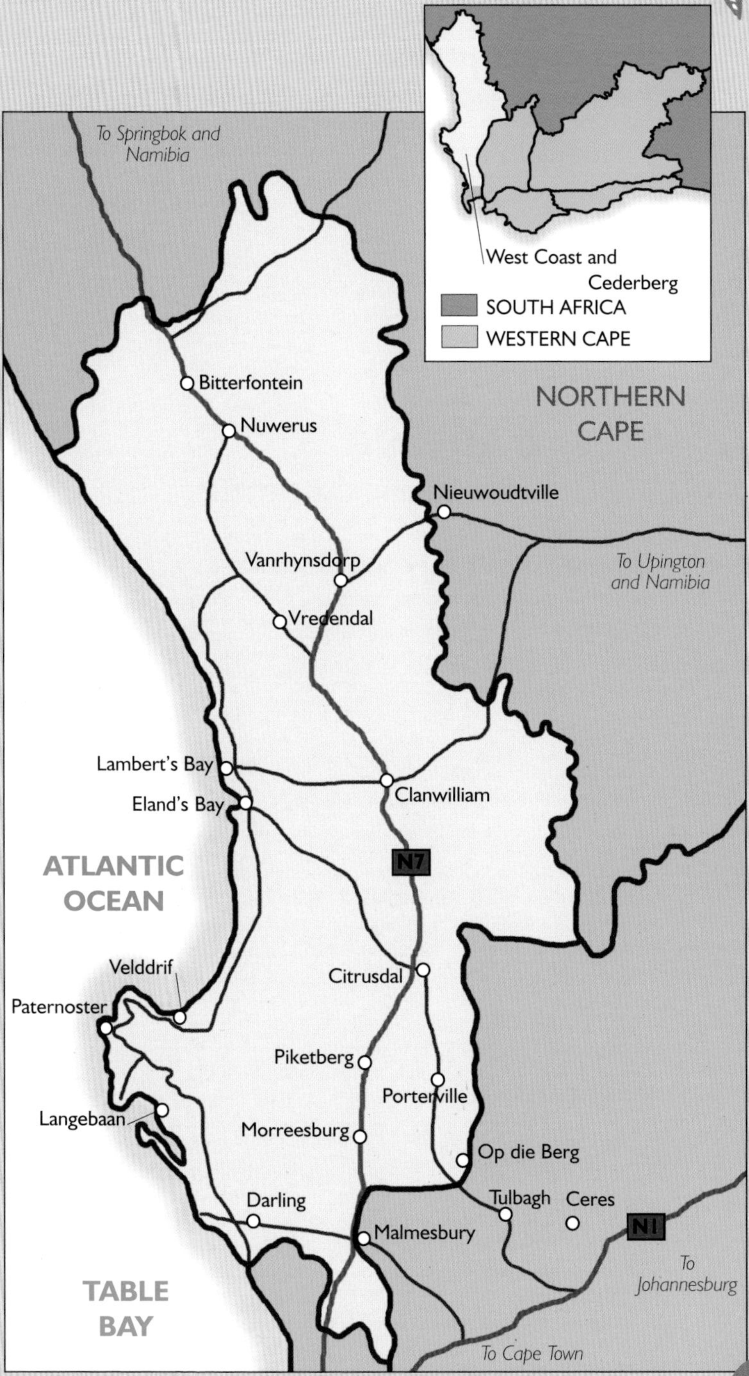

GUIDES AND EXPERTS
NATURE GUIDES

Keith Harrison and Lucille Byrnes, West Coast Bird Club

The West Coast is a cross-over point of migratory routes of both Arctic and Antarctic origins and so offers an astoundingly rich diversity of bird life through the year, with more than 300 birds species recorded along its 230km coastline. West Coast Bird Club members will show you what's what and know all the best spots to track down resident waders and rare visitors alike.

Prices: *R75 for a 3hr birding trip accompanied by club members using visitor's car, incl refreshments.*
Contact: *Call Keith on 022-713-3026*
Or Lucille on 022-742-1944
byrnesmr@xsinet.co.za

DARLING
EATING and DRINKING

Groote Post Winery and Restaurant

Popularly reckoned as making the best wine on the West Coast, the Pentz family also have a fantastic restaurant in the Cape Manor House at Groote Post farm. Filled with antiques and antique glass collections, it serves modern country cooking care of chef Debbie McLaughlin. If not clipped from the garden, ingredients are sourced locally and the à la carte menu changes daily.

Prices: *Tastings free, 8am - 5pm, Mon - Fri, 9am - 2.30pm on Sat. R120 for a 3-course meal, wines sold at cellar price. Open for lunch daily. Picnics must be ordered 24hrs in advance.*
Contact: *Darling Hills Rd, Darling.*
Tel: *022-492-2825*
wine@grootepost.co.za or gpwines@access.co.za
www.grootepost.co.za

Rooibos

Rooibos is a bush that draws its name from the Afrikaans for red bush. You'll see plantations lining the N7 as you head through the Cederberg and will notice that it is distinctly un-red. The leaves are very much green when growing and only turn red when fermented and dried. They're then chopped and packed into the tea bags that find their way onto our supermarket shelves. It's caffeine free and is said to help cure headaches, irritability and tension - making it the ideal drink for long car journeys fraught with navigational issues. Newcomers should definitely give it a try.

DARLING

CULTURE and HISTORY

Evita Se Perron

Evita Bezuidenhout (aka Pieter Dirk Uys) is a character famous across South Africa for 'her' satirical take on the growth of South Africa, the Rainbow Nation. 'She' appears in two cabaret venues at Evita Se Perron and you can check out the programme of shows they offer on the website. Even if there's nothing on, this a great place to stop and delve around in the craft shop and eat traditional S.A. grub en route to the West Coast.

Prices: *Show tickets R55 - R90, meals R35 - R90, arts and crafts R15 - R5,000.*
Contact: *Old Darling Railway Station, Darling.*
Tel: *022-492-2851/2831*
bookings@evita.co.za
www.evita.co.za

LANGEBAAN

EATING and DRINKING

Die Strandloper

Leave plenty of time for dinner at the Strandloper (a good 3 - 4hrs) and be prepared for a seafood extravaganza of some 10 dishes, kicking off with mussels and leading to a climactic crayfish course. All the food is cooked in front of you over open fires, the sea views are fantastic and, though they are licensed, you're welcome to bring your own booze.

Prices: *R140 pp, no corkage charge if BYO.*
Contact: *On Langebaan beach.*
Tel: *022-772-2490*
strandlopers@mweb.co.za
www.strandloper.com

Geelbek

Geelbek started life as a farmhouse built on the shore of the Langebaan Lagoon deep in what is now the West Coast National Park. These days Elmarie Leonard offers traditional dishes for devouring inside or out in the garden looking out to the water. With a post-lunch siesta on the lawn and a stroll along the lagoon an entire afternoon here can easily slip away.

Prices: *56 dishes at R25 - R100+, regional wines R50 - R150. Open 9am - 5pm.*
Contact: *West Coast National Park, off R27 near Langebaan.*
Tel: *022-772-2134*
www.geelbek.com

La Taverna

Piles (and piles) of great seafood on offer here, including prawns and crayfish, as well as a number of eastern dishes. And just to keep you on your toes and Hans in touch with his roots (he came to South Africa some 40 years ago) there are a few old Austrian favourites thrown in for good measure (schnitzels and the like).

Prices: *Average spend R100 - R120.*
Contact: *Cnr Breest St and Wostewal St.*
Tel: *022-772-2870*
mwhwr@mweb.co.za

LANGEBAAN
NATURE and ACTIVITIES

Cape Sports Centre

South Africa's largest water sports centre located on the shores of the Langebaan Lagoon. Here the wind whips across shallow (and so not too wavy) water, making it ideal for learning to windsurf or kite-board. There are kayaks too and everything is for rent or sale. Get some help from the qualified instructors and, even if you haven't got the idea, splash out on the gear in their sports shop.

Prices: *Depends on season, but you can rent kit from R30 per day.*
Contact: *98 Main St, Langebaan.*
Tel: *022-772-1114*
info@capesport.co.za
www.capesport.co.za

West Coast National Park

This park covers the swathe of coastline encompassing the Langebaan Lagoon and it has a million and one things to see from spring flowers to wild eland, bontebok and wildebeest and (even wilder) kite surfers that zip across the lagoon's shallow waters. The bird-watching is particularly good and you'll find a hide at Geelbek (also a restaurant - see above) just made for watching the waders. Eyes peeled for flamingos.

Prices: *R30 entrance. Open all day every day.*
Contact: *Outside Langebaan, off West Coast R27.*
Tel: *Park warden 022-772-2144/5*
www.sanparks.org/parks/west_coast

VRYDENBURG
NATURE and ACTIVITIES

Iziko West Coast Fossil Park

The dig here is a fascinating on-going project that you must see… and you can lend them a hand too. Join in at the sieving station, looking for five-million-year-old fossils, tracing the ancient history of the area. All good archaeologists need an occasional break too, so there's a coffee shop on hand serving home-made meals, with a garden play area for the kids. Mountain bike trails are open to the energetic.

Prices: *Adults R25, students and pensioners R18, kids R12, R60 for a family of four. Bike hire R60, R20 to use your own.*
Contact: *Off R27, just north of Langebaan.*
Tel: *022-766-1606*
pippah@iafrica.com
www.museums.org.za/wcfp

PATERNOSTER
EATING and DRINKING

The Voorstrandt

A traditional West Coast fisherman's house, the building is 108 years old and sits smack on Paternoster's bright white sands, looking straight on to the water. The seafood couldn't be fresher with West Coast lobster a highlight in season, but there are also plenty of other beefy/chickeny/veggie options. Have a starter and glass of wine, stroll on the beach, return for a main course. One of my absolute favourite restaurants in S.A.

Prices: *Meals for R45 - R285. Serving from 10am - 9pm every day, but call ahead to check.*
Contact: *Strandloper St, Paternoster.*
Tel: *022-752-2038*
Cell: *082-211-8619*
voorstrandt@lando.co.za

Café Manatoka

"The best prawns" …and plenty more besides. Though he's lived in S.A. for 20 years (and has the accent to prove it), Mike's a Londoner by origin and brings his experience in French and Italian kitchens to a vibrant menu and bohemian setting here by the sea. "It's nothing fancy, but I like to think it's perfect," he says.

Prices: *3-course meal R150 without drinks. Open for lunch and dinner Mon - Sat, lunch only on Sun.*
Contact: *St Augustine St, Paternoster.*
Tel: *022-752-2090*

PATERNOSTER
NATURE and ACTIVITIES

The Beach Camp

The West Coast is all about the water and at his beach camp Hannes makes the most of it. Guided kayak trips and boat trips head along the coastline of the beautiful Cape Columbine Reserve to nearby seal and breeding bird colonies. You'll also see plenty of dolphins and whales in season. Stick around for a fish braai and paella.

Prices: *2hrs guided sea-kayaking R180, boat trips R180, seafood supper R120, fish braai and paella R65, breakfast R35.*

Contact: *Columbine Nature Reserve, Paternoster.*

Cell: *082-926-2267*

info@ratrace.co.za

www.ratrace.co.za

Paternoster to Swartriet Trail

What better way to appreciate the West Coast than by walking along it. This 17km trail heads north from Paternoster towards Jacob's Bay and the Swartriet holiday complex. If you aim to do it when the tide is out you'll be able to walk on the hard flat sand as opposed to traipsing Sahara-style over the dunes. Do it in spring and you'll have the three-pronged bonus of pleasant temperatures, spring flowers coating the dunes and migrating whales to watch. It's very easy walking and easily do-able in a day. Take a picnic and plenty of sun cream.

Prices: *It is free but you do need to let the Vredenburg Tourist Office know beforehand how many people will be walking and when you want to do it.*

Contact: *Vredenburg Tourist Office, 15 Main Rd, Vredenburg.*

Tel: *022-701-7000 Fax: 022-715-1304*

VELDDRIF
EATING and DRINKING

West Coast Gallery

Relax, admire the bird art and sculpture, play boules under the trees and scoff delicious grub - the very best way to spend a day in Velddrif. From the wood-fired grill comes excellent kingklip and yellowtail. There are also fresh mussels and oysters, springbok salads and the Cento Angelli deli too, so save extra space for biscuits, preserves, chocolate eclairs....

Prices: *Breakfast R32, soups and starters R25, mains R35 - R55, desserts R15. Open 9am - 5pm, Tues - Sat.*
Contact: *6 Kerk (Church) St, Velddrif.*
Tel: *022-783-0942/118*
joanart@mweb.co.za

A Birding Tip...

For a close-up view of myriad water birds go to the Riviera Hotel on Voortrekker Rd in Velddrif and ask for the key to the bird hide on the banks of the Lower Berg River. If your timing is good you may witness the arrival of thousands of Cape and white-breasted cormorants streaming in through the river mouth in the evening to roost on the commercial salt pans. More than 24,000 have been counted - though how they count them is a mystery!

Alternatively... drive 25km north to the Rocherpan Nature Reserve, a wild coastal strip based around a seasonal vlei or pan which is a great place to see great white pelicans, great and lesser flamingos. These are all on the endangered species list but you wouldn't think so. They spend much time feeding here but fly north to Botswana and Namibia to breed. From the bright white beaches here you'll also see whales in season and heavisides dolphins.

Prices: *About R15 pp, open daily from 7am until dusk.*
Contact: *25km north of Velddrif on gravel road towards Eland's Bay*
Tel: *022-952-1727 or 022-931-2900*
www.capenature.org

Guano - a history of poo

Guano (derived from the Peruvian Quechua word for dung as if you didn't already know) or bird poo is intrinsically linked to the history of South Africa's West Coast. Apart from smelling quite fantastically foul it also makes for great fertiliser. Generations of breeding birds left the coastline caked in the stuff and European traders fought tooth and nail to scrape it from the rocks during the 19th century, carefully shipping their "white gold" back to Europe where it sold for a fortune.

AURORA
EATING and DRINKING

L'Aurore

Chef and owner Helmut arrived in South Africa in 1987 via Panama, Australia, Tahiti and the Middle East, so as you can imagine, his menu is pretty international (though with distinct Austrian mementos). The restaurant is in a long and low century-old West Coast house filled to the rafters with antique wood and copper pieces and with a beer garden and pool for cooling off in.

Prices: *Starters R20 - R30, mains R35 - R60, desserts R12 - R18. Open for lunch and dinner.*

Contact: *77 School St, Aurora, off R399 near Piketberg.*

Tel: *022-952-1755*

CEDERBERG
NATURE and ACTIVITIES

Cederberg Wilderness Area

For the hardy hiker, the Cederberg Wilderness Area (all 71,000 hectares of it) offers some of the most spectacular hiking and trekking in South Africa. The wilderness of sandstone scenery is breathtaking and it's a hotspot for San and Khoi rock art sites that can be anything from 300 to 6,000 years old. Trails are unmarked but well-trodden and while there are a number of routes that people follow the emphasis is on forging your own route - a rather adventurous concept. A map is essential for this.

- **Animals:** see plenty of baboons, dassies, duikers, rarely see Cape clawless otter, porcupine, honey badger, very rarely see leopard, though they are common.
- **Plants:** fynbos galore. Watch out for the attractive, purple-blue ridderspoor on the lower slopes and the endemic and rare snow protea on the higher peaks.
- **Birds:** more than 100 species including raptors like black eagles, rock kestrels and jackal buzzards.

Prices: *Adults pay R30 for day hike entry, R60 for overnight hiking, kids R20 for day hiking, R30 overnight. A map is the most essential item and can be bought from the camp in Algeria (which, by the way, was named by a French nobleman reminded of Algeria's Atlas mountains) or by ordering it from the telephone number below.*

Contact: *30km south of Clanwilliam off N7.*

Tel: *022-931-2088*

cederberg@cnc.org.za

www.capenature.org.za

Groot Winterhoek Reserve

Fantastic hiking and rock pool swimming in more than 30,000ha of rugged mountains up to 2,077m (6,814 ft) high, where easily weathered Table Mountain sandstone has created extraordinary rock formations. Fynbos covers the hillside, erica species flower through the year and watch out for red disas along the streams in Jan and Feb. You'll see plenty of antelope and bird species and, very occasionally, leopard, caracal and other predators.

Prices: *Adults pay R30 for day hike entry, R60 for overnight hiking, kids R20 for day hiking, R30 overnight.*
Contact: *Cardouw turn off R44, 2km north of Porterville, park is 33km from town.*
Tel: *022-931-2900/2088*
porterville@cnc.org.za
www.capenature.org.za

Matroosberg Reserve

"God created this beautiful mountain and we must conserve it. But to keep it under lock and key would be pointless," says Cordre Smith. And so his whole family help open up the stunning Matroosberg to visitors. After a cup of coffee in the farm house they'll have you out on 4x4 tours in Bedford trucks, abseiling down the rock faces or taking it easy on a tour of the farm. Extremely friendly people.

Prices: *4x4 excursion R250, abseiling, farm tours R100.*
Contact: *Erfdeel Farm, on R46 35km from Ceres towards Touws River.*
Tel: *023-312-2404*
Cell: *082-809-2935*
info@matroosberg.com
www.matroosberg.com

CLANWILLIAM
NATURE and ACTIVITIES

Elandsberg Eco Tourism

Find out about rooibos on Chris and Annette du Plessis' tea estate. They are extremely welcoming and offer tours of their plantations and processing plant. They also have a unique open-air restaurant serving traditional Cape Malay and West Coast dishes in the shade of an overhanging rock face. For the more energetic there are hiking and mountain bike trails across the farm.

Prices: *Tour of the processing plant R70, breakfast R50, lunch R65, dinner R85.*
Contact: *Elandsberg Farm, Clanwilliam.*
Tel: *027-482-2022*
cduples@mweb.co.za

CLANWILLIAM
CULTURE and HISTORY

Clanwilliam Bushman Art

The San bushman paintings are a fascinating insight into the pre-colonial history of this land. To make the most of it, though, you'll need a guide. Cape Town University helps run the Living Landscape educational project, and you can join them for tours of amazing local rock art sites.

Prices: *Tours from R50. Mon - Fri, 8am - 4pm, Sat 9am - noon.*
Contact: *18 Park St, Clanwilliam.*
Tel: *027-482-1911*

> **Heavisides dolphins**
>
> *These stocky dolphins are endemic to the West Coast and really very little is known about them other than what they look like. They measure up to about 6ft with the front half a light grey sweeping into dark blue-black towards the tail. The belly is a brilliant white and they have a blunt fin and flippers. You'll most often see them in twos and threes, off-shore and they tend to be fairly acrobatic, often following the bow waves of boats.*

VREDENDAL
WINERIES

WestCorp International (Vredendal and Spruitdrift Winery)

Come here to see wine production on a massive scale. On the banks of the Oliphants river, WestCorp is the largest wine co-op in the southern hemisphere, pooling the resources of two wineries and producing wines from more than 100,000 tonnes of grapes a year. Tour the cellars during harvest time and book in for S.A. food at the lapa.

Prices: *Free tastings, open 8am - 5.30pm Mon - Fri, 8.30am - 12.30pm Sat.*
Contact: *WestCorp International, 17 Circle Rd, Vredendal.*
Tel: *027-213-1080*
info@westcorp.co.za
www.westcorp.co.za

LAMBERT'S BAY
EATING and DRINKING

Muisbosskerm Open-air Restaurant

People drive from Cape Town just to eat here. This is the West Coast's original outdoor restaurant, which derives its name from the shelters native herdsmen built from the "muisbos" bush. To the sound of lapping waves yards away, you'll help yourself in a three-hour, scoffing bonanza of every kind of seafood grilled, smoked, boiled or baked in the clay oven.

Prices: *R150 pp, booking absolutely essential for lunch from 12.30pm and dinner from 6.30pm.*
Contact: *5km south of Lambert's Bay*
Tel: *027-432-1017*
muisbosskerm@kingsley.co.za
www.muisbosskerm.co.za

LAMBERT'S BAY
NATURE and ACTIVITIES

Bird Island

The legacy of guano farming, this is the noisiest and smelliest bird-watching you can possibly imagine - but it's a must-see. The island's 3ha are one of only six sites in the world where Cape gannets breed and there are literally thousands and thousands of birds flapping about, performing their odd mating dance and generally making the most astonishing racket. Information boards tell you all about the island and there's a two-way mirror for close-up inspection. Seals, cormorants and 60 penguins also occupy the island... only slightly outnumbered then.

Prices: *Adults R15, kids R7, no booking necessary. Open every day.*
Contact: *Opposite the harbour, Lambert's Bay.*
Tel: *072-133-1440*
www.capenature.org.za

BIRDING BITS

You will see: Southern Black Korhaan, Cape Francolin

You'll be very lucky to see: Protea Canary, Cape Penduline Tit

You might see: Black Harrier, Grey-winged Francolin

Eyes peeled around Aurora and Clanwilliam.

Cape Winelands

For sophisticates - like myself - who have come to expect the finer things in life, the Cape Winelands are the only place to go. They cover a relatively small area of verdant valleys and vertical mountains that spring up out of the sea on the far side of the Cape Flats, about an hour east of Cape Town. Centred around the towns of Stellenbosch, Franschhoek, Paarl, Wellington, Worcester and Robertson, this is the heart of the South African wine industry, encompassing more than 200 wine farms. And where there is wine there is food.... You will also find the best of a myriad of excellent restaurants in this chapter. My spirits were regularly raised in the Winelands (at the expense of my liver) on return stop-offs from long journeys into the hinterland.

Like the wine it's a region best savoured rather than knocked off in a day trip from Cape Town. Allow yourself time not only for the food and wine but also for the landscape itself. There are dramatic individual mountains such as the Simonsberg and the Helderberg, which dominate the surrounding area. And several ranges of mountains make for great walking and birding and there are plenty of well-mapped footpaths available for burning off any overindulgence. Alternatively, make the most of the views by driving to the top of the Franschhoek or Bainskloof passes.

Teetotallers come for the history. The Winelands became one of the early beneficiaries of an expanding Cape Colony when Cape Governor Simon van der Stel first ventured here in the 1670s, modestly dubbing the area Van der Stel's Bush (which became Stellenbosch). Today there's a grand old gabled Cape Dutch house at every turn (of which more later) and many of these now operate as guest-houses.

cape winelands

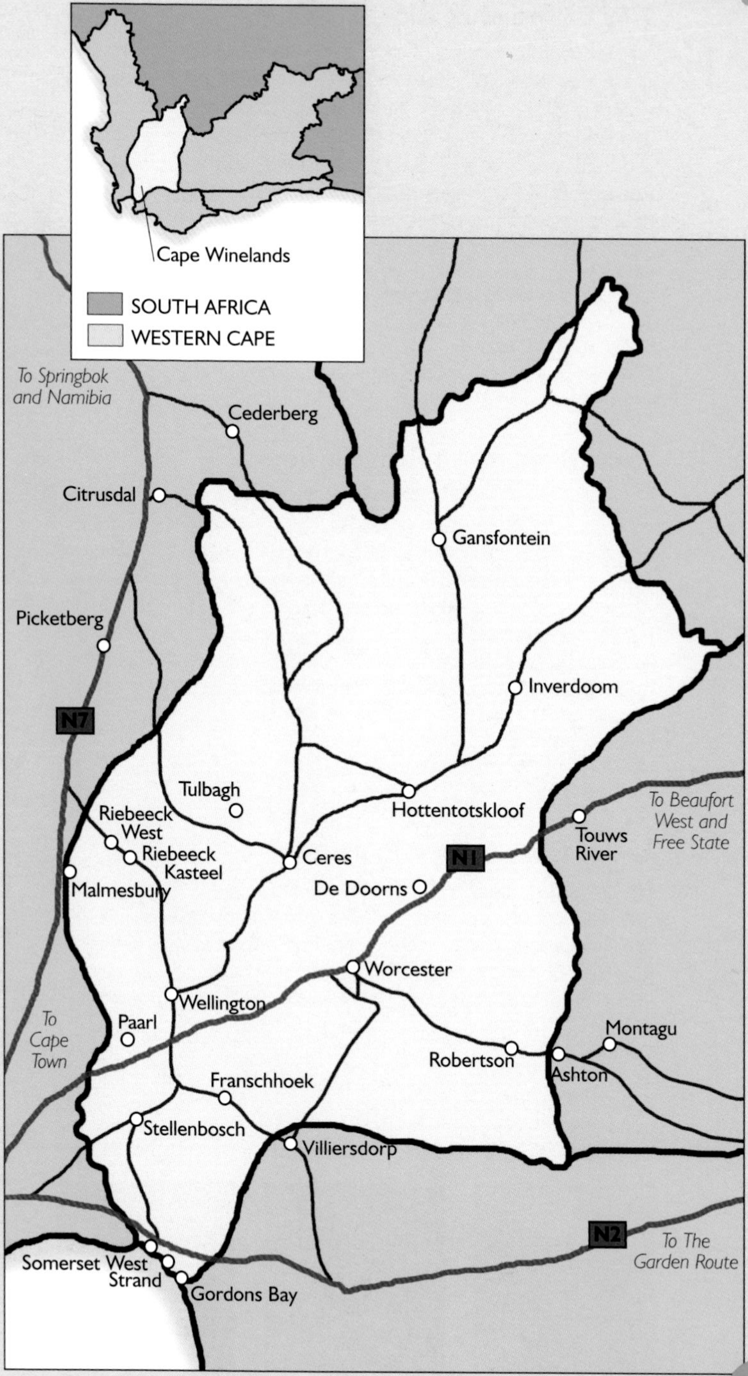
Cape Winelands
SOUTH AFRICA
WESTERN CAPE
To Springbok and Namibia
Cederberg
Citrusdal
Gansfontein
Picketberg
Inverdoom
N7
Tulbagh
Riebeeck West
Riebeeck Kasteel
Hottentotskloof
To Beaufort West and Free State
Touws River
Ceres
N1
Malmesbury
De Doorns
Worcester
Wellington
To Cape Town
Paarl
Montagu
Robertson
Ashton
Franschhoek
Stellenbosch
Villiersdorp
N2
To The Garden Route
Somerset West
Strand
Gordons Bay

GUIDES AND EXPERTS
GENERAL

Nini Bairnsfather Cloete

Nini (also in our accommodation guide) organises private visits to some of the most beautiful houses and gardens in the Cape, including select wineries, artists' studios and thoroughbred stud farms. Meet the owners, taste and talk wine, chat about gardens and history, admire architecture and furniture... and maybe even learn a thing or two as well!

Prices: *From roughly R400 pp per day for a maximum of 8 people to R850 pp per day for 2 people incl transport in an air-conditioned vehicle, guide, private visits, wine tastings and sometimes a light lunch. Complete holiday itineraries can also be arranged.*

Contact: *Longfield House, Eikendal Road, off R44, Somerset West.*
Tel: *021-855-4224*
Cell: *082-365-7554*
ninicloete@longfield.co.za or ninicloete@iafrica.com
www.longfield.co.za

Johan Barnard, La Rochelle Tours

"Yes, yes, yes" all over the place for this tour team who offer specialist wine tours for up to seven people. They're Cape-Wine-Academy-educated and tours include all entrance and tasting fees. Whale trips, Garden Route, Cape Point and Cape Town city tours also available. Accommodation and airport transfers can be arranged.

Prices: *Day tour rates from R395 pp. Day safari rates from R990 pp incl lunch and a game drive. Garden Route Tours from R4,950 pp all incl to R7,900 pp for a Garden Route and Big 5 Safari Tour. Airport transfers from R195 per trip.*

Contact: *Johan Barnard*
Tel: *083-301-6774*
info@larochelletours.com
www.larochelletours.com

Lesley Cox, Amber Tours

Lesley is a tour guide who pulls out all the stops and, as a Winelands specialist, lots of corks too. She'll take you to wineries well away from the crowds and, in fact, anywhere in the Western Cape, tailoring trips to your particular interests.

Prices: *Private tours costs R1,400 incl transport, excludes lunch and nominal tasting fees.*

Contact: *Lesley Cox*
Tel: *021-552-2137*
Cell: *083-448-7016*
ambertours@wol.co.za
www.ambertours.co.za

Gudrun Grünewald, Happy Holidays

"She's amazing," GG B&B owner Tanya Louw says of Gudrun, whose daily wine tours take you off the beaten track (just what we like) to the smaller, more boutique wine farms for tastings and tours with plenty of great scenery and history thrown in too. Cape Town and extended Garden Route trips available too.

Prices: *Wine tours from R300 pp, Cape Town from R350 and Garden Route from R5,500 for a four-day trip.*
Contact: *Gudrun Grünewald*
Tel: *021-876-2160*
Cell: *082-699-3098*
happyholiday@adept.co.za
www.happyholiday.co.za

ACTIVITIES

Judy Elliott, Winescape Tours

For those of you that enjoy the finer things in life, take Judy's three-day, guided walk through the Wellington winelands, olive groves and fynbos. Includes three nights' accommodation on historic Huguenot farms, great wine and olive tastings and gourmet dinners galore… go on, spoil yourself.

Prices: *Walks can be tailor-made and prices vary according to group size, current guest-house and guide rates. Bookings of three to four couples preferred. All luggage transported for you.*
Contact: *Judy Elliott*
Cell: *083-313-8383*
judy@winescapetours.co.za
www.winescapetours.co.za

Shaun Ranwell, Winelands Golf Tours

One of our tipsters "can definitely recommend Winelands Golf Tours above everything"! Shaun and Sean (yes, that's right) love golf and can organise your rounds at the best clubs in the Cape. Once you're golfed out (a meaningless concept for golf addicts, I realise), they can sort you out with everything from heli flips to wine courses and Robben Island tours. Check out their website's 101 reasons to visit!

Prices: *Vary depending on tour so best to ask them yourselves. Half-day wine experience from R350 (R550 for full-day incl introductory wine course). Airport transfers about R400, dinner transfers about R100.*
Contact: *Shop 19A, La Gare Centre, Huguenot St, Franschhoek.*
Tel: *021-876-4042*
info@winelandsgolftours.co.za
www.winelandsgolftours.com

SOMERSET WEST
EATING and DRINKING

96 Winery Road

A buzzing eatery with great views of the Helderberg and Table Mountain. Wooden furniture and walls hung with farm tools. Carnivores will crave the platter of beef cuts, presented for inspection and grilled with your choice of gourmet sauces. Calorie Corner offers indulgent chocolate and apple crumble and you can choose wines from a walk-in cellar (bookable for parties).

Prices: *3-course meal around R150 incl wine and tip.*
Contact: *96 Winery Road, Zandberg Farm, Helderview.*
Tel: *021-842-2020*
wineryrd@mweb.co.za
www.96wineryroad.co.za

Al Forno Pizzeria

Small but bubbly Italian that overlooks the bay and will stuff you with enough antipasti, pizza, pasta and Parma ham to last you for weeks. The set menu is a good deal and relieves the ditherers of any decision-making.

Prices: *Set menu of starter, main course and dessert for R160.*
Contact: *35 Beach Road, Gordon's Bay.*
Tel: *021-856-4021*

L'Auberge du Paysan

Oozing French chic and Provençale flavours, L'Auberge is set deep among the vines. Frederick (a great man) is at the helm and many of his ingredients are fresh from the farm garden alongside a Pinotage from its vineyard. "Cape crayfish bisque, grilled lamb medallions, French crêpe flamed with brandy"... ahh, mon dieu, c'est bon!

Prices: *3-course meal for around R280 plus drinks and a 10% service charge.*
Contact: *Raithby Rd, off the R44 between Somerset West and Stellenbosch.*
Tel: *021-842-2008*
www.aubergedupaysan.co.za

SOMERSET WEST
NATURE and ACTIVITIES

Helderbräu Brewery

A German brewery through and through from the 100% natural German beers to the legendary home-made apple strudels and Schnapps. Cellar tours, beer tasting and private parties all encouraged. Restaurant and bar serving up German and South African food is only open on certain days, so call ahead for current details.

Prices: *From R20 for bar snacks and light meals, lunches/dinners R45 - R70. Pub sells home-brewed beers at R9 - R14 per glass, wines from R45 a bottle and spirits and schnapps usually about R10 per shot.*
Contact: *Mondeor Road, off N2, Somerset West.*
Tel: *021-858-1309*
brewery@telkomsa.net
www.helderbrau.co.za

Hikes around Somerset West and Gordon's Bay 

Give Brian Zeller a call (number below) for accompanied hikes in the Gordon's Bay area. He's a great bloke and flora and fauna fundi who's equally happy to talk politics and history. Otherwise, you can do these walks independently by buying a R10 permit from the Somerset West Municipality before you go (open 8am - 4pm).

- **Gordon's Bay and Danie Miller hike**

A 3km walk through the old village and harbour of Gordon's Bay to the "Whale Watch", followed by a 3km return hike contouring around the mountain on the Danie Miller trail above Gordon's Bay. Exertion: easy to medium.

- **The Steenbras Kloof or Crystal Pools hike**

(4km out of Gordon's Bay en route to Rooi Else)
Hike up the Steenbras Kloof to rock pools and waterfalls. Great views for nature-loving photographers. Return the same route. Takes 2.5 hrs up and 1.5 hrs return, plus any time needed to swim or rest beside the pools. Exertion is medium.

Prices: *Brian charges up to R60 per hour pp (max 6) plus transport costs if needed. Can do Table Mountain trips too.*
Contact: *Call Brian on 021-851-9639 or 082-922-0819. Or visit Somerset West Municipality, ground floor, cnr Andries and Victoria St, Somerset West.*
Tel: *021-850-4521/4311/4441*

Sir Lowry's Pass

You will inevitably take this pass as you head east along the N2, bound for the Garden Route and Eastern Cape. There tends to be a lot of traffic on it, but there's a great (if windy) stop-off point on the top from which you can look over Gordon's Bay and Somerset West, right across False Bay to the back of Table Mountain.

STELLENBOSCH
EATING and DRINKING

Auberge Rozendal

A bio-dynamic farm with working winery, home-grown veggies, cows and happy chickens clucking around its guesthouse. The restaurant sources organic ingredients from the surrounding area producing a simple, high-quality set menu that varies day to day depending on what is freshly available. A very homely atmosphere.

Prices: *3-course menu R130, 4-course menu R150 (may vary by R10). Wines from R60 - R450.*

Contact: *Jonkershoek Valley, Omega Road, Stellenbosch.*

Tel: *021-809-2600*

rozendal@mweb.co.za

www.rozendal.co.za

Cotage Fromage

A thatched cottage at the entrance to Vrede-en-Lust winery, Cotage Fromage (*sic* spelling) is the perfect spot to start or end a day in the Winelands. Man-stopping cooked breakfasts and meaty main meals, savoury pancakes and excellent cheese boards. Eat by the fireside in winter or under the oak trees in summer. Deli products, gifts and pre-order picnic hampers are also available. Open every day 9am - 6pm Dec - Apr, 9am - 5pm May - Nov.

Prices: *Light meals and salads R20 - R50, main meals R50 - R70. Wines R40 - R80.*

Contact: *Vrede-en-Lust Farm, Klapmuts Rd, Simondium.*

Tel: *021-874-8155*

cotage@vnl.co.za

www.vnl.co.za

Fishmonger

"The best food for miles around and utterly unpretentious," sings one happy diner. Fishmonger is a bustling al fresco taverna deep in the Winelands. A great place to enjoy stacks of the freshest seafood, including sushi. Wine list showcases local producers and changes seasonally. Open Mon - Sun 12pm - 10pm. Closed Christmas Day, Boxing Day, New Year's Day and Good Friday.

Prices: *Specialities including seafood thermidor, stuffed kingklip and line fish from R50 - R82. Seafood platters and combos from R60 - R220. Seafood curries, oven bakes, grills and shellfish also available. R7.50 corkage if more than one bottle per couple. Prices increase 10% annually.*

Contact: *Cnr Ryneveld and Plein St, Stellenbosch.*

Tel: *021-887-7835*

fishmonger@adept.co.za

www.fishmonger.co.za

STELLENBOSCH
WINERIES

Cowlin Wines

A kids- (and adults-) friendly winery on a 29-hectare estate. Aside from the usual tastings the Cowlins serve up cracking salmon-stuffed picnic hampers too for feasts on the verandah or umbrella-shaded parties on the lawn, next to the dam. Jungle gym, sandpit and fishing rods will keep the small ones well entertained.

Prices: *White and red wines R30 - R64. Salmon platter for two (incl hot and cold smoked salmon, gravadlax and pâté) around R70, 4 deli meats R55, chicken, cheese and deli or veg platters R40 - R60. Tastings R10.*
Contact: *Klapmuts turning off N1, Simondium.*
Tel: *021-874-3844*
cowlinwines@iafrica.com
www.cowlinwines.com

Dornier Wines

"An absolute must," chant Dornier fans. A real break from the norm, Dornier is a family-owned winery housed in a super-modern face brick and glass creation (not surprising that Christoph Dornier is an artist). A restaurant is planned for 2006. Open Mon - Fri 10am - 4.30pm, Sat 10.30am - 3pm.

Prices: *Wines R65 - R150 per bottle.*
Contact: *Blaauwklippen Rd, off R44, Stellenbosch.*
Tel: *021-880-0557*
visit@dornierwines.co.za
www.dornierwines.co.za

Kaapzicht

"A wine estate for true wine lovers". With four Steytlers hard at work, this is truly a family business. Off the beaten track, with stunning views back to Table Mountain, they've won wine medals galore and are open Mon - Fri 9am - 4.30pm, Sat 9am - 12pm.

Prices: *R10 for tastings (free when you buy wine), wines cost R26 - R150. Cellar tours by appointment.*
Contact: *Steytdal Farm, Bottelary Road, nr Stellenbosch.*
Tel: *021-906-1620*
exports@kaapzicht-wines.com
www.kaapzicht-wines.com

STELLENBOSCH WINERIES

Muratie

"Even the cobwebs here are 300 years old," says Nini Bairnsfather Cloete (see Somerset West). Soak up the history wandering through the farm and garden. Pre-booked picnic baskets soon available and worth spending a little extra for a private tasting with cheese and biscuits. Open Mon - Fri 9am - 5pm, Sat - Sun 10am - 4pm.

Prices: *Tastings R10 - R15 or R35 pp for private tasting.*
Contact: *Knorhoek Rd, Off R44 about 10km from Stellenbosch.*
Tel: *021-865-2330*
muratie@kingsley.co.za
www.muratie.co.za

Overgaauw

Set on the hillside west of Stellenbosch, the farm has been in the family since 1783 and the latest generation of van Veldens oversee informal Overgaauw wine tastings. Phone ahead for a tour of their ancient cellars. Hunt out the green pepper, lime and asparagus aromas in their Sauvignon Blanc.

Prices: *Cellar tours by appointment, R10 for tastings.*
Contact: *Stellenbosch Kloof Rd, Vlottenberg.*
Tel: *021-881-3815*
info@overgaauw.co.za
www.ovegaauw.co.za

Rustenberg

The Barlows don't encourage bus-loads of visitors, and are instead a favourite among wine connoisseurs and keen amateurs. This is one of the oldest wine farms in the Cape (founded in 1682) with beautiful gardens to stroll through and an equally eye-catching herd of Jersey cows.

Prices: *Wines R45 - R360 per bottle. Tastings and tours are free.*
Contact: *Rustenberg Road, Idas Valley, Stellenbosch.*
Tel: *021-809-1200*
wine@rustenberg.co.za
www.rustenberg.co.za

Rust en Vrede

Red wine lovers should make a beeline for this family-owned estate, the first in S.A. to specialise in red wine only (which was served at Nelson Mandela's Nobel Peace Prize banquet). Classic Cape Dutch buildings dating to 1789 are set in beautiful gardens and well worth a look.

Prices: *Cellar tours by appointment, wine tasting free, though R30 pp for groups of 10-15 (max).*
Contact: *Annandale Rd, Stellenbosch.*
Tel: *021-881-3881*
info@rustenvrede.com
www.rustenvrede.com

Thelema Mountain Vineyards

A family-owned and -run winery on the slopes of the Simonsberg just outside Stellenbosch, it's one of the highest (and so coolest) wine farms in the area. Tastings are free and relaxed and everyone's welcome though, regretfully, no pets... "Ours get jealous." Open Mon - Fri 9am - 5pm, Sat 9am - 1pm. Closed on public hols.

Prices: *Red and white wines about R30 - R250.*
Contact: *R310 to Franschhoek, on Helshoogte Pass, 5km from Stellenbosch.*
Tel: *021-885-1924*
barbara@thelema.co.za
www.thelema.co.za

Villiera

Cousins Jeff and Simon Grier began making wine in the 1970s and theirs is one of the larger private wineries, though very much a family business where value for money and environmental awareness rule. The cellars are modern and you can take yourself on a great self-guided tour from Mon - Fri 8.30am - 5pm, Sat 8.30am - 1pm.

Prices: *Whites R24 - R53, reds R29.50 - R80, bottle-fermented sparkling wines R47.50 - R63.50. Free tastings.*
Contact: *Villiera Wines, cnr R304 and R101, Koelenhof, Stellenbosch.*
Tel: *021-865-2002*
wine@villiera.com
www.villiera.com

Warwick Wine Estate

Named after the Warwick regiment in the Anglo-Boer war the winery was founded by Colonel Gordon (of Gordon's Bay fame) and regimented lines of vines produce wines drunk the world over. Soak up some history and sample "Three Cape Ladies" and "Professor Black" under the oak trees. Open Mon - Fri 10am - 5pm, 10am - 4pm Sat.

Prices: *Wines R65 - R120 a bottle. R10 for tastings. No cellar tours.*
Contact: *On R44, 10km from Stellenbosch.*
Tel: *021-884-4410*
cellarinfo@warwickwine.co.za
www.warwickwine.com

Waterford Estate

Famed for its classic reds and wine and chocolate tasting. Belgian delights from chocolatier Richard Von Gesau (see Greyton, Overberg) are intimately matched to the wines. Try Waterford Chardonnay with Lemon Vanilla Milk Chocolate... it's to die for. Free tours on an ad hoc basis.

Prices: *Reds R45 - R120, white R35 - R70.*
Contact: *Blaauwklippen Rd, off R44, Stellenbosch.*
Tel: *021-880-0496*
info@waterfordestate.co.za
www.waterfordwines.com

STELLENBOSCH
NATURE and ACTIVITIES

Stellenbosch University Botanical Garden

The oldest university botanical garden in S.A. with an immense diversity of indigenous and exotic plant life concentrated within 2ha. Aquatics from the Amazon, tropical orchids, insectivores from Borneo, Puya from Chile, Mexican cacti, euphorbias and stapelias from the Karoo… the list goes on and the visitors love it.

Prices: *Free entry, garden brochure R20, garden map R2, garden T-shirts and postcards available. Restaurant and Biobuild garden shop on premises. Open 8am - 5pm every day.*

Contact: *Cnr of van Riebeeck and Neethling Sts, Stellenbosch.*

Tel: *021-808-3054*

vjc@sun.ac.za

www.academic.sun.ac.za/botany/garden.html

Schoonzicht Homestead and Garden

With husband Simon i/c wine (see Rustenberg winery), Rozanne Barlow has created a fabulous garden, which - not excluding butterflies, birds, bees and squirrels - houses a Chartres-style labyrinth and a 25m koi fishpond. Suck in the scents, walk the labyrinth or simply take a rest on oak-shaded benches.

Prices: *Free entry and free wine tasting and tours at Rustenberg.*

Contact: *Rustenberg Road, Idas Valley, Stellenbosch.*

Tel: *021-809-1200*

wine@rustenberg.co.za

www.rustenberg.co.za

Butterfly World

A covered park, showcasing tropical butterflies from Asia, Central America and Africa. Great for kids with other attractions including free-ranging iguanas, marmosets and birds. Plenty of exotic and local spiders, scorpions and other insects to make the little ones squirm. Open every day.

Prices: *Adults R28.50, children R15, pensioners and students R22. A family of two adults and two children pay R70. Group fees are available.*

Contact: *Exit 47 off N1, signed R44 Paarl, Klapmuts, Stellenbosch.*

Tel: *021-875-5628*

esther@yebo.co.za

FRANSCHHOEK
EATING and DRINKING

Delicious

The undisputed local's choice for cool food, hot gossip and the best breakfast in town. Don't miss out on the sticky buns and great salads. Open 7am - 5pm and (for those in the know) for dinner on Wednesdays.

Prices: *Breakfast from R30, paninis R30, sticky buns R10, cake of the day R15 - R20, picnics by arrangement.*
Contact: *38 Huguenot Rd, Franschhoek.*
Tel: *021-876-4004*
www.lqf.co.za

Haute Cabrière Restaurant

Freshest South African ingredients matched seamlessly with Cabrière cellar estate wines - why not combine some food with a cellar tour? Set into the mountainside with a cracking view out over the valley. No starters or mains, just small and large portions of everything.

Prices: *Small portions R40 - R58, large R55 - R100, desserts R26 - R38.*
Contact: *Franschhoek Pass Road, Franschhoek.*
Tel: *021-876-3688*
hautecab@iafrica.com
www.hautecabriere.com

Bouillabaisse Seafood Restaurant and Deli

Visit on an empty stomach and prepare for Camil's nine-course bonanza of the hautest of haute cuisine served with friendly informality. Guests experience "front-cooking", which means the kitchen is based in the restaurant and guests watch the chefs at work while they enjoy seafood taster dishes and wines and champagne by the glass.

Prices: *Serve only a set menu at R295 pp. The 9-course dinner lasts from 7.30pm - 11.00 pm. The 5-course wine selection costs R160 (or choose from the wine list).*
Contact: *38 Huguenot Rd, Franschhoek.*
Tel: 021-876-4430
info@kleinoliphantshoek.com
www.kleinoliphantshoek.com

La Fromagerie

"Stonking restaurant where cheese meets antiques meets great food." The restaurant and shop is set in a 200-year-old barn with a cheese-ophile menu. Eat inside or outside to make the most of the mountain views. Don't miss "Jazz on a Friday" (5.30pm - 8.30pm) with the La Fromagerie Jazz Band. Host Derk sometimes plays the piano at lunchtime too.

Prices: *Cheese tasting R20, starters R45, mains around R70, wines R40 - R120.*
Contact: *13 Daniel Hugo St, Franschhoek.*
Tel: *021-876-2155*
info@lagrange.co.za
www.lagrange.co.za

La Petite Ferme

Dendy-Young family hands combine to run this boutique winery and fantastic restaurant. Wine-maker Mark is often on hand to explain the wine list while you thumb through the menu and soak up the mountain views. If in doubt, opt for the insider's favourite: de-boned, oak-smoked rainbow trout.

Prices: *3-course lunch around R150.*
Contact: *Franschhoek Pass Road, Franschhoek.*
Tel: *021-876-3016*
lapetite@iafrica.com
www.lapetiteferme.co.za

Le Bon Vivant

People from all over the country sing chef/patron Pierre Hendriks' praises. He specialises in European cuisine presented in true gourmet style. For the adventurous the 5-course surprise will guarantee a great food and wine experience. Try and get a table outside when the weather's good enough (that'd be most of the year then...).

Prices: *Starters R30 - R60, mains R58 - R85, surprise menu R250 incl wine or R185 without.*
Contact: *22 Dirkie Uys St, Franschhoek.*
Tel: *021-876-2717*
lebonvivant@mweb.co.za

Reubens Restaurant

"Reuben was just voted the best chef in S.A. yet a nicer, more friendly place you couldn't find," says one Greenwood stalwart. "Wonderful food, nice dog," says another fan. Reuben has worked all over the place and hones all his skills in both classic and contemporary food.

Prices: *Starters R38 - R46, mains R68 - R98, desserts R35 - R45.*
Contact: *19 Huguenot Street, Franschhoek.*
Tel: *021 876 3772*
reubens@mweb.co.za

The French Connection Bistro

More informal than the fantastic Haute Cabrière (which owner/chef Matthew Gordon also runs) this French bistro serves the best aged steaks, fresh fish, mussels and unbeatable fries, all with classic French sauces. Open 12pm - 3.30pm and 6.30pm - 9.30pm every day, booking essential.

Prices: *Starters R26 - R40, mains R38 - R84, desserts R26 - R38.*
Contact: *48 Huguenot St, Franschhoek.*
Tel: *021-876-4056*
french@worldonline.co.za

Topsi and Co.

"I cook and we care about our guests," Topsi tells me - summing up her much-loved eatery in a nutshell. She is a culinary legend in these parts and her restaurant an eclectic and hectic spot. Watch her cooking from your table before devouring heaped salads, fantastic fish and cracking crumbles. Ask about the parrot.

Prices: *Starters R28 - R46, mains R48 - R95. Bring your own wine.*
Contact: *7 Reservoir St West, Franschhoek.*
Tel: *021-876-2952*

FRANSCHHOEK
WINERIES

Boschendal

One of the best-known wineries, recommended particularly for its country-fare-stuffed picnic hampers available through the summer for scoffing in the shade pre- or post-wine-tasting. As well as vineyard tours (Nov - Apr) and cellar visits (May - Oct), you can take tours of the 19th-century manor house, a classic example of Cape Dutch architecture and now a museum.

Prices: *Picnic hampers (Oct - May weather permitting) from Le Pique Nique R95 per adult, R59 per child under 10. Booking essential, collection 12.15pm - 1.30pm. Buffet lunch at Boschendal restaurant R195 pp, dress smart casual, booking essential. Light lunches and tea available at Le Café, no bookings taken.*
Contact: *Boschendal Farm, Pniel Rd, Groot Drakenstein.*
Le Pique Nique Tel: 021-870-4272/3/4/5
Boschendal Restaurant Tel: 021-870-4272/3/4/5
Le Café Tel: *021-870-4282/3*
reservations@boschendal.com
www.boschendal.com

La Motte

One for the culture vultures. Not only can you guzzle great wine here, but they also put on much-lauded classical concerts in the cellar once a month (definitely book, wine and snacks included). Light lunches also available in the seasonal restaurant.

Prices: *Concerts R100 incl wine and snacks. R10 for wine tasting. Prices may increase.*
Contact: *On R43 5km outside Franschhoek.*
Tel: *021-876-3119*
cellar@la-motte.co.za
www.la-motte.com

Môreson Wine Farm and Bread and Wine Restaurant

Môreson is a must for the annual Harvest Festival, usually the last weekend of Feb. Book early and you can hand-pick the grapes and then press them with your feet. Suitably juice-stained, head on to Bread and Wine for slap-up Mediterranean grub. The restaurant is a local favourite open for lunch only from Sept - Mar, Weds - Sun, and from Mar - July Fri - Sun. Closed July 18th to Aug 18th.

Prices: *Harvest festival tickets cost around R200 pp incl food and wine. Môreson white wines R20 - R60, red wines R40 - R110. 3 courses (try twice-baked goats' feta soufflé or pan-fried quail) at Bread and Wine cost around R130 without wine.*
Contact: *Môreson Wine Farm, La Motte, Happy Valley Road, Franschhoek.*
Tel: *021-876-3055 (for restaurant bookings too)*
sales@moreson.co.za
breadandwine@moreson.co.za
www.moreson.co.za

Wine-growing in the Winelands

South Africa is a huge place, but very little of it is suitable vine-growing country. Fortunately the Cape's first Dutch governor, Jan van Riebeeck, picked the right spot when he planted the first vineyard in 1655, and his wine-loving successor Simon van der Stel made good wine from the outset on his Constantia farm on the back of Table Mountain. But the Dutch weren't the greatest of vintners and it was only after the French Huguenots brought their savoir-faire to the Cape between 1680 and 1690 that the wine industry really flourished. As religious refugees, the Huguenots were very short on cash and had to adapt their established wine-making techniques to new conditions. But in time they honed their skills and left a permanent stamp on the industry, which today employs about 257,000 people. The name Franschhoek, meaning French corner, says it all.

Stony Brook

Doctor and former teacher Nigel and Joy McNaught have just 14 hectares under vines and make all the wine themselves on site. They are charming hosts and offer tastings on a tree-shaded verandah (weather permitting) every morning bar Sunday. Afternoons are very busy, but phone ahead and they can generally make a plan.
Prices: *Tastings are R10 pp, with no charge if you purchase a case of wine. Whites for around R40 a bottle, reds R40 - R70, special red aged in new French oak R100.*
Contact: *Stony Brook Wine Farm, Green Valley Road, Franschhoek.*
Tel: *021-876-2182*
info@stonybrook.co.za

FRANSCHHOEK
CULTURE and HISTORY

Bastille Festival

Franschhoek's French heritage is celebrated in this annual festival held on the weekend closest to July 14th each year. Expect plenty of berets, pétanque, music and merriment - plus, of course, good food and wine galore. Book accommodation in advance.
Contact: *Franschhoek Tourist Office, 28a Huguenot Rd, Franschhoek.*
Tel: *021-876-3603*
info@franschhoek.org.za
www.franschhoek.org.za/bastillefestival

Franschhoek Conservation Trust

The trust works for the protection of the Franschhoek valley, its surrounding wetlands and its historic buildings, offering monthly tours of historic venues often otherwise closed to the public. It also organises talks at the village museum, which it runs. Digest all that history with a snack in the tea garden.
Prices: *R5 entry to village museum, which goes to the trust.*
Contact: *Shirley Parkfelt*
Tel: *021-876-2691/4306*
smparkfelt@solvit.co.za

La Motte Classical Concerts

Monthly classical cellar concerts at La Motte winery.
See Franschhoek Wineries.

Music Revival

Chris Duigan of Music Revival in KZN runs two classical music festivals in Franschhoek, at the end of Apr and end of Oct. See KwaZulu Natal, Pietermaritzburg Culture and History.

FRANSCHHOEK
NATURE and ACTIVITIES

Franschhoek Pass Drive and Walks 

• A very windy drive up the pass will reward you with a stunning view over Franschhoek. Buy a R10 permit from the tourist office below first, and you can park the car at the top and hike the Cat se Pad trail.
• The Mont Rochelle Nature Reserve also has great trails. Walk to Breakfast Rock for the best view back to Table Mountain.
• The trail to the top of Du Toits Kop is one for the more adventurous. Ask in the tourist office for permits, maps and details.

Contact: *Franschhoek Tourist Office, 28a Huguenot Rd, Franschhoek.*
Tel: *021-876-3603*
info@franschhoek.org.za
www.franschhoek.org.za

Paradise Stables

Wine-tasting on horseback… the only way to travel. Pieter Hugo leads you on a four-hour trail via two wineries on pure-bred Arabian horses, stopping for half an hour or so at each. Other horse trails are also available and we'd suggest taking a picnic too to really make a trip of it.

Prices: *R350 pp for wine-tasting trip or R100 per hour for riding.*
Contact: *Pieter and Sterna Hugo, Robertsvlei Road, Franschhoek.*
Tel: *021-876-2160*
www.paradisestables.co.za

Para-pax - tandem paragliding flights

See Cape Town Activities Guides.

PAARL
EATING and DRINKING

De Malle Madonna

An owner-run bistro in an historic homestead built in 1837. It has Chagall prints on the walls and is always brimming with locals, in for breakfast, lunch or supper. Grub-wise it's comfort foods with a difference and country cuisine with a Mediterranean flair. Open Weds - Sun 8.30am - 5.30pm and Weds and Sun evenings.

Prices: *Light meals R40 - R50. Hearty meal with a glass of Paarl wine R80 - R100.*
Contact: *127 Main Road, Paarl.*
Tel: *021-863-3925*
mallemadonna@operamail.com

Fairview Wine and Cheese Estate

Award-winning cheeses and wines produced and sold on the farm. Eat and drink them there and then at the "Goatshed" where a variety of fresh-baked breads complement cheeses, farm salads, quiches, desserts and wines. "Delicious and simple food, a lovely atmosphere… and a great black empowerment project."

Prices: *Simple meals for about R45 pp. About R25 for a 200ml carafe of wine.*
Contact: *Fairview Wine and Cheese Estate, Suid Agter Paarl Road, District Paarl.*
Tel: *021-863-2450*
info@fairview.co.za
www.fairview.co.za

Marc's Mediterranean Cuisine and Garden

"Paarl is known for its hot summers and we concentrate on fresh, imaginative ideas for salads, pasta, risotto and cheese platters," says Marc. He lives for wine and is i/c bread-making in his restaurant. It's Provençale all over with comfortable couches, Oregon pine tables and a garden of herb borders and lemon trees. Our tip: save space for a killer chocolate mousse. Open 12pm - 2.30pm and 6.30pm - 9.30pm.

Prices: *Mezze platters and starters R30 - R50, mains R50 - R90, desserts R30 - R40.*
Contact: *129 Main Rd, Paarl.*
Tel: *021-863-3980*
chezmarc@mweb.co.za

Seidelberg

Up on the south-western slopes of Paarl Mountain, this wine farm has one of the most scenic views of the Winelands and Table Mountain, best enjoyed over lunch from its restaurant terrace under 300-year-old oaks. Save time to see the Red Hot Glass studio here too, where artists Liz and David use traditional Venetian glass-blowing methods to create some seriously whacky creations.

Prices: *R12 for 6-wine tasting, R18 for tasting and cellar tour, open all day every day. Restaurant open for lunch 11am - 5pm. Picnic baskets available in spring and summer.*
Contact: *Suid Agter Paarl Rd, off N1 at exit 47, Suider-Paarl.*
Tel: *021-863-5200*
Restaurant bookings: 021-863-5222
info@seidelberg.co.za
www.seidelberg.co.za

Wilderer's Distillery and Restaurant

If you're craving the hard stuff, Wilderer's is the place to go. It's a small, private distillery where you can watch the Wilderers at work producing Grappa and Eau de Vie. On-site eatery specialises in Flammkuchen with great thin-crust, French-style pizzas. Book in for the live jazz, first Sunday of every month.

Prices: *Grappa R120 - R210 for 500ml bottle, lunch dishes R20 - R38.*
Contact: *3 km from Paarl on R45 to Franschhoek.*
Tel: *021-863-3555*
info@wilderer.co.za
www.wilderer.co.za

PAARL
NATURE and ACTIVITIES

Paarl Golf Club

A gem of a course set in the heart of the Winelands. 27 holes with bent grass greens, lush fairways and a blend of parkland and links-like golf that will challenge any handicap. Golf carts, caddies, full driving-range, short game area, bar and food all available.

Prices: *Visitors can expect to pay R300 for a round of golf.*
Contact: *Wemmershoek Road, off N1 as you enter Paarl (2nd Paarl exit).*
Tel: *021-863-2828*
bookings@paarlgolfclub.co.za
www.paarlgolfclub.co.za

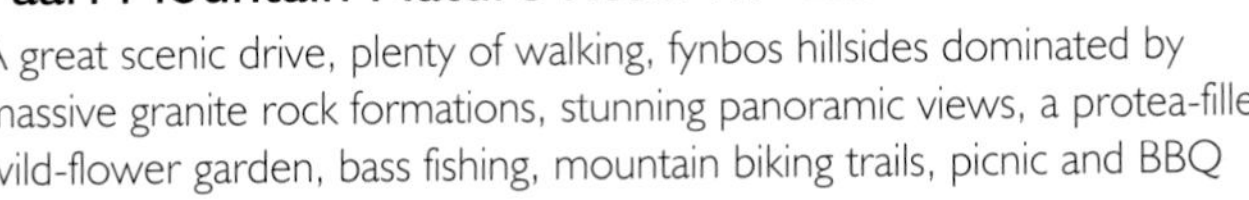

Paarl Mountain Nature Reserve

A great scenic drive, plenty of walking, fynbos hillsides dominated by massive granite rock formations, stunning panoramic views, a protea-filled wild-flower garden, bass fishing, mountain biking trails, picnic and BBQ spots....

Prices: *Nominal entry fee, fishing permits cost R8 for the week and can be bought from Paarl municipality. Open all day every day.*
Contact: *10km out of Paarl on Jan Philllips Drive (turn left off Main Rd). For permits and more information contact Albert van de Merwe, Paarl Municipality, cnr Bergriver Boulevard and Market St, Paarl.*
Tel: *021-807-4500*

Paarl Bird Sanctuary

Set around the sewage works, this may sound horrific, but it's actually a fantastic bird sanctuary run by volunteers who have set up three hides for keen birders, linked by a 3km route.

Prices: *Entry is free and the sanctuary is open all day every day.*

Contact: *On Drommedaris St, between Wellington and Paarl.*
For any more information contact Albert van de Merwe, Paarl Municipality, cnr Bergriver Boulevard and Market St, Paarl.

Tel: *021-807-4500*

> **Vaguely interesting fact**
>
> Paarl Rock is the second largest granite outcrop in the world after Australia's Uluru (or Ayers Rock).

WELLINGTON

EATING and DRINKING

Diemersfontein Wine and Country Estate

By the time you've tasted the wine, ridden the horses and taken a tractor ride through the Diemersfontein vineyards you'll be very much ready for an à la carte Seasons menu of warm duck salad, seared smoked trout and other delights. A whole day here slips down as easily as the wine.

Prices: *Starters about R30, mains R50 - R70, desserts about R30. Wine tasting (Mon - Sun 10am - 5pm) R15, cellar tours R15, horse-riding R100 per hour, tractor ride R35 incl glass of wine.*

Contact: *Off R301, just outside Wellington.*

Tel: *021-864-5050*

hospitality@diemersfontein.co.za

www.diemersfontein.co.za

Nabygelegen

Magnificent setting below the Bainskloof Pass. Nabygelegen is as small and personal as wineries get and tastings and cellar tours are conducted by owner James McKenzie or wine-maker Charles (phone ahead). Claridge's in London share our good taste and have just added James' red to their wine list. Definitely combine this with lunch and a visit to the Holdcrofts' garden next door (see activities).

Prices: *Tastings and tours are free.*

Contact: *Bovlei Valley, Wellington.*

Tel: *021-873-7534*

avalonwines@icon.co.za

www.nabygelegen.co.za

Oude Wellington Wine and Brandy Estate 

As owner Rolf says: "We make wine and brandy and grappa (in this order); we also feed people in our country restaurant, where Nicky is the hot chilli chef. Wine tastings are unpretentious and honest. Our motto: we wine and dine and love company. Anyone with yellow Wellingtons gets a bottle of wine free."

Prices: *Wines R19 - R60, spirits R65 - R190. Restaurant starters R18 - R55, mains R35 - R75, desserts up to R30, cellar tours and tastings R15 - R40.*

Contact: *Bainskloof Pass Rd, outside Wellington.*

Tel: *021-873-2262*

info@kapwein.com

www.kapwein.com

WELLINGTON
NATURE and ACTIVITIES

Bainskloof Pass

Built by master Scots road-builder Andrew Bain, the Bainskloof Pass (part of the R303) winds its way out of Wellington and over the mountains to the fruit-growing town of Ceres. The Wellington side is the steep bit with stunning views back over the town, vineyards and neighbouring Paarl. Once over the top it's a more gradual descent following the river. Good tarmac road all the way and a worthy detour.

Asttack Trust 

The Holdcrofts are fabulous hosts and GG old timers. Theirs is a stunning indigenous garden at the foot of the Bainskloof Pass, nurtured for nine years as a bird sanctuary and home to vines, horses, dogs… you get the idea. Come for lunch and a tour and head next door to Nabygelegen winery afterwards (see Wellington wineries).

Prices: *R100 for lunch with wine and a garden visit by appointment only.*

Contact: *Tim and Caroline Holdcroft, Kleinfontein Farm, Bovlei Valley, Wellington.*

Tel: *021-864-1202*

kleinfon@iafrica.com

www.kleinfontein.com

TULBAGH
EATING and DRINKING

Readers Restaurant

Built in 1754 Readers was the first school in the area but has been a restaurant and gallery since 1997 when Carol Collins first started impressing locals and visitors with a Cordon Bleu menu that changes depending on freshly available ingredients. Bookable too for private functions, fancy dress parties etc.

Prices: *Starters R22 - R28, mains R50 - R65, desserts R15 - R22.*
Contact: *12 Church St, Tulbagh.*
Tel: *023-230-0087*
Cell: *082-894-0932*
readers@iafrica.com

TULBAGH
WINERIES

Twee Jonge Gezellen

Named "Two Young Bachelors" after its founders, TJG is the second-oldest family-owned S.A. wine farm. Best known for sparkling wines made using traditional Champagne methods. Underground cellar tours Mon - Fri 11am or 3pm, Sat and public hols 11am. Tastings Mon - Fri 9am - 4pm, Sat and public hols 10am - 2pm.

Prices: *Wine tastings are free. R15 pp for group cellar tours. Easy-drinking blends cost about R20, Krone Borealis sparkling wine R60.*
Contact: *Twee Jonge Gezellen Road, 6.5km north of Tulbagh.*
Tel: *023-230-0680*
tjg@mweb.co.za
www.tjwines.co.za

Way-out wine fields

Stellenbosch and Franschhoek are the names most synonymous with South Africa's wine production, but it's well worth going a little further afield for tastings too. Try Wellington and Tulbagh or head over the hills to the Worcester and Robertson vineyards. The drive is spectacular and you can really get off the beaten track (something we urge you to do whenever possible).

For wine buffs driving north, there's a string of wineries up the West Coast and also along the banks of the Orange River near Upington in the Northern Cape - so check out those chapters too.

Bianco Wines, Olives and Olive Oil

The Bianco family originated in Piedmont Italy and know plenty about olives, of which there are 22ha here. All sorts of olive products are available to try and to buy with plenty of wines too and there's also a herd of Bonsmara Stud cattle for your inspection.

Prices: *Red wine R36, white wine R26, Olives R14, extra virgin olive oil R34.*
Contact: *On R46 just outside Tulbagh.*
Tel: *023-231-0350*
bianco@lando.co.za
www.bianco.co.za

TULBAGH
NATURE and ACTIVITIES

Bartholomeus Klip Farmhouse

This Victorian homestead and farm is just an hour from Cape Town and surrounded by lush gardens and a 4,000 ha game reserve. Indigenous game includes zebra, buffalo, a variety of Cape antelope and quaggas (a fascinating experiment to reintroduce an extinct zebra species). Whatever you do, don't miss the food. Book ahead and stay the night if you can. Closed June, July and Christmas.

Prices: *Game drive and lunch R250 incl 2hr drive, drinks and 3-course lunch. Bar purchases extra. Game drive only R150 incl drinks. 3-course lunch only R165.*
Contact: *Elandsberg Farm, Hermon, nr Tulbagh.*
Tel: *022-448-1820*
bartholomeus@icon.co.za
www.parksgroup.co.za

Kleinfontein

At 500m (1,640 feet for the non-metric) it's the highest homestead in Tulbagh's Winterhoek Valley and offers several activities for day visitors. The Tolbos Trail takes you from the main house to the very top of Inkrulp Peak, which at 1,380m (4,528 ft) has fantastic views over valleys, vineyards and wheat fields all the way to Table Mountain. It takes about 3 hours to get up there and you need to be reasonably fit. The Bloubos Trail is a circular route of 2 - 3 hours and offers a good mixture of gorges and forested ravines to hill walking and rocky view points.

Prices: *R20 for day visitors. Other activities like fishing on the dam, horse trails, swimming and mountain-biking may cost extra.*
Contact: *Call the farm on 023-230-0731.*
Or contact Tulbagh Tourism, 4 Church St, Tulbagh.
Tel: *023-230-1348*
tulbaghinfo@lando.co.za
www.tulbaghtourism.org.za

Murludi

There are two hiking routes here in the northern part of the Tulbagh Valley best done in Sept - Oct when the spring flowers are often magnificent. The River Route, a 4km walk, meanders through fruit-farming country and mountain fynbos while the 10km Elsbos Route starts on the same path and continues into the lower hills of the Witzenberg Mountains. Plenty of great views (as you would hope) ups and downs, rock features, plains, bridges and freshwater streams for drinking. Keep your eyes peeled for game including duikers, grysbok, klipspringers and look out on a clear day for Table Mountain, 130km away.

Prices: *R20, pre-school kids for free. Open all year, though watch out for the weather in winter.*

Contact: *Call Kobus and Martha van der Westhuizen on 023-230-0732.*
Or contact Tulbagh Tourism, 4 Church St, Tulbagh.
Tel: *023-230-1348.*
tulbaghinfo@lando.co.za
www.tulbaghtourism.org.za

Silverfontein

Depending on how energetic you are feeling there is a one- or two-day hiking trail from this farm. It kicks off heading through blue gum and pine forest, fynbos and shaded kloofs climbing to a saddle and on to the Ontongskop peak at 813m (2,667ft) where the adventurous can sleep the night in a cave. Day two leads you via other peaks to complete the circle and return to the farm.

Prices: *R25 pp. Must take all your own kit, food and water. Trail requires a moderate fitness level and is signed with markers all the way.*

Contact: *17 km past Hermon on the R44 to Tulbagh.*
Call Karin and Bernd Müller on 023-232-0531 or 082-931-8572.
bernd@silverfontein.co.za
www.silverfontein.co.za

WORCESTER
CULTURE and HISTORY

Kleinplasie Living Open-air Museum

A great family outing, this is a living open-air farm museum, depicting the lifestyle of the early Cape pioneer farmers. Watch daily agricultural activities and home industries such as bread-baking, candle-making, wheat-grinding, distilling and forging.

Prices: *Adults R12, pensioners R10.80, students & children R5, school groups R4 pp.*
Contact: *On Robertson road, 1km from Worcester.*
Tel: *023-342-2225*
annalene@kleinplasie.co.za

ROBERTSON
EATING and DRINKING

Fraai Uitzicht 1798

A stunning 18th-century wine farm ringed by vertiginous mountains. People come from far and wide for the irresistible seven-course menu and à la carte choices. Trout salad, springbok carpaccio, beef fillet and others are freshened by herbs and vegetables from the garden. Indulge in the decadent Dream of Africa chocolate cake and leave (like me) with more than one spare tyre in the car.

Prices: *6-course meal R350, 7-course R460, restaurant closed to non-guests Jun - Jul. Lunch and dinner Weds - Sun. Prices may rise.*
Contact: *Klaas Voogds East (Oos), on R60 between 12km east of Robertson.*
Tel: *023-626-6156*
info@fraaiuitzicht.com
www.fraaiuitzicht.com

ROBERTSON
WINERIES

Springfield Estate

"Beautiful setting and great hosts." The fourth hands-on generation of Bruwers to run this wine farm (descended from wine-making Huguenot Bruères) are brother and sister Abrie and Jeanette who do everything from marketing to fork-lift truck driving. Their estate lies alongside the Breede River in the mountain-ringed Robertson valley. Eyes peeled here for springbok (brought down from Namibia 50 years ago).

Prices: *Tasting free, open Mon - Fri 8am -5pm, Sat 9am - 4pm. Guided tours by prior arrangement.*
Contact: *On R317, 2km from Robertson.*
Tel: *023-626-3661*
info@springfieldestate.com
www.springfieldestate.com

Cape Dutch Architecture

So what is Cape Dutch architecture?

You can't move for Cape Dutch buildings in the Winelands - so best that you have some idea of what it is.

As the name suggests, early Dutch settlers were its primary forebears, but there are German, French Huguenot and Indonesian influences in there too.

Importing European ideas, settlers built basic and practical homes using the resources most readily available: clay or thick rubble for the walls, lime-mortar and wild reeds for thatch.

Houses consisted of a single storey of just three rooms, built in a row with a rafter-supported, steeply pitched roof (a snow-shedding European design that never fell by the wayside, so some say). Thick white-washed walls and large rooms helped make sweltering Cape summers more bearable.

As the prosperity of the area grew so the houses became more ostentatious.

A fashion for front gables (often the work of Malay craftsmen) flourished from the early 1700s, and the steady addition of wings over the next century led to U-, T- and eventually the magnificent H-plan houses that you can still see today.

So there you go.

Van Loveren

Home to three Retief generations, this is a beautiful winery surrounded by endless bright red canna plants. The family are warm and friendly people who offer wine tasting inside by the fire in winter or outside in the gardens in summer where you'll get the low-down on Granny Jean's planting plan. Fish Eagle Hiking Trail is a 3 - 4hr circular route through the Van Loveren vineyards, over the Breede River and up into the hills. Rewarded by a fantastic view. The Retiefs will give you a map and say it's a walk best done in the morning, R20 pp.

Prices: *Free tastings, wines R15 - R60, sparkling wine R22.*
Contact: *Klaasvoogds, 15km from Robertson on the Bonnievale road.*
Tel: *023-615-1505*
info@vanloveren.co.za or debtors@vanloveren.co.za
www.vanloveren.co.za

Viljoensdrift Wines

Aside from touring the cellar and tasting the Cabernet Sauvignon, Pinotage or other Viljoensdrift wines, Fred and Manie Viljoen also offer gentle cruises on the Breede river, which runs through their farm. This makes for a great way to see the scenery and a perfect warm up to a picnic lunch of goodies from the farm's deli.

Prices: *Cruises cost R30, last about 1hr leaving at midday (weather permitting) Sat, Weds and first Sun of the month. Cellar open Mon - Fri 8.30am - 5pm, tours by arrangement.*
Contact: *R317 to Bonnievale, 12km from Robertson.*
Tel: *023-615-1901*
Cell: *083 630 9682 or 082 809 2981*
viljoensdrift@lando.co.za or rivercruises@viljoensdrift.co.za
www.viljoensdrift.co.za

ROBERTSON

NATURE and ACTIVITIES

Soekershof Walkabout

Wind your way around the largest hedge-maze in the world, before investigating Soekershof's unique succulent garden (more than 2,200 succulents including cacti), the Philosophers Garden, and Botanical Heaven with more than plant 4,500 different species. Passionate hosts and a real family entertainment with an educational finishing touch.

Prices: *Basic admission R40, kids R20. Full experience including admission, a cup of soup, home-made apple pie and coffee and/or tea R75, kids R55. Closed July 11 - 31.*
Contact: *Klaas Voogds West, Robertson.*
Tel: *023-626-4134*
soekershof@lando.co.za
www.soekershof.com

Fish Eagle Hiking Trail 

See Van Loveren, Robertson Wineries.

BIRDING BITS

Eyes peeled in Somerset West and around Sir Lowry's Pass.

Overberg

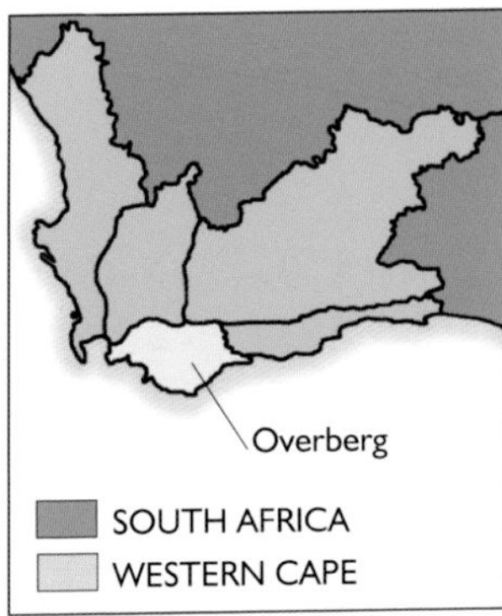

The Overberg is all about the meeting of land and ocean. Agulhas is the southernmost tip of Africa (not Cape Point as is often assumed) and here, where the Indian and Atlantic oceans collide, the sea smashes over rocky and rugged headlands, and washes up on wide, arcing white-sand beaches.

For those visiting between July and December (although August to October is prime time) there's the chance to see migrating southern right whales which, very sportingly, come right into food-rich shallows to calve, making them easily spottable from land. In fact the whole area is wealthy in wildlife, its fynbos-coated slopes home to many birds... so come armed with walking boots and binoculars.

Inland it's traditional Afrikaans farming country, the rolling fields of crops and pastures running between the sea and the Langeberg Mountains. Swellendam is at the centre of all this, a pretty little town founded by the Dutch East India company in 1747 as the administrative base for the Breede River Valley. Definitely make a stop here on your way to the Garden Route and don't - my mum and dad advise me - miss the Old Gaol Café and its milk tart.

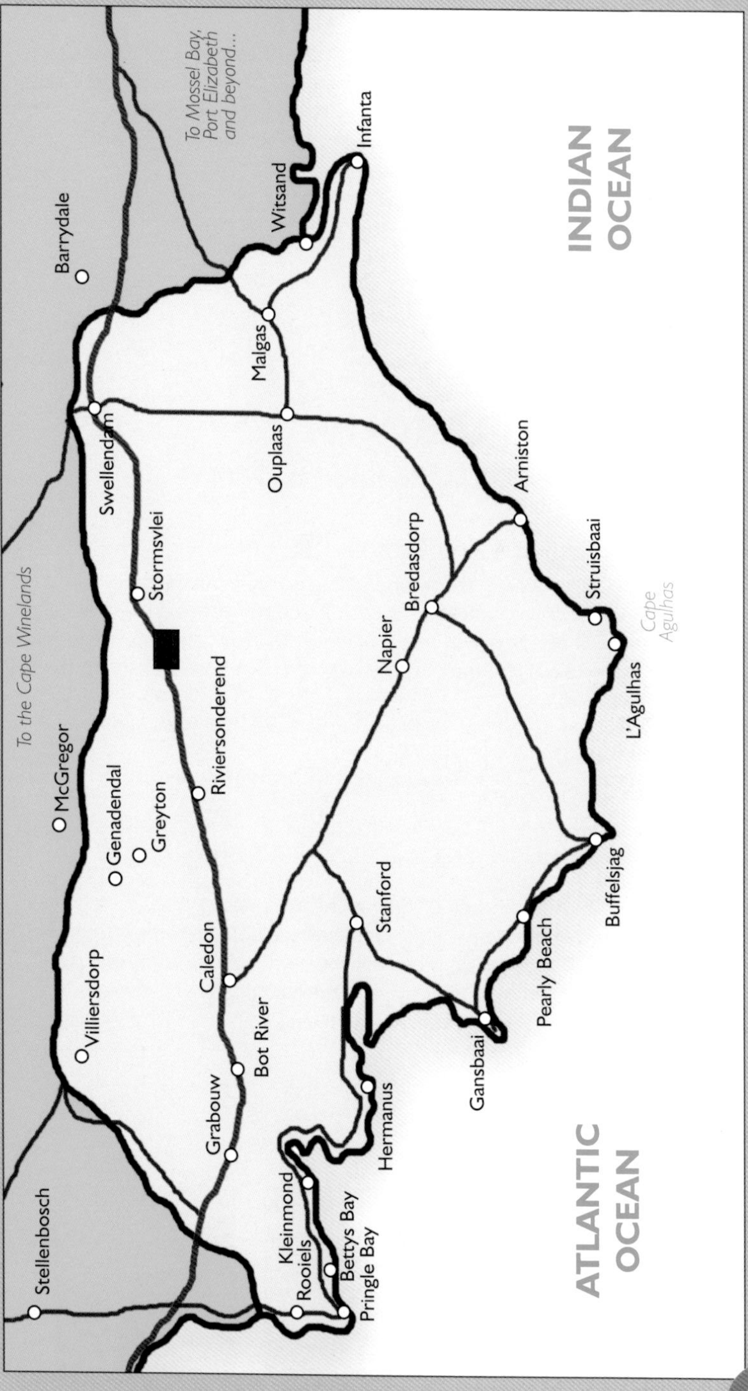

To Mossel Bay, Port Elizabeth and beyond...

To the Cape Winelands

Barrydale

Swellendam

Stormsvlei

Riviersonderend

McGregor

Genadendal

Greyton

Villiersdorp

Caledon

Bot River

Grabouw

Stellenbosch

Kleinmond

Bettys Bay

Rooiels

Pringle Bay

Hermanus

Stanford

Gansbaai

Pearly Beach

Buffelsjag

L'Agulhas

Cape Agulhas

Struisbaai

Arniston

Bredasdorp

Napier

Ouplaas

Malgas

Witsand

Infanta

INDIAN OCEAN

ATLANTIC OCEAN

VILLIERSDORP
ACTIVITIES

Theewaters Cruises

Organise a party with a difference on the Theewater Dam. Romantic sunset cruises, all-out water sports birthday bashes, Theewaters Cruises caters for everything and anything. Cruises last from an hour to an entire day with as much grub as you want from light snacks for 2 to a Champagne-fuelled feast for 32.

Prices: *Prices from R100 per head, excluding food and drink, for a minimum of 20 people for at least a 3hr cruise. Should the number of people be less then there is a bar surcharge. Closed in winter.*
Contact: *Off R321 to Villiersdorp.*
Tel: *028-840-1135*
info@theewatercruises.co.za
www.theewatercruises.co.za

GRABOUW
CULTURE and HISTORY

Paul Cluver Wine Estate

The Cluver family not only produces great wine but they also have an atmospheric amphitheatre buried in a blue gum forest on their 2,000ha estate. Shows here run from November to March and if the performance is going to run late into the night, you can book in beforehand to stay the night.

Prices: *R85 for theatre tickets. Open for free tastings 9am - 5pm Mon - Fri, Sat 9am - 1pm.*
Contact: *Off N2, over Sir Lowry's Pass about 20km from Somerset West.*
Tel: *021-844-0605*
info@cluver.co.za
www.cluver.com

From Paul Cluver, head off on the Green Mountain Wine Route, a 100km trail around the Elgin, Grabouw and Bot River area linking operations focussed on preserving the environment, history and bio-diversity of this area. Wildekrans and Beaumont Winery are also involved. Ask at Paul Cluver for more details.

BOT RIVER
WINERIES

Beaumont Wines

A welcoming troop of hounds will greet you at this, one of the oldest cellars in the Overberg. The Beaumonts themselves are equally friendly and will show you around their cellar and the cellars are open to the public for tastings and wine sales. You should stay here too. The setting is stunning with mountainside for rambling on, a lake for swimming in and Hermanus just a half-hour away.

Prices: *Whites R35 - R70, reds R35 - R80. Tastings free, open 9.30am - 4.30pm Mon - Fri, Sat by appt only.*
Contact: *Compagnes Drift Farm, Exit 92 off N2 to Bot River, Beaumont signed to right.*
Tel: *028-284-9194*
beauwine@netactive.co.za
www.beaumont.co.za

PRINGLE BAY
EATING and DRINKING

Hook, Line and Sinker, Restaurant and Fish Shop

Jackie and Stefan do literally everything themselves here (including spud peeling and washing up). There's space for only 24 people so you MUST book, as it's a crime to miss out on the best paper-wrapped hake and chips in the world (as one happy diner wrote on the wall). Evenings are à la carte with seafood leading the way (lobster thermidor, line fish, crab bisque, Mozambique prawns…). Steaks served on Weds and Sun.

Prices: *Lunch-time hake and chips R30, evening and Sun lunch à la carte starters R25 - R30, mains R60 - R120, crème brûlée and wicked chocolate pot (the only two puds on offer) R20 - R25, corkage R20. Open Tues - Sun lunch and dinner.*
Contact: *382 Crescent Rd, Pringle Bay.*
Tel: *028-273-8688*
Cell: *082-970-6000*

> **Driving tip**
>
> *If you're doing a day trip from Cape Town to the Hermanus area and whale-watching hotspots, take the N2 for a quick journey out there (Sir Lowry's Pass has great views too), but return on the R44 Clarence Drive coast road via Kleinmond and Betty's Bay. This takes longer but is a beautiful drive and, doing it on the return journey, you'll be driving on the sea side of the road, so the views are better.*

BETTY'S BAY
EATING and DRINKING

The Picnic Spot

The picnic spot is so much more than just an eatery. Not only do they turn out fantastic picnic hampers and fresh food take-outs, but they also work in conjunction with local guides and instructors to organise activities all over the area. So once you're loaded up with grub they'll pack you off hiking, rock-climbing, sand-boarding, river-rafting and much, much more besides.

Prices: *R150 - R200 for picnic hampers, open daily 9am - 6pm. Activities start from R70 pp, Multiple all-inclusive activity programmes can be organised from around R1,200 a night.*
Contact: *Village Centre, Betty's Bay.*
Tel: *028-272-9876*
Cell: *072-220-5291*
ccsolutions@telkomsa.net

The Whaling Station Restaurant

A small, family-run restaurant that people drive from Cape Town to eat at. Violet and Gaspard are in every day serving the freshest seafood. Watch the whales from your table (in season) and don't miss the mussels, steamed in their own pot and served with pommes frites, home-made mayonnaise and Dijon mustard. Gaspard, a Belgian, makes chocolates too.

Prices: *Starters R30 - R35, pasta R40 - R50, mains R70 - R110, desserts R30 - R35. Lunch and dinner Tues - Sat, Sun lunch only, open daily in high season.*
Contact: *Clarence Drive, Betty's Bay*
Tel: *028-272-9238*
Cell: *082-394-1016*
gaspard@whalingstation.co.za
www.whalingstation.com

BETTY'S BAY AND KLEINMOND
NATURE and ACTIVITIES

Harold Porter Nature Reserve

You'll be seeing a lot of fynbos if you spend any time in this area, so here's a good place to find out a little more about it. Several kilometres of nature trails wind through these botanical gardens. The reserve covers about 200ha of hillside and coast. 10 of these are cultivated fynbos and there's also a medicinal garden too.

Prices: *R8 for entry, open all day every day.*
Contact: *In Betty's Bay on R44.*
Tel: *028-272-9311*

Ouderbosch to Leopard's Gorge Hiking Trail

This is a great way to reach the Harold Porter Reserve. The reasonably taxing 6km route takes you through a variety of fynbos vegetation (impress your companions with facts from our Fudger's Guide to Fynbos) and has great views of the coastline, shale forests and various sandstone formations. Try and leave before midday to allow enough time to wander the HP Reserve at the other end, where the gates close at 6pm.

Prices: *R20 for the permit. You'll need to work out transport as this is a one-way walk, which takes about 3-4 hours. The trail is limited to 12 hikers and starts from the Ouderbosch in the Kogelberg Nature Reserve 5km from Kleinmond. See the Cape Nature website for other hiking trails in the Kogelberg.*
Tel: *021-659-3500*
capetown@cnc.org.za (they cover the Kogelberg)
www.capenature.org.za

Gravity Adventures

For Palmiet River kayaking in the Kogelberg see Cape Town Activities, Guides.

A couple of good beaches

- Moonlight Bay, at Hangklip (just before Betty's Bay) is a beautiful white sandy beach that faces the Cape of Good Hope from the other side of False Bay. Often deserted and as good a place as any to watch whales.
- Silversands is also a popular one, in Betty's Bay. It's wild and open with high dunes often used for sand-boarding.

HERMANUS
EATING and DRINKING

Asia Restaurant

"Great oriental grub and good feng shui!" Toss Asian recipes into a wok of the freshest South African ingredients and you have the essence of this thumping restaurant. Johan is at the stove and helm, supported by a notably friendly and efficient team of staff.

Prices: *Starters, salads and soups R24 - R58, mains R30 - R80, desserts R17 - R25, cocktails R18 - R30, wines R35 - R200. Open daily for dinner only in winter and lunch and dinner in summer.*
Contact: *Shop A8, Gateway Centre, Main Rd, Hermanus.*
Tel: *028-313-0222*
rustyk@telkomsa.net

Milkwood

A rustic seafood restaurant surrounded by milkwood trees with great views down on to both beach and river bank. Watch the whales, otters, kingfishers (and surfers too) as you chuck back the seafood, whether it be piles of calamari or fresh line fish. Plenty of non-seafood options too.

Prices: *Starters R15 - R30, mains R50 - R80, desserts R15 - R25. Breakfast, lunch and dinner every day.*

Contact: *Beach Rd, Onrus, Greater Hermanus.*

Tel: *028-316-1516*

mwninky@mweb.co.za

The Cuckoo Tree

Named after the tree that once dominated the courtyard, this is one of the longest-surviving restaurants in Hermanus. By day it's all about English breakfasts, light lunches, home-made cakes and tea. In the evening host Craig comes into his own as chef, maître d', receptionist and sometimes even the cabaret. Locals swear by the duck for mains.

Prices: *Breakfast R20 - R40, lunch R25 - R40, dinner R150.*

Contact: *Rothnick Croft Building, cnr High and Dirkie Uys St, Hermanus.*

Tel: *028-312-3430*

craig@hermanus.co.za

African Horse Company

Howard Krut (who is always on horseback when I ring him) welcomes riders of all abilities for horse trails through private farms and nature reserves from one hour to eight days. Gallop on the beaches, trot through pristine mountain fynbos or alongside the river and lagoon and spot southern right whales from your saddle.

Prices: *1hr R150, 2hrs R280, 3hrs R390, all day (6 - 8hrs) R650. Groups up to 8 people.*

Contact: *Mosaic Farm, Stanford, Farm 215, Gansbaai.*

Tel: *028-341-0393*

Cell: *082-667-9232*

omstables@telkomsa.net

www.africanhorseco.com or www.fynbosfarm.co.za

African River Cruises

"Eric is a great character, with long hair and large callused feet that probably never see shoes!" That's because he spends all his time on the boat. Eric and Marlene offer great river cruises on the beautiful Klein River. There are plenty of birds to see if you take your binoculars and there are braai kits supplied for cooking your picnic lunch and the chance to swim too if you get too hot.

Prices: *R50 for 3hr cruise, min 20 people per cruise, max 40, season runs Sept - May.*
Contact: *Cruises leave from the middle of Stanford village.*
Call Eric and Marlene Swart on 082-732-1284.
marlenes@maxitec.co.za

Klein River Cheese

Shelley and Riaan Lourens are cheese-makers and you're welcome to come and taste their produce and watch it being made at the same time. Picnics are available (buy your cheese from the shop) and there's a playground and plenty of farm animals to keep the kids entertained.

Prices: *Cheese-tasting is free, open 9am - 5pm weekdays, Sat 9am - 1pm.*
Contact: *Klenrivierskloof, 7km from Stanford on R326.*
Tel: *028-341-0693*
kleinriver@telkomsa.net

A birding note

Birders and nature-lovers should stop at the Kleinmond Estuary (just next to the town). An important all-year wetland, it heaves with about 160 bird species (many of them water birds) and regularly holds some 30,000 individual birds.

A Fudger's Guide to Fynbos

Fynbos vegetation covers a vast area of South Africa from Nieuwoudtville in the Northern Cape to Port Elizabeth in the Eastern Cape, and, a great deal of noise is made about it. So what's all the fuss about? I turned to botanists at the University of the Western Cape for answers: The word fynbos comes from the Dutch for fine-leaved and these plants do indeed have small leaves that are leathery and tough to the touch. Elegant ericas and proteas (South Africa's national plant is the king protea) are the most conspicuous, but in total fynbos contains some 7,700 species of which 70 percent are found nowhere else on earth. As such fynbos constitutes a recognised "floral kingdom". There are only 6 of these in the world usually occupying vast areas like Australia or most of the northern hemisphere. Despite being the smallest of these kingdoms, the Cape Floral Kingdom is the richest with 1,300 species per 10,000km2. The South American rainforest runs a distant second with 400 species. Fynbos is at its best during late winter and spring (the best time to see whales too by coincidence). If you're hungry for more information check out www.botany.uwc.ac.za/envfacts/fynbos.

Mosaic Farm

This is a peaceful eco-activity centre where you can make the most of the proclaimed bird sanctuary, lagoon frontage and fynbos on foot, horse-back or in a kayak. The views of the Overberg are fantastic and from the high points you can see the Atlantic and even Cape Point on a clear day.

Prices: *Guided birding, horse-riding, kayaking R140 pp per hour, guided sundown/breakfast 4x4 trips R320 for 2 hrs.*
Contact: *Mosaic Farm, 10km from Stanford.*
Tel: *028-313-2814*
Cell: *082-740-8046*
info@mosaicfarm.net
www.mosaicfarm.net

The New Junk Shop

"A fascinating shop to spend a while and part with some serious cash if the fancy takes you." The only thing The New Junk Shop doesn't have is space. It's packed wall-to-wall and floor-to-ceiling with antiques. "I buy and sell antiques from as far back as the Big Bang up to 1960," says Erwin, and I can almost believe him.

Prices: *Items from R1 to R50,000 and above.*
Contact: *9 Queen Victoria St, Stanford.*
Tel: *028-341-0797*
junkshop@standfordlocals.co.za

GANSBAAI
NATURE and ACTIVITIES

Dyer Island Cruises

A very popular whale-watching operation. Guides are well trained and knowledgeable and with the diversity of the local sea life you won't just see the legendary southern right whales (in season) but often penguins, seals, seabirds, dolphins and even great white sharks too. Trips last about 2.5hrs.

Prices: *R650 pp, prices may increase.*
Contact: *Trips leave from Kleinbaai harbour, nr Gansbaai.*
Tel: *028-384-0406*
bookings@whalewatchsouthafrica.com
www.dyerislandcruises.co.za

Ivanhoe Sea Safaris

Rudy runs boat-based whale-watching in Walker Bay, Hermanus, which in the season (June - Dec) heaves with the southern right whales that come here every year to mate and raise their calves. He guarantees close-up sightings on every trip and you may also see humpback and bryde whales, Cape fur seals, penguins and possibly sharks too. Trips take two hours, with 40 - 70 minutes with the whales.

Prices: *R600 pp, kids 10 and under R300, prices may increase.*
Contact: *Operates out of Gansbaai harbour.*
Tel: *Rudy Hughes on 028-384-0556*
balaena@kingsley.co.za

Gansbaai Scuba and Adventure

"Really professional service and not one of these sausage machines that pumps clients through as fast as possible." For water- and land-based activities in Gansbaai, Fred is your man. For up to 10 people at a time, he offers everything from whale-watching, diving and fishing charters to rock-climbing courses and 4x4 adventures.

Prices: *Scuba dive R250 pp, full kit hire (wetsuit, dive boots, mask and snorkel, B.C.D., cylinder, weights) R450 pp, tank and weights hire only R100. Charter fishing R450 pp incl gear, bait and soft drinks. Bring warm clothes.*
Contact: *24 Buitekant St, Gansbaai.*
Tel: *Fred de Pauw on 028-384-1509 or 082-957-9698*
info@gansbaaiscuba.co.za
www.gansbaaiscuba.co.za

What's so right about a southern right whale?

This whale's name originates from early hunting days when it was simply considered the "right" whale to hunt, because they lived close to shore, and, moving slowly, were easy to approach. If you visit the Western Cape between July and December you are almost certain to see southern right whales. In winter and spring they use the shallow coastal waters to mate and rear their calves. If you're there between August and October and you don't see any whales, you're seriously unlucky. Yup, that's you I'm talking to.... The Overberg is the area everyone flocks to but you will spot whales from the KZN coastline all the way around to the Cape Peninsula and West Coast (we watched them every day from our flat in Kalk Bay). Despite swimming slowly they are pretty acrobatic. Their favourite moves include: flipper slapping, breaching (driving up out of the water, often up to 10 times in a row), lobtailing (slapping the water with the flukes) and sailing, when they hang vertically upside down and use their tail as a sail. Adults grow to 11 - 18m (36 - 59ft) long and weigh between 30 and 80 tonnes. They are browny black in colour, with a white belly. Hunting pushed southern rights almost to extinction, with some 45,000 estimated to have been killed in the first half of the nineteenth century. Today's population is reckoned at up to 4,000. On a lighter (or heavier) note, right whales have the heaviest testes in the animal kingdom with each pair weighing in at up to a tonne, roughly the weight of a small car.

Gansbaai Golf Club

This is one of the friendliest courses you'll come across, and a great place to meet the locals, be it in the clubhouse or on the immaculate greens. An informal 9-holer at present, it's in the process of expanding to 18 holes. There are golf buggies available too for those reluctant to do it all on foot (or who just want the fun of driving one).

Prices: *Green fee R60, golf buggy R150.*
Contact: *Perlemoen St, about 5km east of Gansbaai.*
Tel: *028-384-1441*
joelu@telkomsa.net

Klipgat or Duiwelsgat Hiking Trail

A great walk for combining fynbos inspection and whales. It's a 7km there-and-back path along limestone and sandstone shoreline, which starts at the caravan park in Gansbaai and heads to the entrance to the Walker Bay Nature Reserve and the famous Klipgat Cave, finding-place of 80,000 year-old archaeological remains. It's fairly easy going and, if you fancy some local insight, Lionel Paeper will accompany you on the path and show you the various caves en route, explaining their history and geology. This will take about three hours.

Prices: *It's free to walk while Lionel's tour will cost about R100 pp (negotiable).*
Contact: *Gansbaai Tourist Office, Cnr Main and Berg Rd, Gansbaai.*
Tel: *028-384-1439*
ganbsaaiinfo@telkomsa.net

Heidehof Farm

Passionate about plants, Mathia is an expert on the medicinal values of coastal fynbos (on which she has written a book and gives regular talks). She'll take you on a guided tour of their 200ha farm (part of it at least) discussing the plant life you will see, and invites you to bring a picnic or braai to gobble under the milkwood trees afterwards. Wear stout shoes.

Prices: *R250 pp for 3 - 4 hr trail, 175 pp for short trail. Mathia can offer drinks, but bring your own food. Book in advance.*
Contact: *Heidehof Farm, 20km from Gansbaai, off R43 nr. Pearly Beach.*
Tel: *Mathia Schwegler on 028-388-0073*
Cell: *082-901-5070*
schwegler@telkomsa.net

GREYTON
EATING and DRINKING

The Post House

A truly English pub of warped walls and huge fireplaces, swept up and plonked in the Overberg. The Post House started life as just that and now operates as a hotel and restaurant serving magnificent food. I guiltlessly gorged on pan-fried sole and chocolate terrine before a final snifter from the bar's endless choice of single malts.

Prices: *Starters and desserts about R20 - R30, mains R50 - R80. Open for breakfast, lunch and dinner.*

Contact: *22 Main Rd, Greyton.*

Tel: *028-254-9995*

info@posthouse.co.za

www.posthouse.co.za

Von Gesau Chocolates

This is one for anyone in need of some serious, sweet-toothed indulgence. Richard and Terry are chocolatiers (a most enviable job title) and they use the best Belgian and Swiss chocolate to create their cocoa wonders. They also make gift boxes and their chocolates are matched with wines for combined tastings at Waterford Wine Estate (see Stellenbosch, Cape Winelands).

Prices: *Slabs from R20, gift boxes from R35 and truffles from R3 each.*

Contact: *19 Main Rd, Greyton.*

Tel: *028-254-9100*

vgv@mweb.co.za

GREYTON
NATURE and ACTIVITIES

Greyton - McGregor Walk

This stunning hike along the Boesmanskloof Trail winds its way through the Riviersonderend Mountains that separate the two villages, passing the 750m (2,461ft) high point of Uitsigpunt and leading you to your destination via a series of waterfalls and pools that are great for swimming. En route you will see plenty of fynbos and protea and erica species. On the mammal front, keep your eyes peeled for baboons, klipspringers, common duikers and perhaps a caracal, while birds-wise there should be malachite sunbirds and Cape sugarbirds, black and booted eagles and jackal buzzards.

Prices and Details: *It's a reasonably strenuous 14km hike that you can do in a day. Alternatively, do the "out and back", staying the night in either Greyton or McGregor and walking back the next day (see the Post House, Greyton). Permits cost R25 pp per day and must be bought at one of the tourist offices, where you can also pick up the map. Dogs, fires and camping are not allowed. Booking ahead is essential. Note that on the McGregor side the route starts/ends 14km south of town at Die Galg so you will need to arrange transport.*

Contact: *Greyton Tourist Office, 29 Main Rd, Greyton.*
Tel: *028-254-9414 / 9564*
greytoninfo@mweb.co.za
McGregor Tourist Office, Main Rd, McGregor.
Tel: *023-625-1954*
info@mcgregor.org.za
www.mcgregor.org.za

CAPE AGULHAS
ACTIVITIES

EcoQuad

Experience nature with just a twist of adventure and adrenalin. Working on the rugged coastline of Africa's southern-most point, Henry Steyn takes you on eco tours of this stunning spot on easy-to-ride quad bikes or buggies. All trails are guided and you will be fully filled in on everything from the flora and fauna to the history and people of the area... oh, and on how to ride a motorbike.

Prices: *1hr trail R200, 2hr R300, 4hrs R500. 1- and 2-day self-drives also available.*
Contact: *Crescent Drive, Struisbaai, Cape Agulhas.*
Call: *Henry Steyn on 082-854-5078*
ecoquad@icon.co.za
www.ecoquad.co.za

BREDASDORP
NATURE

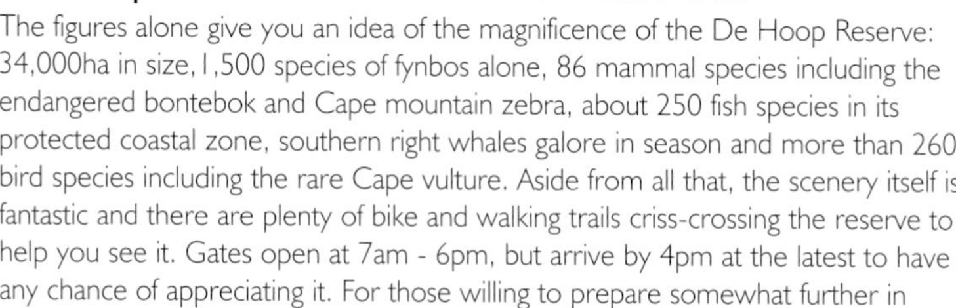

De Hoop Nature Reserve and the Whale Trail

The figures alone give you an idea of the magnificence of the De Hoop Reserve: 34,000ha in size, 1,500 species of fynbos alone, 86 mammal species including the endangered bontebok and Cape mountain zebra, about 250 fish species in its protected coastal zone, southern right whales galore in season and more than 260 bird species including the rare Cape vulture. Aside from all that, the scenery itself is fantastic and there are plenty of bike and walking trails criss-crossing the reserve to help you see it. Gates open at 7am - 6pm, but arrive by 4pm at the latest to have any chance of appreciating it. For those willing to prepare somewhat further in advance, the Whale Trail is not to be missed.

• The Whale Trail.

This is probably the most popular hiking trail in South Africa and as such you have to book it a long, long, long way in advance - in fact, book as soon as you know you are going to South Africa. The path runs for 54km and, with plenty of allowance made for inspecting flora and fauna and relaxing, it includes five overnight stops at fully-equipped cottages plugged into the Potberg mountainside or the coastline. Days one and two head out through mountainous fynbos while the last three are strung out along the coast with a chance, in season, to see dozens of whales (and get lots of sand in your boots).

Timing and Prices: *Bookings are limited to groups of 6 - 12 people - so find a gang to go with. Price-wise: Aug '05- Jul '06 R690 pp, R250 pp for porter service, Aug '06 - Jul '07 R850 pp, R290 for porter service. Prices include a lift back to the start.*

Contacts: *Reach the reserve from either Bredasdorp or Swellendam (last 50km on dirt). For Whale Trail bookings contact Bredasdorp Reservation Office.*

Tel: *028-425-5020*

capenature@tiscali.co.za

For De Hoop info call 028-542-1253

www.capenature.org.za

STORMSVLEI
EATING and DRINKING

Zanddrift Restaurant

This is a new venue for Edwina Kohler but the formula is the same: great country food cooked as you want it, when you want it. "You want breakfast at 4pm? I'll make it. If you want a vegetarian dish, I'll pick them straight from the garden," she says. Food is served to your table on shared platters with always at least three choices with bread, pâté and salad coming as standard. Walk off the food in the garden.

Prices: *R100 for a full meal. Open 9am - 5pm every day bar Sat. There's also wine tasting and a dried flower seller on site who will talk you through the garden.*
Contact: *In the centre of Stormsvlei, 40km west of Swellendam off N2.*
Tel: *028-261-1167*

SWELLENDAM
EATING and DRINKING

Jan Harmsgat Country Restaurant GG

These GG stalwarts run a true country restaurant for dinner only in an old wine cellar (c1723) set among pecan, almond and fruit orchards. The four-course menu is simply superb and the wine list just as good. Judi and Brin are very hands-on hosts and have trained their fantastic staff, drawn from the local farm-worker community, to cook, run the show and make home-made breads and cheeses.

Prices: *4-course menu R190. Book before 11am on the day and tell them of any food preferences or allergies.*
Contact: *On R60, on right 24.5km from Swellendam.*
Tel: *023-616-3407*
brinreb@iafrica.com
www.jhghouse.com

The Old Gaol Coffee Shop

My mum loved this place. Set in the grounds of the Drostdy Museum (see separate entry) this fantastic coffee shop and empowerment project is run by local Xhosa ladies who produce the most fantastic breads and milk tarts cooked over the coals in the tradesmen's yard of the museum. Home-made lemonade, roast vegetables, smoked springbok carpaccio, local cheeses, cajun chicken....

Prices: *Snack meals about R40 - R60. Coffees R10, cakes R18, muffins and scones with jam and cheese R15. Open every day 8.30am - 5pm.*
Contact: *26 Swellengrebel St, Swellendam.*
Tel: *028-514-3847*

Wildebraam Liqueurs

After stuffing down a huge lunch in Swellendam you'll need a digestif of some form, so pay a visit to Wildebraam on the outskirts of the town. It's set on a stunning young-berry farm surrounded by mountains and they use the berries to produce their fiery liqueur. Visitors are welcome for tours and tastings and there's a deli selling jams and berry vinegar.

Prices: *Tastings are free, liqueur costs R35 for 250ml, R80 for 750ml. Open Mon - Fri, 8am - 5pm, Sat 8am - 3pm.*
Contact: *Wildebraam Liqueurs, Farm S4, Hermitage South Lane, Hermitage Valley, Swellendam.*
Tel: *028-514-3132*
wildebraam@telkomsa.net
www.wildebraam.co.za

SWELLENDAM
CULTURE and HISTORY

Bukkenburg Pottery Studios

David and Felicity are two extremely friendly and highly successful South African potters who work from their studio producing a huge range of hand-made pottery including table ware, enormous floor jars, fountains and even wash basins. They're almost always in the studio and can teach you their craft in workshops for up to 8 people.

Prices: *Pots R80 - R10,000+. Pottery workshops R250 - R600 pp per day. Call ahead if visiting from distance to make sure they will be there.*
Contact: *8 Hermanus Steyn St (next to Drostdy Museum), Swellendam.*
Tel: *028-514-1644*
Cell: *082-342-5453*
bukkenburg@sdm.dorea.co.za
www.pottery.co.za

Drostdy Museum

The Drostdy swims in South African colonial history. A former office for the Dutch East India Company it has well-preserved Cape Dutch buildings and its own gaol. Traditional trades are on display in the yard and there's a working water mill producing flour for bread-making in the outdoor oven. Wander the rose gardens and definitely eat lunch in the Old Gaol Coffee Shop (see Swellendam Eating and Drinking).

Prices: *R15 for adults, R4 for kids. Guided tours by appointment. Open weekdays 9am - 4.45pm, weekends 10am - 3.45pm.*
Contact: *18 Swellengrebel St, Swellendam.*
Tel: *028-514-1138*
info@drostdymuseum.com
www.drostdymuseum.com

All aboard for the Malgas ferry… well, almost all

En route to De Hoop, this is the last hand-pulled ferry in the country and with a one-car berth you'll have the run of it as it crosses the Breede River. Runs every day except if it's too windy or there has been a lot of rain. Heading east, follow signs right off N2 to Malgas/Infanta 2-3km before Swellendam or turn right off N2 7km after Swellendam at BP garage.

SWELLENDAM NATURE

Bontebok National Park

Once the colourful Bontebok was reduced to just 17 in number. Now there are some 3,000 with 200 living on this 3,000ha reserve. Aside from four-legged creatures there are 200 bird species here and the Breede River, on the park's western border, is the perfect spot for watching them, swimming, picnicking and fishing.

Prices: *R15 pp entry for South Africans, R20 pp for foreigners. Buy fishing permits at the entrance.*
Contact: *Off N2, 6km west of Swellendam.*
Tel: *028-514-2734*
www.sanparks.org/parks/bontebok

WITSAND
NATURE

Witsand is a winner for whales

This is pretty out of the way, but so worth the trip. While each town claims to host more whales in season than its neighbour, it seems that Witsand, which looks over San Sebastian Bay and lies next to De Hoop Reserve, is the most likely victor. The bay is known as the whale "nursery" and you can regularly see up to 70 at once!

Witsand lies 30km south of the N2.

BIRDING BITS

You will see: Blue Crane, Jackal Buzzard

You'll be very lucky to see: Knysna Woodpecker, Hottentot Button-quail

You might see: Southern Tchagra, Denham's Bustard

Eyes peeled around De Hoop Nature Reserve and Bredasdorp.

Garden Route

This area is world-famous due to some strong marketing to overseas tourists, but I don't think that all who pass through necessarily enjoy it to the full. This is mainly because the best it has to offer requires some effort from you. The Garden Route is a narrow strip of coastline, hemmed in and well watered by rain falling on the seaward side of a wall of mountains that runs parallel to the coast. (The Klein Karoo on the other side is a virtual desert.) The unusually high rainfall (for South Africa) allows for deep forests and lush vegetation (thus the "Garden Route") and there are many permanent rivers.

Its real treasures are only accessible by foot, whether you walk into the forests for bird-watching, secluded picnics and fresh-water swimming; or along the ravishing coastline with its gorges, cliffs, lagoons and the first bit of warm-enough sea-water to swim in as you go east from Cape Town. Boat trips and birding, kayaking and canyoning, it's all on offer. Don't miss one of the dolphin or whale trips and set aside time for beach walks and braais.

The only logical, and therefore best, route to take if coming from Cape Town (which almost everyone will be) is to skip along the N2 from west to east, stopping off wherever you fancy until you reach the magnificent Tsitsikamma Forest at Storms River. From here you can hop north over the mountains and return to Cape Town via the Klein Karoo, making for a perfect round trip of about a week to 10 days that takes in several very contrasting regions.

Mossel Bay's auspicious history

Mossel Bay marks the first recorded meeting point of Europeans and Africans on Southern African soil. Portuguese explorer Bartolomeu Dias landed here on February 3rd, 1488 after a great storm swept him straight past the Cape of Good Hope. He originally christened the cape Cabo das Tormentas or Cape of Storms, but it was later renamed when it was found to unlock the route to the east.

See a model of the caravel he sailed in the town's Maritime Museum on Market St, open daily, tel: 044-691-1067.

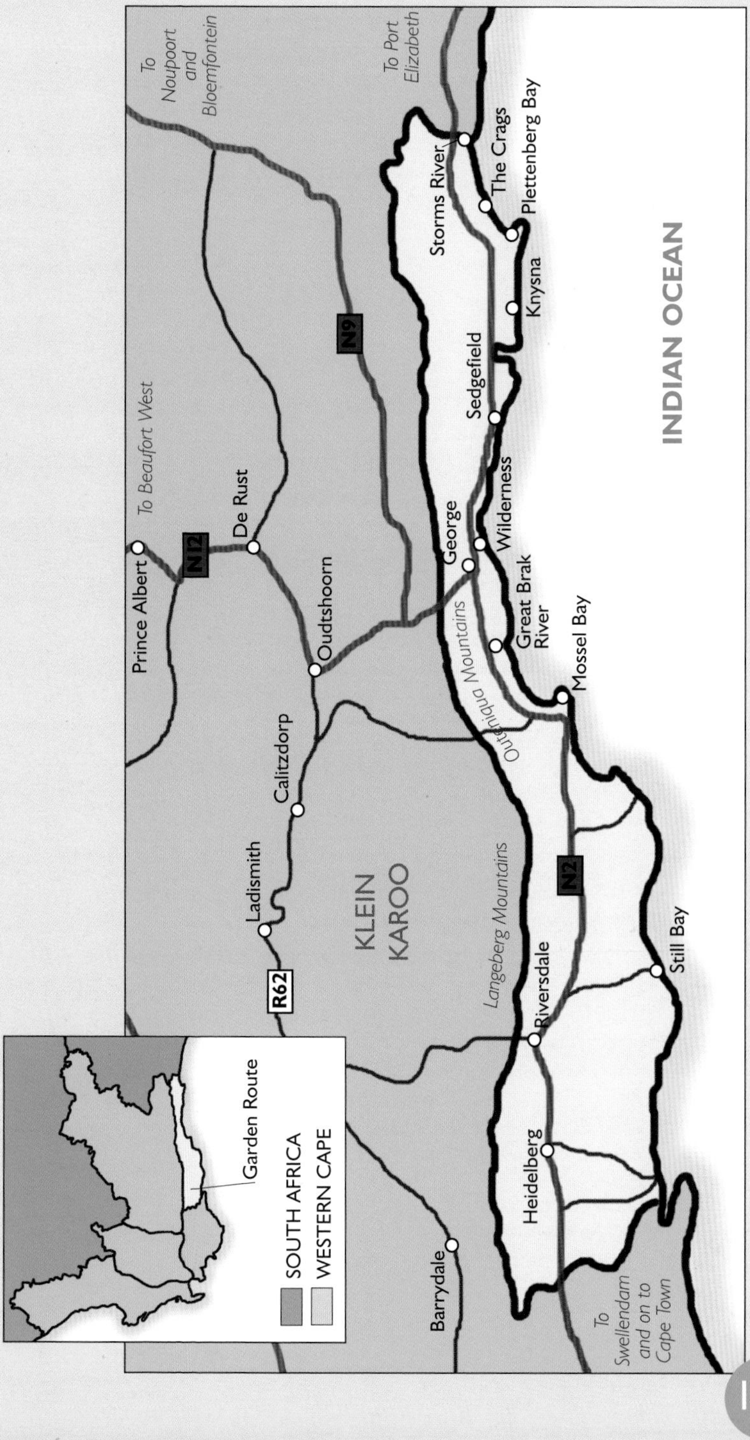

Garden Route
SOUTH AFRICA
WESTERN CAPE

Prince Albert
To Beaufort West
To Noupoort and Bloemfontein
N12
De Rust
Ladismith
R62
Calitzdorp
Oudtshoorn
N9
KLEIN KAROO
To Port Elizabeth
Barrydale
Storms River
George
Outeniqua Mountains
Sedgefield
Langeberg Mountains
The Crags
Wilderness
Great Brak River
Knysna
Plettenberg Bay
Heidelberg
Riversdale
N2
Mossel Bay
To Swellendam and on to Cape Town
Still Bay
INDIAN OCEAN

GUIDES AND EXPERTS

GENERAL GUIDES

Antoinette Stear, Origins from Africa

Little did you expect to come on holiday and follow in the footsteps of early man. Antoinette is fascinated by South Africa's first inhabitants and will take you to the best rock art sites the Garden Route has to offer. She'll also show you all the usual tourist hot spots and will happily organise pretty much anything that tickles your fancy.

Prices: *Depend on length of tours and activities chosen.*
Tel: *044-382-4440*
Cell: *082-872-4805*
stearage@yebo.co.za
www.originsfromafrica.com

ACTIVITIES GUIDES

Mark Andrews, African Ramble

Whales are huge, an obvious fact best appreciated from the air. So call Mark at African Ramble to do just that. He offers airborne whale-watching in season, as well as scenic flights around Plett' and Knsyna. With another base at Addo Elephant Park he'll take you there too, or indeed, all over the Eastern Cape and Garden Route. Fly-in safaris, vintage tiger moth trips… it all sounds rather romantic, doesn't it?

Prices: *Scenic flights R400 pp (min 2), vintage tiger moth flight R950 pp, Addo day trip incl flights from Plettenberg Bay, safari, lunch at Shamwari Lodge R4,300 pp.*
Contact: *Based at Plettenberg Bay airport.*
Tel: *044-533-9006*
Cell: *083-375-6514 or 083-231-9529*
aframble@mweb.co.za
www.aframble.co.za

Dave and Cheryl Griffiths, Outeniqua Adventure Tours

For a "wheely" good time (humble apologies), call Dave and Cheryl. They love the scenery of the Garden Route and Karoo and arrange 2-10 day cycling routes along quiet country roads in order to share it with you. If you don't fancy that, they run more traditional tours that focus on spending the minimum time in the vehicle and the maximum time exploring.

Prices: *Day trips R400 - R550, about R500 - R600 per day for extended tours.*
Contact: *29 Tarentaal St, Denver Park, George.*
Tel: *044-871-1470*
outntour@mweb.co.za
www.outeniquatours.co.za

Blue Crane Farm Stall

As you whizz down the N2 make sure you stop at this small but very popular farm stall, café and bakery that sells nothing but local produce including home-made breads, jams and cakes, dried fruit, biscuits and cold meats. Theo offers a simple coffee-shop menu of home-style cooking that will fill you up and set you on your way again.

Prices: *Breakfast R18 - R40, lunch R15 - R45. Open 8am - 5pm every day.*
Contact: *Signed off N2, 3km before Heidelberg.*
Tel: *028-722-2651*
tpienaar@iafrica.com

Grootvadersbosch Nature Reserve 

This reserve covers 250ha of forest in the Langeberg. With some 200 recorded species including the rare narina trogon, the bird-watching is fantastic and there are 56km of hiking and cycling trails winding through forest and fynbos. Bushbuck and Cape grysbok are present as well as lots of baboons, a subspecies of the ghost frog and a unique forest emperor butterfly. An adjoining 14,400ha, mountain wilderness area and world heritage site offer more fantastic hiking.

Prices: *R20 pp per day, bring your own bikes.*
Contact: *23km from Heidelberg, signed from N2.*
Tel: *028-722-2412*
gvbosch@telkomsa.net
www.capenature.org.za

Bonniedale Farm

Rock art to rock pools, horse-riding (for beginners and beyond) to hiking, you can do so much at Bonniedale that you won't want to leave. Friendly hosts Nico and Danette offer a true back-to-nature experience in the middle of some of the most pristine fynbos-coated surroundings. What more need I say?

Prices: *Horse-riding R150 per hour, bushman painting tours R350 per hour per group, mountain bikes R60 per hour.*
Contact: *West off R328 25km from Mossel Bay, then right after 8km.*
Tel: *044-695-3175*
bonniedale@mweb.co.za
www.bonniedale.com

MOSSEL BAY
CULTURE and HISTORY

Barnyard Theatre Mossel Bay

Based on London's Globe, this theatre is housed in a 148-year-old stone-built barn that seats about 200 at wooden tables downstairs and in two galleries upstairs. There's a cash bar and snack platters and meals available, but general practice is to arrive loaded down with a picnic and your own drinks. Actors tend to join you at the bar after the show and expect festivities to continue well after the curtain falls.

Prices: *High season R90 - R120 every night (bar Christmas) Dec 10 - Jan 10, fortnightly for the rest of the year, R80 - R100.*
Contact: *1km down R327 (Habertsdale Rd), off N2 14km west of Mossel Bay.*
Tel: *044-698-1022*
info@thebarnyard.co.za
www.thebarnyard.co.za

GREAT BRAK RIVER
EATING and DRINKING

De Oude Stasie

De Oude Stasie in English translates as The Old Station, and it's this building that J.D. Bredenkamp renovated to create his restaurant serving traditional S.A. cuisine. It's surrounded by trees, with great views of the lagoon and ocean and there's live music every night on the baby grand piano. J.D.'s also opened a deli just around the corner.

Prices: *Dishes R16 - R150. Open Tues - Sat, 6pm - 10pm, Sun lunch 12pm - 2pm. The Purple Onion deli is open Mon - Sat, 8am - 5pm.*
Contact: *1 Morrison Ave.*
Tel: *044-620-4163*
Cell: *083-452-7770*
deoudestasie@telkomsa.net
The deli is at 41 Long St.

Riversyde 

Dora is a long-time GGer and serves the most fantastic teas and dinners (by appointment only) at her elegant house on the river bank. Stuff down home-baked cakes beneath water-side coral trees after a stroll around the village and estuary (see Great Brak River walks), then come back for dinner in the evening. The menu is fresh, selective and utterly delicious. I had the most fantastic baby sole and fillet steak.

Prices: *R160 for three courses with coffee (not including wine), tea and cakes for about R25.*
Contact: *2 Long St, Great Brak River.*
Tel: *044-620-3387*
Cell: *082-784-5885*
riversyd@mweb.co.za
www.riversyde.co.za

GEORGE
EATING and DRINKING

Meade House Emporium and The Conservatory at Meade House

Whether you're the "shop first, eat later" type or the exact opposite, it doesn't matter here as you can do both. 91 Meade St is not only a fabulous home-maker's shop of linen and limited edition prints, gifts and books, but it's also a restaurant serving breakfast and lunch or tea and home-made cakes in an English garden.

Prices: *Business breakfast R21, eggs Benedict R34, Caesar salad R35, Irish stew R38, Thai chicken curry R39, Franschhoek trout R42.*

Contact: *91 Meade St, George.*

Tel: *044-874-1938*

info@meadehouse.co.za

www.meadehouse.co.za

GEORGE
NATURE and ACTIVITIES

Garden Route Botanical Gardens 

Two dams built in 1811 water these lovely gardens, a showpiece for the huge diversity of vegetation found in the southern Cape from Karoo succulents to the endless fynbos species. There's a medicinal plants mound, an educational Khoi maze, a herbarium and sales of your favourite plants. Found at the feet of the Outeniqua Mountains, hiking and walking trails have been cut into the mountain fynbos next to the gardens.

Prices: *Free entry, R100 for guided tours of about an hour for a group of up to 10 people. Plans are in the pipeline for a small restaurant.*

Contact: *49 Caledon St, George.*

Tel: *044-874-1558*

info@botanicalgarden.org.za or scherb@pixie.co.za

www.botanicalgarden.org.za

Outeniqua Choo-Tjoe

Enjoy some classic steam travel and some great views too along the Garden Route to Knysna. The train leaves George and follows the coast to neighbouring Victoria Bay before ducking inland past Wilderness Lagoon and Sedgefield to Knysna. Spend a couple of hours (lunching) in Knysna at the other end and then come back the same way.

Prices: *R80 for adults. R60 for kids 6 - 16 years old, under 6s for free. Train leaves George at 9.30am, arrives Knysna 12pm, returns to George 2.15pm and back by 5pm. Only does George - Knysna leg in winter.*

Contact: *Trains depart from the Outeniqua Railway Museum, 2 Mission St, George.*

Tel: *044-801-8288*

Or call George Tourism on 044-801-9295

www.transnetheritagefoundation.co.za/ct_content.asp

GEORGE
CULTURE and HISTORY

If you're passing...

Stop in to look at George's Dutch Reform church most notable for its amazing yellowwood pillars and the pulpit of carved stinkwood. The church's cornerstone was laid in 1832 (followed promptly by a celebratory feast for the bricklayers and plasterers who worked on it) and it was consecrated in 1842. It's open on weekdays and Sundays.

WILDERNESS
EATING and DRINKING

Serendipity

Rudolf and Lizelle Stolze have space for just 26 diners in their restaurant and focus on giving you a South Africa-inspired gourmet experience you won't forget. Rudolf will be looking after you while Lizelle works culinary wonders preparing a five-course table d'hôte menu that changes regularly. "Not cheap but so, so worth it."

Prices: *5-course menu (with vegetarian options) R179, wines R65 - R350. Mon - Sat dinner only.*
Contact: *Freesia Lane, Wilderness.*
Tel: *044-877-0433*
chef123@mweb.co.za

The Riverside Kitchen

As you would imagine, the Riverside Kitchen steals the show for positioning, smack bang on the river bank, its cool wood, thatch and glass design underpinning that wilderness feel. The sea is just a hop, skip and a jump away too, so get in the marine mood by ordering a cocktail on the deck and attacking their great seafood platter.

Prices: *Starters R28 - R42, mains R65 - R160 (seafood platter), desserts R25 - R35. May rise 12% or so by end 2006. Closed Mon and Tues in winter.*
Contact: *Off N2, Wilderness.*
Tel: *044-877-0900*
Cell: *072-124-7375*
riverside@lantic.net

WILDERNESS
NATURE and ACTIVITIES

Eden Adventures

Try this for size: paddle 40 minutes through indigenous forest up the Touw River, park your canoe, then hike a forest trail for another 40 minutes to a perfectly-placed waterfall for picnic and swimming. That's just one of the options at the excellent Eden Adventures, where you can abseil, kloof and canoe to your heart's content. Medicinal plant walks, birding and lots of advice on the area also available.

Prices: *2-seater canoes from R35 per hour or R100 per day. Tours from about R200 for a half-day and R405 for a full day. Prices may increase 10% per year.*
Contact: *Chris Leggatt*
Signed off N2, 2km east of Wilderness Lagoon bridge.
Tel: *044-877-0179*
Cell: *083-628-8547*
tours@eden.co.za
www.eden.co.za

Wilderness Craft Market

If you're short of presents to take home, drop in at this craft market on the banks of the Touw River on the last Sunday of each month.
Contact: *Wilderness Tourist Office on 044-877-0045*

Garden Route, Klein Karoo or Karoo?

Navigation and life in general will become much easier once you know the difference between these three areas. They are essentially divided by two waves of mountains that run east to west, parallel to the coast. The Garden Route is the band of lush greenery that runs along the coast itself. The ocean is an obvious attraction and the walking here is particularly good. Heading inland to the north you will cross the Langeberg and Outeniqua Mountains (say from George to Oudtshoorn) into the Klein (or Little) Karoo.

This long tongue of land is home to many of South Africa's soft fruit farms and famous too for its ostrich-farming heritage. The R62 is increasingly marketed as the tourist route that whisks you through this part of the world, but the area still has a wonderfully off-the-beaten track reality that is sometimes hard to find nearer the sea. Head north again over the Swartberg range though, into the Groot (Great) Karoo and you really do escape the crowds. Prince Albert, just the other side of the hairy Swartberg Pass, makes a great first stop through this vast, arid expanse of veld that spreads hundreds of kilometres into the Northern Cape and north towards Johannesburg.

Seven Passes Road

If you can spare a leisurely couple of hours, the Seven Passes Road is a great drive that takes you along a back route roughly parallel to the N2 from Wilderness to Knysna via incredible scenery and (believe it or not) seven passes. Turn off N2 at Wilderness to pick it up and emerge at Rheenendal N2 exit, west of Knysna. It's all dirt road, so take it easy at the wheel and make sure you have plenty of camera film too.

The Malachite Hide

Birdlife on the Wilderness Lagoon is great and for the best view head to the malachite hide, a thatched rondavel at the end of the waterside boardwalk, which is left permanently open.

SEDGEFIELD
ACTIVITIES

Wild Oats Farmers Market

This Saturday market bursts at the seams with local produce. Do your bit to encourage small-scale organic farming, promote rural town links and stimulate job opportunities and, moreover, get stuck into fantastically fresh farm produce. Make a note to reward your early start with a croissant. Market opens 7.30am - 11am in summer, 8am - 11.30am in winter.

Contact: *Cnr of N2 and Jan van Riebeeck St, Sedgefield.*
Tel: *044-883-1177*

KNYSNA
EATING and DRINKING

34° South

A deserved reputation as a great all-round eating, drinking and meeting place. Come here to savour the seafood (fresh oysters, east coast sole, crayfish and prawns…) with influences from Spain, Portugal and Greece. Listen to the clinking of halyards on masts and enjoy the daily bustle of marina life.

Prices: *Fresh oysters R12 - R20, salads from R30, fish from R34, stir-fry R45, desserts and cakes from R15.*
Contact: *Shop 19, Waterfront, Knysna.*
Tel: *044-382-7331*
info@34-south.com
www.34-south.com

The Knysna Oyster

You'd think oysters were long embedded in Knysna's history as they seem to pop up everywhere, in restaurant names and menus all over town, but actually their's is a short history. The Knysna Oyster Company say cultivation was initiated only 60 years ago by a Mr. Bright, a retired wine merchant from the U.K.

De Oude Fabriek

Dennis and Marlene have built up a six-year reputation for really authentic South African cuisine. "Of course you can have your chicken and steaks, but people come here for the game," says Dennis. Springbok, kudu, wildebeest, crocodile, ostrich - you name it, you can eat it. Put that with a great S.A. red and Zulu bread and you're in for a treat.

Prices: *R150 for 3-course meal with wine. Open from 9am every day, dinner only on Sun.*
Contact: *Cnr of Main Rd and Gray St, Knysna.*
Tel: *044-382-5723*
oudefabriek@iafrica.com

île de Pain

As expected with a name like "Bread Island", the breads, cooked in a wood-fired oven, feature regularly alongside seasonal ingredients on the breakfast and lunch menus here. For those arriving later drinks, desserts and pastries are on hand and, for takeaways, there's a shop open all day selling not only the chef's food but the tools of the trade too. Aprons, knives, bread bags....

Prices: *Breakfast menu items R20 - R40, lunch R35 - R60, pastries R5 - R20, wines R70 - R150 (and by the glass) breads R10 - R60. Prices may rise 10% a year. Open 7am - 5pm, closed Mon and August.*
Contact: *10 The Boatshed, Thesen Island, Knysna.*
Tel: *044-302-5707*

Paquitas

Embedded in the seaside rocks of the Knysna Heads, the water will be practically lapping at your feet at this busy family restaurant, grill and pizzeria. Seafood leads the way on a long menu of hearty portions. Come for lunch to make the most of the great view and surroundings.

Prices: *Starters R30 - R50, seafood R65 - R350, grills R60 - R90, pizza/pasta R35 - R55, wines R50 - R300. Open from 12pm every day.*
Contact: *George Rex Drive, Knysna.*
Tel: *044-384-0408*
syjan@mweb.co.za
www.paquitas.co.za

The Oystercatcher

Holidaying can sometimes be a bizarrely stressful business so, to unwind, grab a table at the casual and friendly Oystercatcher, order a glass of champagne and watch the sun set… bliss. It's open from 11am and gives top billing on a menu buckling with seafood to its Knysna oysters which I'd heard about even before leaving Cape Town.

Prices: *Menu items R15 - R100. Most people order a barrel-load and then share them.*
Contact: *Smallcraft Harbour, The Waterfront, Knysna Quays.*
Tel: *044-382-9995*
oystercatch@mweb.co.za

The Phantom Forest Eco Reserve

Get ready for a whole evening's magical dining experience. Phantom Forest is a world unto itself, privately owned and set in a 137ha reserve in the hills above the river. This is a place for dreamy treats and culinary delights in the form of a seven-course menu eaten in a traditional boma, literally built into and out of the indigenous forest. You will be taken up to the restaurant by 4-wheel drive from the entrance at the bottom of the mountain. Very atmospheric.

Prices: *R225 for 7-course menu, evenings only. Booking essential.*
Contact: *Phantom Pass Rd, 7km west of Knysna.*
Tel: *044-386-0046*
phantomforest@mweb.co.za
www.phantomforest.com

KNYSNA
NATURE and ACTIVITIES

Forest Horse Rides

Liz Hattersley runs great horse trails through pine plantations and indigenous forest, up and down hills and across rivers. All rides are supervised and don't worry if you can't ride, as the horses are docile and well schooled. Picnic rides can be arranged too. Booking essential.

Prices: *R150 pp for 1.5hr forest ride, prices rise 10% annually.*
Contact: *Highway West, Rheenendal, Knysna.*
Tel: *044-388-4764*
ashgrove@lantic.net

Pezula Championship Golf Course

By golfing standards, the Pezula course really is a stunning creation. Teetering on the Knysna cliff tops it's near enough the Indian Ocean for a nasty slice to find its way into a seriously large water trap! Championship standard, the course is flanked by indigenous forest and flora and really isn't one for beginners.

Prices: *Nov '05 - May '06 R775, R575 for referrals/groups, May '06 - Oct '06 R550, referral/groups R450. Prices include locker and golf cart. Booking essential.*
Contact: *Lagoon Drive, Knsyna.*
Tel: *044-302-5300*
golf@pezula.com
www.pezula.com

Knysna Elephant Park

Great family fun to be had here with a unique opportunity to touch and feed African elephants and their babies. There are elephant walking safaris available, sunrise or sunset ele-accompanied sorties and if you really are mad about these tusked giants, you can sleep beside them too in the elephant boma!

Prices: *Daily tours every half hour from 8.30am - 4.30pm, adults R100, kids R50. 2.5hr walking safari adults R395, kids R195.*
Contact: *On N2, 22km east of Knysna.*
Tel: *044-532-7732*
info@knysnaelephantpark.co.za
www.knysnaelephantpark.co.za

KNYSNA

CULTURE and HISTORY

Knysna Arts Festival

Visit Knysna from the end of September to early October for the annual arts festival. Theatre demonstrations, art and drama workshops, music master classes, cultural lectures, food and wine tastings, exhibitions, cooking classes and more.

Contact: *Knysna Tourist Office, 40 Main St, Knysna.*
Tel: *044-382-5510*

Knysna Oyster Festival

Though oysters do feature, this is more a celebration of the good life and centres around sport. There's plenty to see and participate in (golf, running, cycling, kids' fashion shows, naval displays…) so if you're in Knysna during the first ten days of July ask at the tourist office about what's going on.

Contact: *Knysna Tourist Office, 40 Main St, Knysna.*
Tel: *044-382-5510*
www.oysterfestival.co.za

A note on Noetzie

Definitely worth a minor detour. Noetzie is a highly picnic-worthy sandy beach just east of Knysna. The beach is bisected by a small river, but its most remarkable feature is a row of castles, set into the hillside looking seaward and reachable only by padding across the sand on foot. They're private homes and guest houses, none of them particularly old, but all utterly intriguing. To get there head 4km east of Knysna on N2 and turn right to Noetzie. Follow the road all the way to the car park at the end and walk down to the beach.

PLETTENBERG BAY
EATING and DRINKING

Blue Bay Restaurants

Three great restaurants in one. The main room is white tablecloth fine dining with a menu of Mediterranean/Asian (Mediterrasian?) dishes. Attached is a courtyard (perfect for summer evenings) serving the same dinner menu plus breakfast, lunch and tea while "Le Bijou" a deli-style café, offers light meals inside or on street-facing decks.

Prices: *Breakfast R20 - R40, lunch R20 - R60. Dinner R45 - R250 (for some seafood platters), desserts R25 - R40, picnic baskets R60 - R90. Specialities include springbok carpaccio, seared tuna and fillet steak with Parma ham and parmesan.*
Contact: *Lookout centre (opposite ABSA bank), Main St, Plettenberg Bay.*
Tel: *044-533-1390*
magalan@telkomsa.net

Fifty7 Kloof

"Cracking specials and dance lessons after Sunday lunch." No promises to dance on demand, but Simon does play the piano for guests on most evenings. By day, Fifty7 Kloof has a café/bistro air about it with windows and doors thrown open to the views of the bay and mountains, while at night, candle-lit and linen-clothed tables have a more sophisticated feel. Menus revamped fortnightly.

Prices: *Average dinner per head R100. Warm chicken salad R35, seared tuna with citrus sauce R59, sticky apricot pudding R28.*
Contact: *Shop 57, Melville's Shopping Centre, Plettenberg Bay.*
Tel: *044-533-5626*
eat@fifty7kloof.co.za

The Med Seafood Bistro

"Not only is the seafood excellent, but the kudu's great too." Dave and Marianne have been filling appreciative tummies for some 20 years and have built up a great rapport with locals and visitors alike as a known constant on an ever-morphing restaurant scene - "no fusion/confusion food here," she says.

Prices: *Starters, mezze, salads R25 - R35, pastas R50, seafood R55 - R225, meats and grills R69 - R95. Open 12pm - 2pm, Mon - Fri, from 6pm Mon - Sat.*

Contact: *Village Sq, Main St, Plettenberg Bay.*

Tel: *044-533-3102*

info@med-seafoodbistro.co.za

www.med-seafoodbistro.co.za

PLETTENBERG BAY

NATURE and ACTIVITIES

Barefoot Festival

A September weekend town festival that includes a charity barefoot ball, a calamari cook-off, golf and rugby matches, and a fun run and triathlon.

Contact: *Plettenberg Bay Tourist Office, Melville Centre, Plettenberg Bay.*

Tel: *044-533-4065*

info@plettenbergbay.co.za

www.plettenbergbay.co.za

Harkerville Saturday Market

Every Saturday morning between 8am and noon you can visit the open-air market at Harkerville next to the N2. With a wide range of fresh farmers produce on offer, it's where the chefs and locals go to stock up on the edible goodies.

Contact: *Plettenberg Bay Tourist Office, Melville Centre, Plettenberg Bay.*

Tel: *044-533-4065*

info@plettenbergbay.co.za

www.plettenbergbay.co.za

Old Nick Village

Old Nick Village showcases some of SA's best arts and crafts work in 10 independent galleries and studios. Once you've invested time or money in artwork, treat yourself to a slap-up lunch and a wander through the surrounding indigenous gardens. Expect special exhibitions, lazy afternoons on the lawns or encounters with the odd vervet monkey.

Prices: *From R10 for a piece of hand-made soap to R35,000 for a bronze by a sought-after South African sculptor. Galleries, shops and restaurant open daily 9am - 5pm.*

Contact: *Off N2 about 2km east of Plettenberg Bay.*

Tel: *044-533-1395*

info@oldnickvillage.co.za

www.oldnickvillage.co.za

The Old House Shop

A warren of rooms crammed with homeware, linen and clothing, The Old House Shop is also a popular eatery for breakfast, brunch and lunch that's been pulling in the locals for more than 10 years. It's a historic monument and one of the oldest buildings in town, built on Stand no.1. Think of scrambled egg and smoked salmon breakfasts and chicken pie lunches.

Prices: *Breakfast R20 - R40, R30 - R45 for lunch. Open Mon - Fri 9am - 5pm, Sat 9am - 1pm except high season when open all day.*
Contact: *Kloof St, Plettenberg Bay.*
Tel: *044-533-2010*
oldhouseshop@mweb.co.za

Dolphin Adventures

Martin Fraser Smith offers environmentally friendly sea-kayaking and sailing charters in Plettenberg Bay. Kayaks are one of the best ways to get close to whales and dolphins when they are around and Martin's fans like his personal touch and insistence on taking small groups only.

Prices: *Sea-kayaking 2-3hrs R200 pp. Sailing 3-4hrs on a 42ft catamaran R300 pp.*
Contact: *Trips leave from central beach, Plettenberg Bay.*
Cell: *083-590-3405*
martin@dolphinadventures.net
www.dolphinadventures.net

Know your stinkwood from your yellowwood

Both of these are found in the abundant forestry of the Garden Route, but they are both protected trees. Generations of settlers hacked down these hardwoods like there was no tomorrow, using the magnificent timber to build the floors, ceilings and furniture that you will still see today in many old houses across the country.
Stinkwood (ocotea bullata) is an evergreen that has a pungent rotten-socks smell when it is felled but, as you can't chop it down, try and recognise it from the blisters or bubbles (hence bullata) on the upper side of its leaves. These trees grow to about 25-30m tall with a trunk about 1.6m in diameter. The bark starts smooth grey or pink and turns rough and dark as it matures.
Yellowwood (podocarpus falcatus) whose timber is a deep golden yellow when varnished is a much larger tree, growing up to a massive 60m high. Identify it by its dark purple-brown bark that flakes in round patches.

Ocean Blue Adventures

Plett' is a haven of marine life and activities and you can see and do pretty much all of them with Ocean Blue. On boat-based tours they have spotted up to 7 different marine mammals and for the birders (or those who just like the idea of a lazy river trip) they organise cruises up the nearby Keurboom River.

Prices: *Marine tour R300, whale-watching R495, may increase 10% by end of 2006.*
Contact: *Central Beach next to Beacon Island Hotel.*
Tel: *044-533-5083*
info@oceanadventures.co.za
www.oceanadventures.co.za

Ocean Safaris

These guys will take you right up to the whales and dolphins that visit Plettenberg Bay. They also run trips from Knysna and guides in both locations are highly trained and always friendly. With the emphasis on responsible tourism, the proceeds from the trips they offer are pumped back into research and education.

Prices: *2-2.5hr whale-watching trip R520 adults, R300 kids, 2hr dolphin discovery tour R350 adults, R150 kids.*
Contact: *Trips leave from central beach (Beacon Island) Plettenberg Bay or from Thesen Island, Knysna.*
Tel: *044-533-4963*
Cell: *082-784-5729*
For Knysna trips call 082-852-9402
info@oceansafaris.co.za
www.oceansafaris.co.za

Rhino Base Camp

You don't expect, on the Garden Route, to see a white rhino grazing grassy tufts... until you visit Rhino Base Camp. A two-hour game drive in an open Landrover offers you the excitements of the northern game parks, deep in the south. There are more than 700 wild animals on its 2,000ha, including hippo, giraffe and even lions roaming in a separate camp.

Prices: *Drives cost R150 per adult and R65 per child.*
Contact: *On R340, off N2 12.5km from Plett.*
Tel: *044-535-0000*
Cell: *084-444-4407/8*
kathy@rhinobasecamp.co.za
www.rhinobasecamp.co.za

Robberg Nature Reserve 

You can't miss this reserve if you're in Plett'. It occupies the Robberg Peninsula, a rocky headland that juts out from the coast and has three circular walking routes that give you great views out across the ocean and back to town (see the walks section for more detail on these). The Nelson's Bay Cave has interesting archaeological finds and there's a huge seal colony to look out for too.

Prices: *Buy entry permits at the gate for R20 adults and R10 kids. Open 7am -5pm and until 8pm in Dec and Jan.*
Contact: *About 8km south of Plett', follow airport road and look for turn-off left.*
Tel: *(044) 533 2125/85*
robkeur@mweb.co.za

THE CRAGS
ACTIVITIES

Face Adrenalin

If you're going to do a bungy jump, do Bloukrans Bridge. It's officially the highest in the world at a whopping 216m and an experience you will never forget. Those with less of an appetite can also leap off the Gourits Bridge - it's (only!) 65m high. Zip lines, bridge walking and plenty of other terrifyingly fun activities also available.

Prices: *Bloukrans bungy from R580, Gourits bridge from R170. Open daily 9am - 5pm.*
Contact: *Bloukrans Bridge, The Crags.*
Tel: *042-281-1458*
info@faceadrenalin.com
www.faceadrenalin.com

STORMS RIVER
NATURE and ACTIVITIES

Stormsriver Adventures

The best way to see the Tsitsikamma Forest is from close up. Stormsriver Adventures organise fantastic treetop canopy tours and will have you on a zip line inspecting the foliage, 100ft above the forest floor. Among all sorts of other activities you can abseil into and tube down the river and cycle and walk pretty much anywhere.

Prices: *Tree canopy tour R395, tubing R345, abseiling R175.*
Contact: *Storms River, Off the N2 east of Plettenberg Bay.*
Tel: *042-281-1836*
adventure@gardenroute.co.za
www.stormsriver.com and www.treetoptours.com

Dolphin Trail

For those slightly put off by the rigours of the Otter Trail this is the answer. Starting in the Storms River Mouth it's a 2-day, 3-night hike - well more of a luxury ramble actually - where you'll carry nothing but your day-sack east along the Tsitsikamma coast, through 21km of pristine marine wilderness. After an indulgent first night, the programme is fairly leisurely with time allocated on day one for a Storms River boat trip, forest picnic and tidal pool snorkelling before a couple of stiff climbs to escarpments. A second night of serious comfort and then day two, which leads you along the water's edge spotting oystercatchers and whales in season and listening to the crash of Indian Ocean waves. The prospect of a slap-up 4-course farewell dinner should spur tiring legs on to the end and you'll be dropped back at the start via an exciting 4x4 ride the following morning. Strenuous stuff!

Price: *R2,700 pp for whole package include meals, guide and transport. Max 12 per group.*
Tel: *042-280-3699*
info@dolphintrail.co.za
www.dolphintrail.co.za

GARDEN ROUTE WALKS

I am sure you have covered clothing and footwear needs etc and the wisdom of walking as a group in isolated areas.

To those who whizz down the N2 via a quick stop-off in Knysna and Plettenberg Bay, it's often difficult to fathom quite what's so special about the Garden Route. To really get the idea, you need to stop the car, get out and walk. Only then can you really appreciate the astonishing diversity and greenery of the thick forest and fynbos that clothes this southerly strip of the country.

There are literally thousands of walking paths to choose from, so to make it a little easier, here are the details of a few routes that we have enjoyed or which have been particularly recommended to us. They vary in length from a few hours to a few days; some are guided, some are not; all - we hope you'll find - are hugely satisfying. Further details of each can be obtained from the tourist offices mentioned.

Make sure you take sun hats and water in summer, raincoats and decent hiking shoes in winter and cameras and binoculars all year round.

MOSSEL BAY

Contact: *Mossel Bay Tourism, Market St, Mossel Bay.*
Tel: *044-691-2202*

Cape St. Blaze Trail

This is one for lovers of coastal magnificence, a reasonably strenuous 13.5km in each direction with great views of towering cliffs and rocky bays and coves. It begins at the Cape St Blaize lighthouse with a fairly steep climb on a wooden walkway/steps to the ridge above. The trail then heads along the coast to Dana Bay, 13.5km away. People tend to judge the length they want to walk in total and turn back when they are ready. Or walk the entire length and get a taxi from Dana Bay back to their car. Jordan Taxis are on 082-673-7314.
Price: *Free, no permit needed.*

Oystercatcher Trail

Like the neighbouring Whale Trail in the Overberg, this two- or four-day coastal route leads you through some of the best scenery of the Garden Route. It's fully guided and portered leaving you to plod happily along, investigating ancient caves and rock pools, learning about flora and fauna or soaking up views of the Indian Ocean from the cliff tops.
Prices: *R2,800 for 2-day to R5,800 for 4-day trip for groups of 2 - 4 people, R2,300 and R4,800 for larger groups. Prices are all-inclusive. You must book well in advance.*
Contact: *Trips start at Mossel Bay Museum or at Boggomsbaai.*
Call: *Fred Orban on 044-699-1204 or 082-550-4788*
forban@mweb.co.za
www.oystercatchertrail.co.za

Skaapplaas Trail

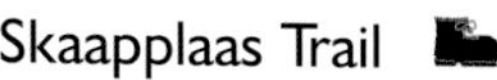

This is a beautiful 10km hiking trail which should take you about 5 to 6 hours leading from the fynbos-coated hills outside Mossel Bay down to the banks of the Kouma river. 600-year-old yellowwoods and stinkwoods provide the shade (that the tree ferns like too) and there are amazing waterfalls and swimming spots to picnic by. Watch out for rock art too.

Prices: *R35 pp. Ask about the half-way hut to overnight in to really draw out the pleasure.*

Contact: *Hannes and Anmalise van Rensburg.*

Skaapplaas Farm, take R328 to Oudtshoorn/Hartenbos off N2, pass Ruiterbos after 22km and turn L at primary school to Haelkraal, turn R after 3km.

Tel: *044-631-0035*

skaphiking@telkomsa.net

GREAT AND LITTLE BRAK RIVER

Contact: *Great Brak River Tourist Office, Amy Searle St.*

Tel: *044-620-3882*

Glentana Beach Walk

If there's nothing you like more than padding along on the seafront, brain in neutral, admiring your surroundings then head for the parking area near the Sea Side Café at Glentana. Walking east from there this easy low-tide 6km route leads you east to one of this coastline's many wrecks. Once you've reached it, patted yourself on the back and taken some photos you can turn around and walk back. I usually prefer circular walks but the rocky beach and caves are worth seeing twice and things can look very different when walking in the opposite direction - plus, of course, you won't get lost. Allow 3 hours.

Prices: *Free, no permits needed. The Sea Side Café is in Little Brak 15-20 mins east along N2 from Mossel Bay.*

Great Brak River Village Walk

A very easy 5km circular walk around the Great Brak River estuary. Start close to the library on Long St and head over the bridge in town. The path takes about an hour and returns across another bridge just downstream. Watch out for cormorants and other bird life around the river and estuary.

Prices: *Free, no permits needed. 044-620-3882, Great Brak Tourist Office, in Amy Searle St.*

GEORGE

Contact: *Outeniqua Nature Reserve*
Tel: *044-870-8323*
George Tourist Office
Tel: *044-801-9295*

TV Tower 

This may not sound particularly glamorous but it's a great 5km walk up onto the Langeberg that gives you a fantastic view back over George and the neighbouring mountains. Starting at the entrance to the Outeniqua Nature Reserve (1.5km out of George on Oudtshoorn road) follow the clearly marked route all the way up the mountain, stopping for a picnic on top before coming back the same way. Allow 2 to 3 hours.
Prices: *Free, but you must stick to the marked route.*

WILDERNESS

Contact: *Wilderness Tourist Office, Milkwood Centre, Beacon Rd, Wilderness.*
Tel: *044-877-0045*

Wilderness Heritage Trail

From the petrol station in Wilderness walk across the railway line and onto the beach and then, in a westerly direction, re-cross the railway line and walk under an elevated section of the N2 National Highway to the Kaaimans River mouth. Then walk up the estuary before crossing under the N2 to a steep climb up an old wagon track - you can actually see part of the tracks. This leads you to a ridge which brings you to the 'Map of Africa', rock formations that look just like… yup, you guessed it. The 'map' is formed by the meandering Kaaimans River. From here and for the remainder of the route along the ridge you have magnificent views over mountain and sea before descending through farmland. It'll bring you back into town after about 7km or three hours and is an easy walk offering great birding for those with keen eyes or binoculars.
Prices: *Free.*

KNYSNA

Contact: *Knysna Tourist Office, 40 Main St, Knysna.*
Tel: *044-382-5510*

These 3 forest walks all start off the Rheenendal road, off the N2 just west of town.

Woodcutters Trail

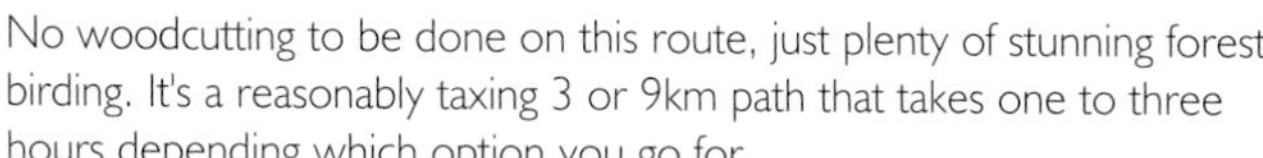

No woodcutting to be done on this route, just plenty of stunning forest birding. It's a reasonably taxing 3 or 9km path that takes one to three hours depending which option you go for.
Prices: *Self-issued permit (R6) from the hut at the start of the route - it has a map on the back. Walk signed beyond Rheenendal, 28km from N2, starting and ending at Krisjan se Nek picnic site.*

Jubilee Creek Forest Walk

A circular walk again that's just 3.6km long and should take you about an hour. For those feeling overheated it's blessed with a stream and cooling swimming hole as well as forest shade. The forest is wonderful containing a wide variety of indigenous trees and tree ferns as well as a massive blue gum that begs to be photographed - although the scale of the thing will probably not come through. You cross the stream several times before reaching the swimming hole and there are old mining excavations on the route, which you can view but not enter!
Prices: *Self-issued permit (R6) has detailed map of the walk. Buy this in the parking area where the walk starts and finishes. Route starts about 10km beyond the Woodcutters Trail.*

Millwood Goldmine

This starts at the Millwood picnic spot and ends up in the same place 5.6km or two hours or so later, following a moderate path that passes the remains of the old mining village and graveyard as well as plenty of the ever-present fynbos and forest plantations. At the start (or end) of the walk are a museum and a delightful coffee shop.
Prices: *Self-issued permit (R6) at the start. Route starts about 5km beyond the Jubilee Forest Trail.*

PLETTENBERG BAY

Kranshoek Coastal Walk

A choice of a 3km or 9km circular route. It's strenuous (but exciting) going with plenty of ups and downs and will need 2 hours for the short route and 5 for the longer one taking you through forest plantations and fynbos and along coastal escarpments, down towards a rocky beach and back. It is on this sort of walk that the Garden Route comes into its own.
Prices: *Sign the register and pay a small entrance fee at the starting point picnic site.*

Robberg Nature Reserve

The three circular walks of 2.2, 5.6 and 9.2km all start and end in the parking area and become increasingly difficult with length. The first walk is very easy - a stroll. The second (and probably the most popular) takes you down a spectacular sand dune (which cuts right across the peninsula) to the beach. This is fairly strenuous and entails some walking along rock faces. The third - which goes all around the peninsula - is a serious walk. On both the second and third, you should be aware of the tide movement. It is best to do both at low tide. Allow 45mins for the short route and about 4 hours for the longest. Take water and a sun hat and be wary of the sea. That said, make sure you enjoy it too as the views are spectacular!

Prices: *R20 entry for adults, R10 kids.*

NATURE'S VALLEY

Nature's Valley is about as beautiful as the Garden Route gets, a deep valley of thick, thick forest fringed by rocky cliffs and sandy beaches. The views are stunning, the bird life is too and there's a network of footpaths offering 1 - 6km routes that will take up to three hours for lingerers taking the longest route.

Prices: *Maps (R5) are available at the camp in Nature's Valley. To get there turn R off the N2 (if coming from Plett) 1km after The Crags (so about 16km from Plett). The camp is about 500m beyond the entrance to Nature's Valley on the right and is open from 7am - 5pm.*

Contact: *Call the camp on 044-531-6700.*

STORMS RIVER

Dolphin Trail

A luxury three-day hike that heads east along the coast. See p.129.

Forest and Fynbos Walks

Bob and Louise Reed are salt-of-the-earth folk who offer walking tours through the forest and fynbos of the Tsitsikamma. They are both registered guides, mad keen on their birds (eyes peeled for narina trogon and Knysna lourie), and with such a rich profusion of vegetation and wildlife along the Garden Route you'll be glad of someone to explain it all.

Prices: *R100 pp for 1-3 people, R60 for 4-10 and R40 for 11 or more.*

Contact: *88 Saffran St, cnr Darnell St, Storms River.*

Tel: *042-281-1936*

Cell: *072-299-1760 or 082-787-1598*

rreed@oldmutualpfa.com

The Otter Trail

This is probably the best known (and consequently most popular) of the Garden Route trails, a coastal walk alongside the magnificent Tsitsikamma Forest. It is extremely popular so, like the Overberg's Whale Trail, book your place as soon as you possibly can (up to a year in advance sometimes). Bear in mind that the reservation cost does not cover accommodation before or after the walk.
The trail itself covers 42km of rough and rugged coastline with booming breakers on one side and virgin indigenous forest on the other. Getting lost is difficult as the paths are clearly marked with blue otter signs but walking-wise it's challenging stuff. You'll need to be fairly fit to carry all your own cooking kit and sleeping bags up steep inclines and along steeper cliffs and over 11 river crossings. Four overnight stops are spent in bunk-bedded huts that sleep six and on day five you'll reach Nature's Valley, tired but inspired.

Prices: *R500 pp.*
Tel: *012-426-5111 for reservations.*

Storms River Mouth Trails

Starting from the parking area of the Tsitsikamma National Park you can walk a selection of 1 - 5.6km trails around the Storms River mouth. Head up to the plateau via the Indiana Jones-esque suspension bridge, follow a slice of the Otter Trail along the rugged coastline and caves, and dive into the forest. Allow up to three hours for the longest walks and much longer for picnics and swimming stops.

Prices: *Entrance fee to the national park R80 for adults, R40 for kids per day. The entry point is at Storms River off the N2.*
Contact: *Call the National Park Office on 042-281-1607.*

BIRDING BITS

You will see:
Knysna Turaco, Sombre Bulbul

You'll be very lucky to see:
Narina Trogon, White-starred Robin

You might see:
Chorister Robin-chat, Terrestrial Brownbul

Eyes peeled around Wilderness.

Klein Karoo

and Karoo

Admiring the success of the Garden Route's megalithic tourist marketing machine, much effort is being made at the moment to promote the R62 tourist route that runs through the Klein (meaning little) Karoo. This is still, however, in its infancy, which is ideal as the real charm of this region lies in the fact that it remains, for the greater part, "undiscovered", despite being so close to Cape Town.

On any journey through this part of the world there is therefore plenty of scope for the unexpected. For me the Klein Karoo was a mine of holiday gems worth digging for: guest houses set on sprawling, off-the-beaten-track fruit farms, restaurants tucked away in quiet little towns like Montagu or Barrydale and intriguing wildlife experiences, like my sunrise expedition with the Meerkat Man of Oudtshoorn. A meerkat researcher for 10 years, he took me out at dawn armed only with two plastic garden chairs, a large stick for warding off aggressive ostriches and an astounding self-taught repertoire of meerkat calls (see further details below).

The pace of life here is relaxed, the travelling easy, the distances short and really it's a region to potter through. Wend your way towards or from Cape Town along undulating valley floors where twisting rivers feed fruit, wine and ostrich farms and springtime brings a sea of blossom.

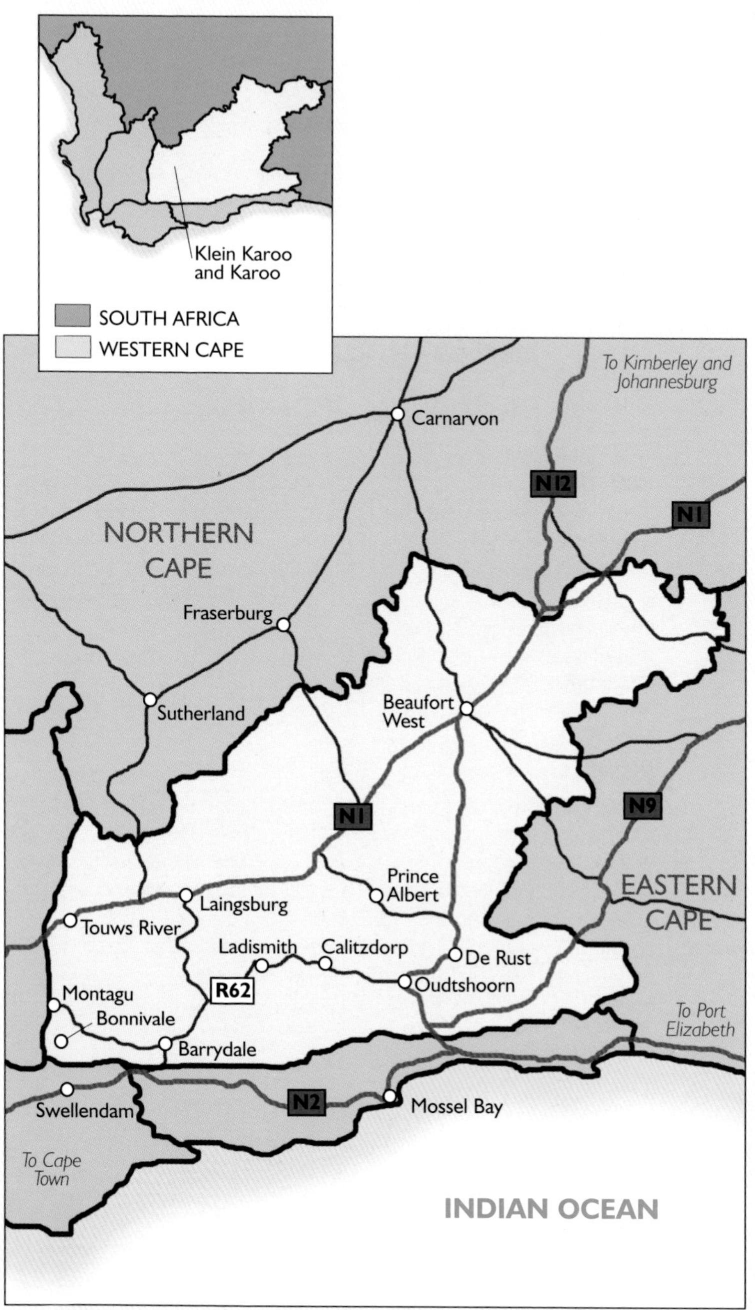
Klein Karoo
and Karoo
SOUTH AFRICA
WESTERN CAPE
To Kimberley and
Johannesburg
Carnarvon
N12
N1
NORTHERN
CAPE
Fraserburg
Sutherland
Beaufort
West
N1
N9
Prince
Albert
EASTERN
CAPE
Laingsburg
Touws River
Ladismith
Calitzdorp
De Rust
Oudtshoorn
R62
Montagu
Bonnivale
Barrydale
To Port
Elizabeth
Swellendam
N2
Mossel Bay
To Cape
Town
INDIAN OCEAN

BONNIEVALE
NATURE and ACTIVITIES

Breede River Goose

The Breede River oozes its way through the fruit farms of the Klein Karoo just begging to be boated on. And that's what Kelvin Phillips does. He'll take you for waterborne bird-watching, bass fishing and swimming trips or simply to watch this beautiful part of the world slide lazily past.

Prices: *Adults R50, kids R25, min of 10 adults or R500. Braais available.*
Contact: *Kelvin Phillips, Farm Eureka, Gelukshoop Rd, Bonnievale.*
Tel: *023-616-2175*
Cell: *082-759-5727*
breederivergoose@xsinet.co.za or janephillips@xsinet.co.za

MONTAGU
EATING and DRINKING

Die Stal

Indulge in simple pleasures and enjoy Suzanne Venter's delicious country grub at this farm restaurant just outside the pretty town of Montagu. The view from the verandah over the Karoo countryside is great and it's open all day, so even if you're passing early in the morning, you can drop in for fresh-baked breakfast goodies.

Prices: *Breakfast R40, lunch R45 - R65, open Tues - Sun, 8am - 5pm.*
Contact: *Kruis Farm, on R62 just outside Montagu.*
Tel: *082-324-4318*

Jessica's

Rainer and Shaye have been in the restaurant game for years and as testament to their success, have been listed among the country's top 100 eateries. I sent my folks there, and they came back with glowing reports of a chic but unpretentious haven of excellent food from Karoo lamb and roast duck to fresh fish and Thai dishes.

Prices: *Starters R25 - R35, mains R55 - R90, desserts R25 - R30, wines R45 - R120, corkage R20*
Contact: *47 Bath St, Montagu.*
Tel: *023-614-1805*
jessica@lando.co.za

Mimosa Lodge

Fida and Bernhard Hess haven't been long at Mimosa's helm but they're doing a cracking job. Dining at this two-storey Edwardian town house is a real treat with Bernhard's own Mimosa blend wine soon to accompany his four-course menu, which changes daily depending on ingredients most freshly available (many of them selected from the 200 plant species in the garden).

Prices: *Dinner R165 - R185.*
Contact: *Church St, Montagu.*
Tel: *023-614-2351*
Cell: *083-787-3331*
mimosa@lando.co.za
www.mimosa.co.za

MONTAGU
NATURE and ACTIVITIES

Montagu Nature Garden

A pretty, indigenous garden that strives to preserve wild flowers of the Karoo. Potter by the stream, march around the circular walking trail and keep your eyes open for black eagles soaring over the surrounding Cape Fold mountains. A great place to mug up on your floral knowledge, particularly over tea of a Tuesday morning.

Prices: *Free entry but donations happily accepted! R5 for tea and nibbles (10am - 11.30am, April - Nov - too hot in high summer!).*
Contact: *Van Riebeeck St, Montagu.*
Tel: *023-614-2304*
murray@lando.co.za

Swartberg Pass

It's generally a safe bet that if it says "pass" on the map the drive will be thrilling, but the Swartberg Pass is something special. This 27km road connects the Klein Karoo to the Karoo between Oudtshoorn and Prince Albert, zig-zagging up the Swartberg range to 1,583m and then down the other side. It's a dirt road all the way and can make for treacherous driving. If the weather is bad road signs at either end tell you if it's closed. Pay attention to these - it may be a beautiful day in Prince Albert or Oudtshoorn, but it can be a different story on the pass. I did it in a little hire car and even in drizzle I was sliding about in the mud. That said, it was utterly magnificent and I took dozens of photos of panoramic views, plunging drops and huge, contorted rock faces.

De Bos

The best way to get to grips with the fantastic Karoo landscape. Stuart Brown offers rock climbing and instruction and guided walks all over this region and, given that what goes up must come down, he offers abseiling too, as well as via ferrata (fixed protection climbing paths which do not require climbing gear). Living in the area, he knows its geography and weather like the back of his hand (which, being a rock climber, he probably knows pretty well).

Prices: *Guided rock climbs: full-day R900 for 1 person, R600 for 2, R450 for 3-4. Half-day R600 for 1, R450 for 2, R350 for 3-4.*
Contact: *De Bos Guest Farm, 8 Brown St, Montagu.*
Tel: *023-614-2532*
Cell: *082-332-5453*
sdbrown@mweb.co.za
www.debos.co.za

Simonskloof Mountain Retreat and Gecko Trail 

If you've been a little over-indulgent in the Winelands, this is the place to work it off. Plenty of exercise in stunning rocky Karoo surroundings. Jurgen offers hiking trails (30mins - 3hrs), biking trails (5 - 40km), kloofing, abseiling and geo-caching (a modern treasure hunt using a GPS receiver to locate hidden caches in the bush).

The Gecko Trail

A relatively strenuous 21km hike that connects the vine-covered plains of the Nuy Vallei near Worcester, via the spectacular Nuy River Gorge, to the fruit-growing Koo Valley west of Montagu. It takes 6 - 9hrs and there's accommodation at both ends. Get R25 permits and maps from the farm.

Prices: Abseiling R95 per session, mountain biking R25 for map and day permit, kloofing R850 for 2 nights, R980 for 3 nights fully catered and guided.
Contact: *Simonskloof Farm, Koo Valley, 40km west of Montagu.*
Tel: *023-614-1895*
info@simonskloof.com or info@geckotrail.co.za
www.simonskloof.com or www.geckotrail.co.za

Fruit farms

I think the best time to drive through this part of the world is spring. The Klein Karoo is the heart of South Africa's soft fruit growing industry and in September the whole region is awash with the scents and colours of millions of blossoming fruit trees, the air vibrating with the buzz of zillions of pollinating bees, hard at work.

So what exactly is "kloofing"?

An adventure sport that takes the direct route following a river down a mountain. Kitted out in a wet suit and helmet you'll abseil, bushwhack, swim, boulder hop (or clamber depending on your agility) and raft your way down the course of a river.

Tractor Ride

An unmissable trip if you visit Montagu, this takes you up the mountainside by tractor to get the best views of the Klein Karoo for the least effort. Once back down there's also the option for a traditional Afrikaans lunch cooked over the fire in a potjie (pronounced poy-kee) three-legged pot.

Prices: *R50 for ride and additional R50 for lunch for adults (less for kids). Prices may well increase.*

Contact: *Montagu Tourism, Bath St, Montagu.*

Tel: *023-614-2471*

montour@lando.co.za

BARRYDALE

EATING and DRINKING

Clarke of the Karoo

The perfect one-stop shop on the Cape Town/Oudtshoorn drive. On one side of the road are the restaurant and excellent deli farm stall and, opposite, the wine shop and café. Meals for all appetites include traditional cuisine of Karoo lamb curries and bobotie to light organic salads and humungous sandwiches. Plenty of local wines. Ask about the "Karoo oysters".

Prices: *Curry R75, bobotie R60, burgers R32 - R42, sandwiches R42, jams R29, olive oils R65 to R85, rootstock R28. Open 8am - 5pm Sun - Tues, 8am - 8.30pm Weds - Sat.*

Contact: *On R62 in Barrydale.*

Tel: *028-572-1017*

clarkekaroo@telkomsa.net

BARRYDALE
WINERIES

Joubert-Tradauw Private Cellar and Deli

Yes, Cape vine-growing does stretch this far. Alongside the Joubert is a boutique cellar producing four great wines and piles of deli (-cious) products to accompany them. Expect platters of meats and cheeses with local musical accompaniment!

Prices: *Glass of wine R15, bottles R50 - R80, platter of deli produce (cheeses, salamis, peppers, breads...) R70. All deli produce available to buy. Mon - Fri 9am - 5pm, Sat 10am - 2pm. R10 for wine tasting*
Contact: *Joubert-Tradauw, Tradouw valley, on R62 52km east of Montagu.*
Tel: *028-572-1619*
joubert.r62@lando.co.za
www.joubert-tradauw.co.za

CALITZDORP
EATING and DRINKING

Rose of the Karoo

A charming little Calitzdorp café and restaurant that bubbles with life and serves traditional South African meals (best followed by the ice cream). If you're not hungry enough for the whole three courses there's a variety of home bakes, farm cheeses and gourmet coffees. Don't leave without some deli snacks for the road too.

Prices: *3-course meal R85 - R90, light R40 - R50. Open every day 7am - 10pm, closed Sun evening.*
Contact: *Voortrekker Rd, Calitzdorp.*
Tel: *044-213-3133*
sunshine1@xsinet.co.za

OUDTSHOORN
EATING and DRINKING

Kalinka

Olga is Russian (how she ended up in Oudtshoorn I never found out - answers on a postcard) and has a reputation in town for her divine cakes. But there's so much else here too. Light lunches, vegetarian treats, lamb, quail and game from crocodile to kudu. The wine list is lengthy, the vodka list long too and there's a pretty garden to slurp/chomp it all in.

Prices: *Starters R30 - R35, garnished mains R55 - R95, desserts R30. Dinner every day, lunch Weds - Sun.*
Contact: *93 Baron van Reeda St, Oudtshoorn.*
Tel: *044 279 2596*
kalinka@mweb.co.za

OUDTSHOORN
ACTIVITIES

Balloon Drifters

Probably the most tranquil way to see the Klein Karoo and one of those expenses that, at some stage in life, one just has to splash out on. Charl Erasmus is a top bloke (he'd have to be to persuade you to get out of bed for sunrise) and will take you floating over the ostrich country of Oudtshoorn or the astonishing Red Stone Hills near Calitzdorp. You'll fly at 1,000 - 2,000ft, sinking to tree-top level for close-up inspections of this stunning scenery.

Prices: *R1,700 pp for about a 1hr flight. Bookings of at least six for Red Stone Hills flights.*
Tel: *044-279-4045*
Cell: *082-784-8539*
charl@balloondrifters.co.za
www.balloondrifters.co.za

Red Stone Hills 

These amazing geological formations are well worth a detour from the R62. They date to the enon-conglomerate period, formed 65 million years ago when the earth twisted and a torrent of sanguine mud-stone settled and solidified; a few million years later, bushmen hid in the hills' stone pockets and painted wildlife. A chap from Roberts (the ultimate S.A. bird book) identified 185 birds here, including eagles, black stork and five varieties of kingfisher.

The hills lie half way between Calitzdorp and Oudtshoorn on the R62. Head west from Oudtshoorn for 28km, then take Kruisrivier turn-off. Red Stone is 6km down this road. Check out the Potgieters at Red Stone Hills in our accommodation guide for somewhere to stay.

Meerkat Magic

You simply can't miss this. Grant has been studying meerkats for an unhealthily long time and has even learnt all of their calls. Head out with him on a dawn or dusk visit and watch as he starts chirruping and chirping. The meerkats come streaming out to see what's going on and you get the most fantastic close-up inspection of these intriguing animals as well as an amazing explanation from "The Meerkat Man" on their social structures and behaviour.

Prices: *R300 pp. Max of 4 people in the Meerkat Machine but 10 max on the tour if you have your own transport. Book ahead.*
Tel: *044-272-3077*
Cell: *082-413-6895*
gmmcilrath@mweb.co.za
www.meerkatmagic.com

PRINCE ALBERT
EATING and DRINKING

Millers

Millers sits opposite Albert's Mill, built in 1842 and now home to Johan's cigar bar (great for a late-night digestif) and his sister's gallery. The cogs and wheels grind the flour used to make Miller's pasta and breads. Those compliment a menu that features great Karoo lamb and ostrich (try lamb shanks in figs and onion) while for the non-carnivorous Johan couriers in fresh line fish three times a week

Prices: *Starters R22 - R28, mains R44 - R72, desserts R20 - R24. Open lunch and dinner every day Nov - Feb, Mar - Oct dinner only closed Tues.*
Contact: *Christina de Wit St, Prince Albert.*
Tel: *023-541-1112*
Cell: *084-457-5300*
vectornewton@absamail.co.za

Onse Rus

Lisa and Gary's 150-year-old Cape Dutch house is totally charming, as are they, and after the Swartberg Pass there's nowhere better for some nerve-calming lunch. In winter it's warming stews and fresh-baked bread while in summer a salad on the ash-shaded verandah is a deliciously lazy affair, best polished off with fig ice cream and a good book.

Prices: *Lunch every day except Weds and Sun, roughly R50, fully licensed.*
Contact: *47 Church St, Prince Albert.*
Tel: *023-541-1380*
Cell: *082-629-9196*
info@onserus.co.za
www.onserus.co.za

PRINCE ALBERT
NATURE and ACTIVITIES

Weltevrede Guestfarm

Suzelle Koorts farms figs, peaches and citrus fruits out here in the dry Karoo and you're welcome to visit her to inspect the farm, take a tour through the orchards and find out how they pick, work and dry the fruit... and no doubt take some away with you too.

Prices: *R35 by appointment only.*
Contact: *Weltevrede Farm, signposted at cemetery, 25km from Prince Albert.*
Tel: *023-541-1715*
Send an email via princealberttourism@intekom.co.za

Oudtshoorn and its ostriches

Ostrich feathers have been used throughout history to denote nobility and authority, worn by Egyptian pharaohs, Roman generals and Zulu warriors alike. They became a Europe-wide fashion accessory in the 19th century and an ostrich feather export industry quickly grew up in the Cape Colony. Over-hunting and predation had greatly reduced ostrich numbers and the feather price rose dramatically, sparking a rush into ostrich farming, particularly around Oudtshoorn.

Farmers became very wealthy and built ostentatious 'feather palaces' that still stand in and around the town. Ostrich plumage by the early 1900s had expanded into S.A.'s fourth largest export, but the market collapsed at the start of World War One and it was not until the end of Word War Two that farming ostriches for their meat and leather became established. The world's first ostrich abattoir was erected in Oudtshoorn in 1963.

Today you'll see flocks of these huge birds across the Klein Karoo and Overberg and they are still central to the region's economy. Aside from the meat, the eggs make for huge omelettes, the leather for chairs, clothes, handbags and wallets, and even the eggshells are used to make decorative lampshades.

Vital statistics

- *An ostrich's eye is bigger than its brain.*
- *Ostriches don't need to drink. They can internally produce their own fluid and get the rest from vegetation.*
- *Ostriches live for up to 40 years.*
- *An ostrich has intestines 14m long to get the most from the tough plants it eats.*

Prince Albert Golf Club

One of the smaller golf clubs of South Africa with just a couple of dozen members. But it's a fun desert course for those looking for a very different round of golf and the sand-oil greens can make for interesting putting!
Tel: *023-541-1841 or phone the butcher (023-541-1470) where the club secretary works. Alternatively ask the tourist office for details on 023-541-1366.*

BEAUFORT WEST

NATURE and ACTIVITIES

Lemoenfontein Game Lodge 

The perfect stop on a long drive up or down the N1. Lemoenfontein was built in the shadow of the Nuweveld Mountains as a hunting lodge in 1850 and is now a wooden-verandahed game lodge and reserve, home to antelope and zebra and to guests contentedly munching on Ingrid's fabulous dinners. Make sure you're one of them.
Prices: *3-course dinner R120, game drive R75 for 2hrs.*
Contact: *Signed off the N1, 2km north of Beaufort West.*
Tel: *023-415-2847*
lemoen@mweb.co.za
www.lemoenfontein.co.za

BIRDING BITS

You'll be very lucky to see:
Cinnamon-breasted Warbler, Rock Pipit

You might see:
Verreaux's Eagle, Ludwig's Bustard

Eyes peeled en route to Beaufort West.

Eastern Cape

The Eastern Cape, a huge expanse of land with 800km of coastline, is home to much of this country's history, both ancient and modern. Its earliest inhabitants left their mark in rock art sites across the area while European settlers of the 1700s stamped their own signature in the forts and garrisons from which they attacked resident Xhosa tribes. More recently, the Eastern Cape has bred many of the most influential names of the modern South Africa - Nelson Mandela, Thabo Mbeki and Desmond Tutu to name but a few.Most visitors arrive via the Garden Route and it's worth stopping off at some of the great sandy beaches that line the coast for seafood, sunbathing and perhaps even a spot of surfing around St. Francis Bay. (Surfing is for some an exciting schuss down the slopes of steepling waves. For others, like me, it is an exhausting and painful way to half-drown yourself.)

Other highlights are historic Grahamstown which hosts the country's largest annual arts festival, and travelling on past East London you'll reach the rolling green Wild Coast, perhaps the country's most spectacular seafront.

Away from the coast the landscape rises through once fought-over pastures into the wilds of the Winterberg Mountains (an area I am personally particularly keen on) and, further north, the southern reaches of the Drakensberg. Agoraphobics beware, this is South African wilderness at its gigantic best. Public and private game reserves span much of this country, with Addo Elephant Park an institution in the world of wildlife conservation.

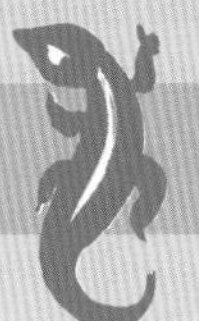

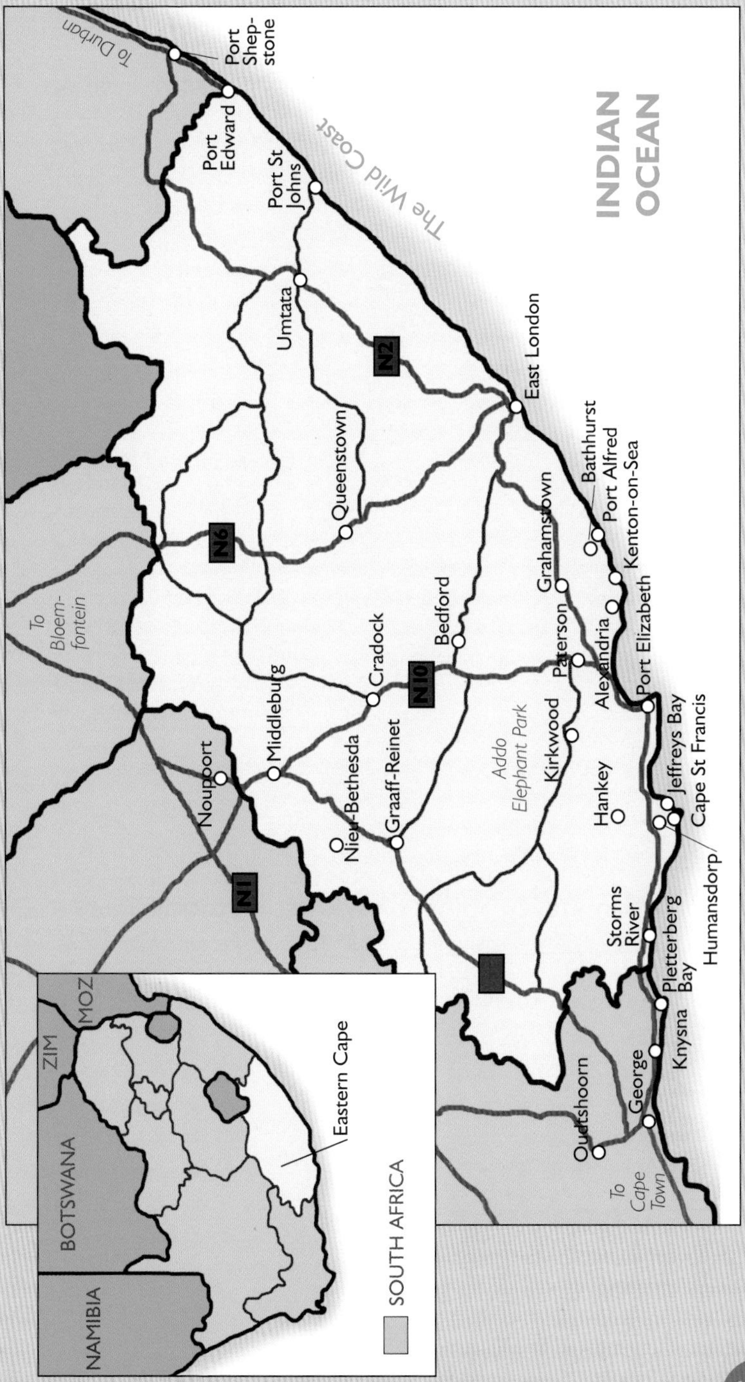
To Durban
Port Shepstone
Port Edward
Port St Johns
The Wild Coast
INDIAN OCEAN
Umtata
N2
East London
Queenstown
Bathhurst
Port Alfred
Kenton-on-Sea
Grahamstown
N6
Bedford
To Bloemfontein
Paterson
Alexandria
Port Elizabeth
Cradock
N10
Addo Elephant Park
Kirkwood
Jeffreys Bay
Cape St Francis
Middleburg
Noupoort
Nieu-Bethesda
Graaff-Reinet
Hankey
Humansdorp
N1
Storms River
Plettenberg Bay
Knysna
George
Oudtshoorn
To Cape Town
MOZ
ZIM
BOTSWANA
NAMIBIA
Eastern Cape
SOUTH AFRICA

GUIDES AND EXPERTS
CULTURE and HISTORY GUIDES

Sithembiso Foster, eZethu Cultural Tours

Sithembiso comes highly recommended by owners from our accommodation book who regularly send their guests out with him. He'll take you all over the Eastern Cape from the townships and a history tour of Port Elizabeth to Addo Elephant Park and the frontier country. He can also take you to cultural shows and does a great talk on Xhosa values and traditions.

Prices: *4hr township tour R280, 4hr city tour R250, 6hr Addo visit R450, full-day frontier country trip R600.*
Tel: *041-463-3698*
Cell: *083-493-8741*
ezethu@hotmail.com

DTours

Johnnie Morgan and Marianne Lear of "DTours" are THE people to contact for off-the-beaten-track tours in the Eastern Cape (although they do cover the whole Southern African region). Their specialities are listed under the following headings: art and architecture, gardens (including "a wonderful combination of South Africa's most beautiful botanical gardens, specialized nurseries and the exquisite private gardens along the route between Cape Town and Port Elizabeth"), bird-watching and eco (concentrating on the wonderful wilderness areas, such as the Winterberg, and coastline of the Eastern Cape), farm activities, Frontier and Anglo-Boer wars in the Eastern Cape. This is a small, friendly operation whose interests match up perfectly with our own.

Contact: *Johnnie Morgan, DTours, Ventor, PO Box 137, Tarkastad, 5370*
Tel: *045-848 0152*
www.dtours.co.za
info@dtours.co.za

Alan Weyer, Spirits of the Past Historical Tours

If you think you knew little of South Africa before coming here, just think about the droves of Europeans who set sail for these lands in the 1880's. The colonisation period is a fascinating story of adventure and hardship, of determination and gritty humour and it's one Alan Weyer tells captivatingly. He's a knowledgeable historian and a great raconteur.

Prices: *Half-day tours R350 pp - R450, full-day R600 - R850, 2-day package from R2,500.*
Tel: *046-622-7896*
info@spiritsofthepast.co.za
www.spiritsofthepast.co.za

ACTIVITY GUIDES

Paul Davies, Boma Helicopter Adventure Tours

The most exciting way to travel. Paul Davies is a one-man band who'll take you on thrilling helicopter rides. From photography tours and fly-fishing trips to game capture and scenic flights, each comes with an insightful running commentary and of course "a damn good lunch or two". Paul and Karen also own and run Rivermead in Grahamstown.

Prices: *Roughly R4,000 per flying hour for the helicopter, seats up to 4 people. More "grounded" trips are also available as well as fixed-wing flights.*

Contact: *Call Paul on 046-636-2727 or 082-659-0254*

helbom54@global.co.za

www.bomahelicopters.co.za

www.rivermead.co.za

NATURE GUIDES

Cliff Hopkins, Turaco Tours

Cliff runs specialist birding, nature and all-round eco-tours and will take you off into the wilderness as far from civilisation as possible for a taste of an African ecology unchanged for centuries. He's a highly respected ornithologist and a great bloke besides.

Prices: *Birding from R700 pp for a day tour. Wilderness adventures from R2,000 pp for 2-day trip. Discounts for groups of more than 2 people.*

Tel: *041-365-4832 (office hours) or 041-379-1406*

Cell: *082-784-3242*

turacotours@mweb.co.za

www.turacotours.co.za

NIEU-BETHESDA
NATURE and ACTIVITIES

Ganora Guest Farm and Excursions

J.P. and Hester's working farm is steeped in history and fascinating stories on everything from the Boer War to fossil remains and the early settlers who left their print in the rock art sites that you can visit on guided walks. There's a network of hiking, birding and biking trails best rewarded with rock-pool swims and lunch in the garden (by prior arrangement). Stay the night to make the most of it all.

Prices: *Activities incl rock art walk R35, woolshed visit R15, museum entry R15, fossil walk R45, lunch R45.*

Contact: *Off N9 between Graaff-Reinet and Middleburg, turn towards Nieu-Bethesda (second turning to Nieu-Bethesda if coming from Graaff-Reinet).*

Tel: *049-841-1302*

Cell: *082-698-0029*

info@ganora.co.za

www.ganora.co.za

NIEU-BETHESDA
CULTURE and HISTORY

The Owl House Foundation

What started for Helen Martin as a plan to brighten up her typically Karoo-style home became an artistic homage to light and colour through vibrant paints and crushed glass. Outside some 500 sculptures crowd the yard. It is an intriguing place and from the Owl House you can also take a donkey-cart tour of the village or township.

Prices: *Adults R15, kids and pensioners R10. Open all day every day.*

Contact: *Martin St, Nieu-Bethesda (off N9 between Graaff-Reinet and Middleburg).*

Tel: *049-841-1733*

owlhouse@intekom.co.za

www.owlhouse.co.za

HUMANSDORP
EATING and DRINKING

Le Chameleon

"An absolute gem! This is a boutique-style café whose food is as beautifully presented as it tastes," sings one happy diner. Famed for their home-baked Chelsea buns, Rudi and Helga produce imaginative salads, massive burgers, decadent cakes and mighty breakfasts. There's also a boutique selling crystal glasses, S.A. pewter ware, books etc.

Prices: *Breakfast R32, salads R30, burgers R25, cakes R15. Some 80 wines in stock. Open every day.*

Contact: *53 Voortrekker Rd, Humansdorp.*

Tel: *042-291-0262*

le.chameleon@agnet.co.za

Surfer's survival kit

Learn the following terms by heart and drop them nonchalantly into conversation at the local bar. Let the kudos - like the waves - roll in.

- *Beach Break - Waves breaking on the sandy seabed - best to start surfing on (not that you're a beginner or anything...)*
- *Point Break - Waves breaking onto a rocky point. Swaze/Reeves film named after this impressive formation.*
- *Reef Break - Wave breaking over a coral reef or a rock seabed. A classic surfing wave - unforgiving if you Muller (see below) but most rewarding in their perfection. Cloud Break is an extreme reef break.*
- *Tube - The hollow centre of a breaking wave, and the place to be. Also called a barrel.*
- *Mullering - Wiping out in spectacular style - inevitable.*

Waves are either Left or Right depending on which direction the wave breaks from the point of view of the surfer (never from that of the beach observer).

Wind is the ultimate deciding factor between a really 'A1' day's surfing or a non-day. An onshore wind is the worst, dude! The wind blows from out to sea and ensures that all the waves crumble and have no shape, making the waves unsurfable. An offshore wind is the best, ensuring the waves rolling in are well formed.

HANKEY
CULTURE and HISTORY

Pure Afrikan Tours

As genuine a township tour as you will find. Richard Mashangoane takes you not only to the streets of Hankey township, but to its homes, schools and shebeens as well. And if you're hungry there's African food available too. Richard also has plans for tours of the surrounding region. There must be thousands of jokes you could make about the name Hankey but I just can't think of one now....

Prices: *R175 for 3hr tour, R45 for food, R50 for dance display. Book ahead.*
Contact: *Hankey is signed off the N2 along R330 or R331.*
Call Richard Mashangoane on 042-284-0516 or his wife Gloria at the Hankey Tourism Office on 042-284-0543.

CAPE ST. FRANCIS
NATURE and ACTIVITIES

Cape St. Francis Lighthouse

Commissioned in 1878, this beautifully restored lighthouse was declared a national monument in 1984 and sits on a protruding, rocky point looking over the Indian Ocean. Visitors can go on regular guided tours and the views from the top are spectacular. There is also the coffee shop and the surrounding protected reserve makes for a great leisurely walk. And if you really love it here, you can stay the night.

Prices: *R15 entry.*
Contact: *On R330 from Humansdorp to Cape St. Francis.*
Tel: *021-449-2400*
salato@npa.co.za
www.npa.co.za (navigate to lighthouse tourism)

JEFFREYS BAY
EATING and DRINKING

The Walskipper

Literally metres from the sea, the floor of Philip and Grace's super-relaxed restaurant is sand and you're welcome to pitch up barefoot for the best seafood around (the calamari special is a particular favourite). Put your order in and watch it being cooked in front of you over an open fire, or even go for a swim to build up your appetite while you wait.

Prices: *Meals R60 - R150, booking essential. Open from noon, closed Sun evening and Mon in low season.*
Contact: *The Marina Martinique, Seafront, Jeffrey's Bay.*
Tel: *042-292-0005*
Cell: *082-800-9478*
wals@inetcom.co.za

Surfing

J'Bay as it's known is, along with St Francis Bay, the Mecca of the South African surf scene, renowned for its supertubes (see survival kit) and the point that creates rides hundreds of metres long. The town has changed substantially since the surf scene really took off in the 1960s, but the swell still arrives every year and is at its best from June until August. Come in July to witness the major surfing competitions.

PORT ELIZABETH

EATING and DRINKING

Wicker Woods

Joel Malkinson taught himself to cook and having got to grips with South Africa's traditional cuisine has given it a good shake-up in his own restaurant, an old house with open fires in winter and essential air-con in summer. An innovative menu is chalked up on a blackboard and there are seafood and grills galore.

Prices: *Average spend for 3-course meal and drinks R90 - R100.*
Contact: *99 Cape Rd, Mill Park, P.E.*
Tel: *041-374-8170*
malkies@iafrica.com

Homeleigh Farmyard

A kids' delight. Farmyard animals to pet and investigate (sheep, emus, cows…), horse-rides, tractor rides - for the more mechanically-minded nipper - and even a bouncy castle. Parents meanwhile can lunch in the Thatchwoods, pick up some farm produce or opt simply to relax with some tea in the garden and enjoy, if they're lucky, a little time away from their own pint-sized wildlife.

Prices: *Entry R15, kids under 2 for free, meals at Thatchwoods from R80. Open Tues - Sun 9am - 4.30pm.*
Contact: *Homeleigh Farmyard, off Kragga Kamma Rd, P.E.*
Tel: *041-379-2901*
starters@mweb.co.za

Truly the Rainbow Nation

South Africa's most famous statesman Nelson Mandela is from the Eastern Cape's Transkei area. He is a Xhosa, just one tribe in a country that has 11 official languages. This makes for a complex racial, cultural and linguistic make-up, which needs some explaining. So (deep breath) here goes:

Population: 44,344,136 (when I last counted! No, actually, according to the CIA factbook):

- *African/Black - 75.2%*

Although the majority of the population is African or black, it is neither culturally nor linguistically homogenous and, aside from Afrikaans and English, South Africa has nine other official languages: Ndebele, Pedi, Sotho, Swazi, Tsonga, Tswana, Venda, Xhosa and Zulu. These belong to the different tribes, although Xhosa and Zulu are probably those that you will hear most about on your travels.

- *White - 13.6%*

The white population descends largely from the colonial immigrants of the 17th, 18th and 19th centuries - Dutch, German, French Huguenot and British. Linguistically whites are generally divided into Afrikaans and English-speaking groups.

- *Coloured - 8.6%*

The label "coloured" is a controversial one, but still largely used for the people of mixed race descended from slaves brought in from the East and central Africa, the indigenous Hottentots and Bushmen and indigenous African blacks and whites. The majority speak Afrikaans.

- *Indian/Asian - 2.6%*

Asians mostly arrived from India, brought in by the British to work the sugar cane plantations of KZN. There is also a large Chinese immigrant population.

About two-thirds of South Africans are Christian, mainly Protestant. They belong to a variety of churches, including many that combine Christian and traditional African beliefs. Many non-Christians espouse these traditional beliefs. Other significant religions are Islam, Hinduism and Judaism.

Seaview Game and Lion Park

A great chance for all the family to get really close up to more than 40 of South Africa's biggest wildlife stars including giraffe, zebra, wildebeest, impala, monkeys and above all the lion. It's also a 120ha wildlife sanctuary for injured or orphaned animals. Handling lion cubs is surely an irresistible opportunity.

Prices: *Adults R30, kids R12, lion cub handling R40. Open daily 9am - 5pm, lion feeding at noon on Sun.*

Contact: *Signed off N2, 25km west of P.E. city centre.*

Tel: *041-378-1702*

Cell: *084-444-4702*

seaview@isat.co.za

www.seaviewgamepark.co.za

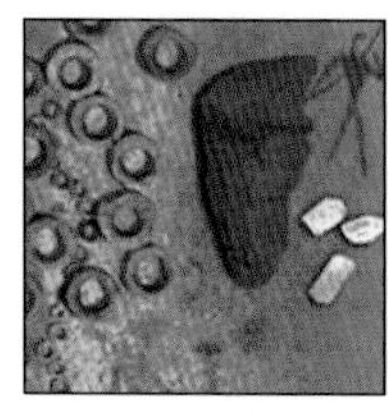

PORT ELIZABETH

CULTURE and HISTORY

Calabash Tours

Paul Mediema and his team run township tours in Port Elizabeth that focus on understanding contemporary urban black culture and unravelling the social history of this area. It's great fun and you will genuinely come away feeling enlightened. No wonder they've won bags of prizes for ethical and responsible tourism.

Prices: *Tours cost R250 - R350 pp leaving daily at 10am and 4pm. Book ahead, tours can be tailored to particular interests.*

Contact: *7a Hunt St, P.E.*

Tel: *041-585-6162*

Cell: *083-303-7553*

calabash@iafrica.com

www.calabashtours.co.za

KIRKWOOD
NATURE and ACTIVITIES

African Everose

The Maske family run a citrus farm but with a serious sideline in flowers. Tinie grows roses and lavender for sale and for preserving (an intriguing technique) and as well as showing you the flower beds, greenhouses and drying rooms, her team serve great lunches and teas in the sprawling and elegant garden and country house.

Prices: *R150 for a tour and tea, R200 for the tour plus 3-course lunch with wine.*
Contact: *Waverley Farm, Sundays River Valley, half way between Addo and Kirkwood.*
Tel: *042-230-1303*
info@africaneverose.com pmaske@iafrica.com
www.africaneverose.com

PATERSON
NATURE and ACTIVITIES

Amakhala Game Reserve

This you can only really do as a day and night excursion and it's great. A personal "Big 5" game experience, an awesome river cruise with cheese and wine, an African bush dinner in the middle of the reserve followed by a night drive - and, eventually, a great night's sleep!

Prices: *R650 pp for a maximum of 18 people.*
Contact: *Take N2 60km from P.E. towards Grahamstown, turn L to Paterson.*
Tel: *042-235-1608*
Cell: *082-783-2506*
reedvalley@bulkop.co.za
www.amakhala.co.za

ADDO ELEPHANT PARK

The park itself

One of the greatest attractions in the Eastern Cape and rightfully so. Not only is Addo home to herds of African elephants, but the park contains the other four Big 5ers too. You can see them all on game drives and guided walks or horse trails. The park conserves five of South Africa's seven flora and fauna communities or biomes and you can watch whales and dolphins along its coastal strip (the largest coastal dune system in the southern hemisphere).

Prices: *R80 entry fee per day (kids under 12 half price, under 2s for free). Guided game drives R140 - R220, 1-5hr guided horse trails R90 - R170 (no under 16s), Zuurberg mountain walking is free except for normal entry fees.*

Contact: *Head towards Grahamstown from P.E. on N2, turn L towards Motherwell and Addo.*

Tel: *021-428-9111*

reservations@sanparks.org

www.sanparks.org

Eyethu Hop-On Guides

Support the local community and get a guide on board - literally. Backed by Addo, the Eyethu guides all come from the villages around the park and run their own small business as affordable and very knowledgeable guides who join you in your car for a lap around the park.

Prices: *R100 - R300 charged per vehicle for a 2hr guided drive. Guides operate from 8am - 5pm every day. You can book a guide by contacting the park, or you can find them at the main gate (subject to availability of course!).*

Alexandria Hiking Trail

This is a 36km, two-day circular walk. Day 1 (19.5km) winds through ancient indigenous forest, home to bushbuck, the rare nocturnal tree dassie (as opposed to the very common rock dassie) and the beautiful Knsyna turaco. The path then meanders down onto the beach with kilometres of unspoilt coast. Trail your toes in the surf and look out for the bottlenose dolphin and southern right whale. A climb up the coastal cliffs and a stretch through fragrant coastal fynbos brings you to a welcome rest at the Woody Cape hut. The second day starts off strenuously through the dunes of the largest coastal dune field in the southern hemisphere. Once through the dune field, the indigenous forest beckons again and leads you to the end of the trail, where the newly-refurbished Langebos huts will provide rest for weary bones at the trail base.

Prices: *R50 pp per night. Hikers also have to pay a daily conservation/entry fee of R80 per adult. These prices may rise. Hikers must carry their own provisions and equipment. The hike is not guided, but is well signposted. Min of 3 per group, max 12.*

Contact: *Bookings for the trail administered by Camp Matyholweni.*

Tel: *041-468-0916/8*

matyholweni@sanparks.org

Trail base office: Woody Cape office at Addo National Park.

Tel: *046-653-0601*

For flights to and from Addo and other airborne adventures contact Mark Andrews at African Ramble. See Garden Route Activities Guides.

ALEXANDRIA
NATURE and ACTIVITIES

Quin Sculpture Garden and Gallery 

"Perfect synergy between sculpture and garden." Come and marvel at the array of beautiful sculptures that stand on plinths, peek from behind trees, graze on the lawn, guard a fountain or glower down from walls. Maureen is known nationwide and you must visit her studio to watch her at work (and then maybe even pick up a purchase from the gallery).

Prices: *R10 entry incl self-service tea, coffee or home-made lemon squash sipped in the tree shade.*
Contact: *Etienne and Maureen Du Plessis, 5 Suid St, Alexandria on R72.*
Tel: *046-653-0121*
Cell: *082-770-8000*
info@quin-art.co.za
www.quin-art.co.za

BEDFORD
NATURE and ACTIVITIES

Cavers Country Guest House

An Eden of mature, well-watered lawns and vivid flowers and a fifth generation working farm. Rozanne and Kenneth are great hosts and you are welcome to come and tour the garden or opt for the more energetic pursuits they can organise like horse-riding, fishing, or maybe even a spot of cricket!?

Prices: *Garden tour and tea R50, fishing R50, riding R100.*
Contact: *8km from Bedford on the R63 towards Adelaide.*
Tel: *046-685-0619*
Cell: *082-579-1807*
ckross@intekom.co.za
www.cavers.co.za

GRAHAMSTOWN
EATING and DRINKING

La Galleria

Italian elegance at its finest. Esme has been running this very popular restaurant for 14 years and serves the freshest pastas (i.e. four different ones made fresh every day) that you can even wash down with Italian wine (quite a rarity in a country with so much of its own great booze). Definitely opt for starters and desserts too, which arrive on a trolley for you to take your pick from.

Prices: *R120 for 3-course meal without wine. Open Mon - Sat for dinner.*
Contact: *Constitution St, Grahamstown.*
Tel: *046-622-2345*

Madhatters Coffee Shop

A bustling coffee shop often busy with university staff and students and quirkily decorated with murals depicting scenes from Alice In Wonderland. Alice would have wondered at the great selection of baked goodies (muffins, scones, cakes…) and no doubt started with their breakfast and come sharply back for lunch too (kudu, beef, ostrich…).

Prices: *Drinks from R6, breakfast R30 -R40, lunch dishes R20 - R40. Open all day Mon - Sat, plus Fri evening, closed Sun.*
Contact: *118 High St, Grahamstown.*
Tel: *046-622-9411*
j.mcdougall@ru.ac.za

Norden's Restaurant, The Cock House

Here at Norden's Belinda Tudge's team manage to wrap together South African, European and Asian food and then fold it into a fine dining restaurant within a cosy and friendly pub atmosphere. The building is heading for its 190th birthday and its yellowwood bar, is a favourite with locals.

Prices: *Starters R25 - R60, mains R58 - R78, desserts R20 - R30.*
Contact: *10 Market St, Grahamstown.*
Tel: *046-636-1287*
Cell: *082-820-5592*
cockhouse@imaginet.co.za
www.cockhouse.co.za

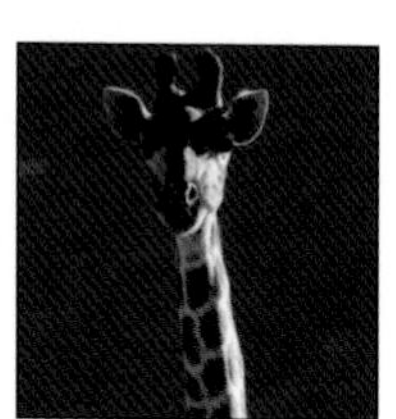

GRAHAMSTOWN
NATURE and ACTIVITIES

E.P. Sky Divers

The Eastern Cape is pretty massive, so get a good view of it from the air - albeit while hurtling towards the ground at great speed! Don't worry if you have no experience. Joos and his fellow instructors will be strapped to your back in tandem and in control (well, just one of them). An unforgettable experience (unless this is somehow the norm for you), but just in case you do (forget) you can get the dvd and photos to remind you of it.

Prices: *Tandem skydive R1,300. Dvd R450, photos R100.*
Contact: *Grahamstown airport.*
Cell: *082-800-9263*
joosvos@eastcape.net
www.epskydivers.co.za

GRAHAMSTOWN
CULTURE and HISTORY

Albany Museum

This is the second oldest museum in South Africa and today consists of a family of six buildings that specialise in natural history and sciences and Eastern Cape history (including the 1820 settlers). It also includes the Observatory Museum, a multi-storeyed Victorian building with a unique camera obscura - the only one ever built in South Africa.

Prices: *Obsevatory Museum R8 adults, R5 kids and pensioners, Natural History Museum R15 adults, R4 kids and pensioners. Natural History Museum open Tues - Fri and Sat morning, Observatory Museum open Mon - Fri and Sat morning.*
Contact: *Somerset St, Grahamstown.*
Tel: *046-622-2312*
l.webley@ru.ac.za
www.ru.ac.za/affiliates/am/info

Frontier Country

Boer and Zulu war history pervades much of the country's cultural background, but the Eastern Cape was also the scene of violent cultural clashes where British and Boer settlers collided with the resident Xhosa. The Eastern Cape was an area of rich grazing land, ripe for colonial expansion, but the Great Fish River that fed it also divided it, becoming a bitterly fought over frontier. Over almost a century, from 1779 - 1878, nine frontier wars were fought and today the region is littered with old forts and buildings of historical interest. Grahamstown itself has more than 70 heritage sites and its Albany Museum makes a good starting point for avid history hunters.

National Arts Festival Grahamstown

Dance, drama, opera, jazz, crafts, books, films and basically art of every and any shape and form… You name it and you can see it at this South Africa's best-known arts festival that takes Grahamstown by storm every year from the end of June to mid-July. A sort of Edinburgh Festival for the southern hemisphere.

Prices: *Ticket prices R20 - R80. Many events are free.*
Tel: *046-603-1103*
info@nafest.co.za
www.nafest.co.za

Valley of Ancient Voices

Visit a valley once sacred to its ancient inhabitants, the San and Khoi people. A three-hour walking tour takes you to rock art sites hidden in towering cliffs that are home to plenty of animals and birds including the magnificent black eagle (so don't forget those binoculars). You'll be transported in by 4x4 through a game reserve and given a backpack with a picnic lunch and water.

Prices: *R250 pp for 3 or fewer, R150 for 5 - 10 people.*
Contact: *From Grahamstown head 18km towards Bedford on R350, turn L and its 9km down R400 to Riebeek East.*
Tel: *046-622-8511*
info@ancientvoices.co.za
www.ancientvoices.co.za

KENTON-ON-SEA
EATING and DRINKING

Kenton-on-Sea for a reason

No wonder they built Kenton where they did, sandwiched between the Kariega and Bushmans rivers, it has some of the best beaches in the Eastern Cape. Sand is whiter than white, the bird life is fantastic and there are some great restaurants beside them too:

Homewood's Restaurant

It is small wonder that John chose to pitch his stand right on the sand. At the mouth of the Kariega River the setting really is remarkable and the restaurant specialises in seafood and steaks. Spoil yourself with the queen prawns or seafood bisque.

Prices: *Queen prawns R70, seafood bisque R55, calamari R50, line fish R55, mussels R44. Open from 11am, closed Sun night and Mon.*
Contact: *1 Eastbourne Rd, Kenton-on-Sea.*
Tel: *046-648-2700*
swootton@mweb.co.za

Sand Bar Floating Restaurant

Birders and nature lovers should keep eyes open for kingfishers and fish eagles at this restaurant which, as the name would suggest, bobs about on the Bushmans River. With the ocean a stone's throw away it specialises in seafood and neither the calamari nor a sundowner on the deck are to be missed.

Prices: *Salads and starters R15 - R30, light meals R13 - R40, fish R35 - R110, beef R45 - R65. Booking essential, open Tues - Sun.*
Contact: *Signed off R72, Bushmans River, Kenton-on-Sea.*
Tel: *046-648-2192*

Stanley's

Rodney and Dot Long run this farmhouse restaurant with a casual and friendly touch that goes perfectly with the great food. Sunday lunch is particularly popular with the locals so make sure you book ahead. The view from the deck over the Kariega River and bush is simply spectacular and there's bags of space for kids to exhaust themselves in.

Prices: *Sunday lunch R60 - R70, à la carte starters R20 - R25, seafood R50 - R80, steaks R55 - R80, lunches and light meals R30 - R40, desserts R20. Lunch and dinner every, closed Sun evening, breakfasts on request.*
Contact: *Eve's Retreat, 3.5km from Kenton-on-Sea on the Grahamstown road.*
Tel: *046-648-1332*
Cell: *082-774-9326*
stanleys@imaginet.co.za

BATHURST
EATING and DRINKING

Pig 'n Whistle Hotel

Built in 1831, the Pig 'n' Whistle (which started life as the Bathurst Inn) is more than 170 years old and the pub and restaurant ooze ancient and convivial charm. A huge menu of very affordable grub from fresh veggies from the garden and fresh fish to huge steaks.

Prices: *Nothing over R55 on the menu. Serving food every day from 8am - 9pm.*
Contact: *Cnr of York and Trappes St, Bathurst.*
Tel: *046-625-0673*
carzel@tiscali.co.za
www.pigandwhistle.co.za

PORT ALFRED
EATING and DRINKING

Milk Shed Restaurant, Green Fountain Farm

The Milk Shed (yes, once a milk shed) makes a great venue for breakfast for the early risers or lunch. All the dairy products come from the farm and there's something for everyone, pastas, steaks, curries and a pub menu too. Wander the farm, pick up some goodies from the stall or investigate the cheese factory.

Prices: *Starters and salads R20 - R35, mains R39 - R69, steaks R59 - R75. Open 8am - 5pm every day.*
Contact: *7km east of Port Alfred on R72.*
Tel: *046-624-5859*
robg@paparadise.co.za

PORT ALFRED
NATURE and ACTIVITIES

Anne Williams Bird-watching Tours

Praise came in from all corners for Ann's birding tours. She has an intimate knowledge of a 20km stretch around Port Alfred and has personally recorded 309 species there. But she's not purely a birder and, offering an ecological walk too, is just as happy talking flora, fauna and history. With access to private land, escaping the crowds is guaranteed.

Prices: *Birding tours R200 - R250 per hour for a group of max 6, ecological walk R80 pp for min 6, video presentation R250. Gift vouchers for all tours are available.*
Tel: *046-675-1976*
Cell: *083-719-4950*
birders-babble@eject.co.za
Read her Birder's Babble column on www.talkofthetown.co.za

Fish River Sun Golf

This is an 18-hole championship course designed by South African golfing legend Gary Player, and as such, it's pretty tricky stuff! The greens are fiendishly crumpled, the indigenous cactus-like euphorbia trees and rough bush are definitely to be avoided and the river is a ball-magnet. So pack your courage and plenty of spare balls, and let rip.

Prices: *Green fees for non-members R300 for 18 holes. Booking is essential.*
Contact: *On R72, 28km east of Port Alfred.*
Tel: *040-676-1002*
fishsun@sunint.co.za
www.suninternational.com

Great Fish Point Lighthouse

Bang on the estuary of the Great Fish River, this lighthouse is not the tallest of South Africa's 45 operational lighthouses (just 9m high) but, painted with black and white stripes, it stands out from the land around it like a sore thumb. You can visit it for tours and there's also a walking trail and even a pool and jungle gym here too.

Prices: *R15 entry.*
Contact: *24km from Port Alfred on mouth of Great Fish River.*
Tel: *021-449-2400*
salato@npa.co.za
www.npa.co.za (navigate to lighthouse tourism)

River Rufanes Horse Rides

Dave and Alison Legg take you horse-riding through rolling hills and pristine milkwood dune forest, then down to the ocean's edge for thrilling beach rides. The game and bird life are great, the guides are experienced and can cope with riders of all standards in the same group and the horses (most importantly!) are very well behaved.

Prices: *From R120 pp for 1.5hr ride. Prices will increase.*
Contact: *5km from Port Alfred*
Tel: *046-624-1469*
Cell: *082-697-1297*
davel@border.co.za

EAST LONDON
EATING and DRINKING

Ernst's Chalet Suisse

The seafood in the Eastern Cape is a speciality, particularly if Ernst is preparing it (don't miss his saddle of lamb either). Being Swiss, he has an international approach to his food which, combined with a cracking view onto the Indian Ocean, makes for a great meal all round. Come at the weekend for live entertainment and a wonderfully indulgent dining experience.

Prices: *Starters R24 - R40, mains R50 - R98, desserts R17 - R33. Lunch and dinner Mon - Fri, Sat dinner only, Sun lunch only.*
Contact: *Esplanade, Orient Beach Complex, East London.*
Tel: *043-722-1840*
steidl@iafrica.com

THE WILD COAST
NATURE and ACTIVITIES

The Wild Coast

This is one of South Africa's most unspoilt areas of natural beauty where the green slopes tumble off rocky cliffs into the Indian Ocean's crashing surf. For those who make it this far east there are some very rewarding coastal walks to be had. Starting at Port St. Johns you can take routes north or south from a few hours up to a few days, sleeping overnight in villages en route. The tourist office has local trail maps as well as all the information on longer hikes such as the five-day route to Coffee Bay. It strongly recommends that you do not do these alone. Ask them for details of local guides who will accompany you.

Prices: *A local route map will cost R10 from the tourist office, while guides cost around R150 per group per day. The tourist office is open every day, 8am - 4.30pm.*
Contact: *Port St Johns Tourism, at the entrance to the town.*
Tel: *047-564-1187*
tourismpsj@wildcoast.co.za
www.portstjohns.org.za

BIRDING BITS

You will see: Black-headed Oriole/Forest Buzzard

You'll be very lucky to see: Roseate and Bridled Tern

You might see: Red-necked Spurfowl/Emerald Cuckoo

Eyes peeled around Cape Recife and Port Elizabeth.

KwaZulu Natal

CRAZY ABOUT KZN

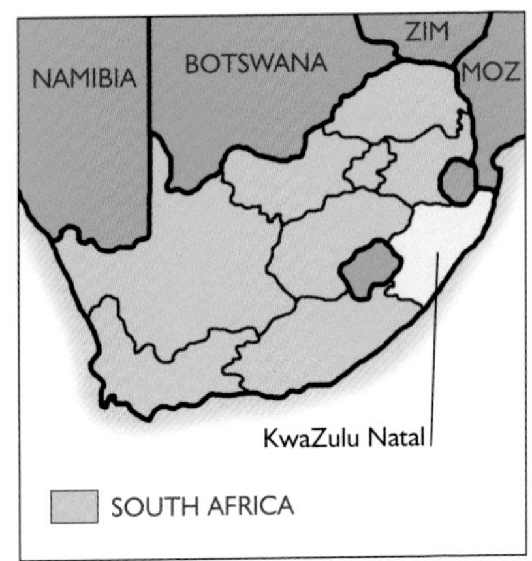

With other areas like Cape Town, the Garden Route and The Kruger Park already so firmly on the map KwaZulu Natal often doesn't get as much press as it deserves - so we are going to unashamedly blow its trumpet.

For anyone looking for a real range of activities from their holiday, this huge region offers as complete a package as you'll find anywhere in the country. KZN offers a perfect two- to three-week adventure.

Beaches: the entire coastline from Mozambique to the Eastern Cape is lined with white sand and blessed with warm Indian Ocean waters.

Mountains: the Drakensberg is a remarkable range that caters for fishing, riding, birding, hiking, rafting… and basically any outdoor activity.

History: the Boer War and Zulu battlefields such as Rorke's Drift, Isandhlawana and Three Tree Hill - but there are dozens more.

Culture: Zululand

Kids: the coastal and Midlands nature and activity parks are ideal for families who want activities other than the beach.

Food: Durban for great grills and Indian spices, the coast for seafood, the Midlands for gourmet retreats.

Game and nature: some of the finest reserves in the country from the lush hills of Umfolozi, to the coastal reserves of St Lucia Wetlands and Kosi Forest.

Navigation

When cross-referencing this chapter with the map note that we have firstly run south from Durban and then west as far as the Sani Pass. From there we start from Durban again and follow the N3 to the Free State border before arcing north-east to the Mozambique border and back down to the coast - a rather lumpy circle.

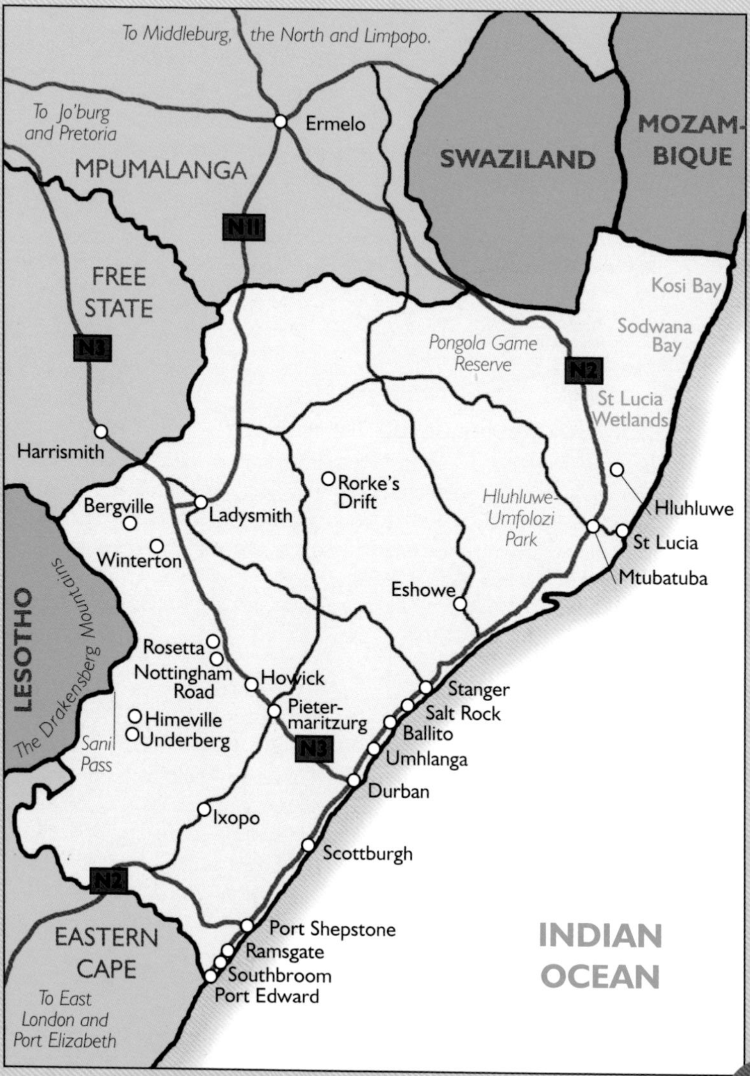

GUIDES AND EXPERTS

CULTURE and HISTORY GUIDES

Kian Barker, Shakabarker Tours

Kian weaves Zulu culture into his specialised trips around the Greater St Lucia Wetland Park, a 328,000ha park with five major eco-systems. Depending on your timing you could see migrating whales or loggerhead and leatherback turtles and, of course, plenty of birds. Try a night drive or a big five game trip.

Prices: *Big 5 trip R475, eastern shores and night drive trip R265, night drive R225, turtle tours R650, whale-watching R475, guided walk with Zulu guide R95.*

Contact: *Call Kian on 035-590-1162 or 082-445-6462.*

info@shakabarker.co.za

www.shakabarker.com

Graham Chennells, Zululand Eco-Adventures

Forget mock-up, mud-hutted villages, and come and experience real Zulu life with Graham Chennells - a born and bred Zululander (and, by the way, former mayor of Eshowe, paratrooper and sailor!). He'll take you to weddings, coming of age rites or sangoma healing ceremonies. Alternatively head to villages deep in Zululand to meet the people and find out about their politics, history and religion.

Prices: *Zulu traditional ceremony trip R350, 3-5-hour Zululand outback tour R450 - R650 min 3 people.*

Tel: *035-474-2298*

info@eshowe.com

www.eshowe.com

Ron Gold, Stonehaven Tours

Ron specialises in battlefields - which is a bonus, as there are dozens of them in KZN. He covers the Anglo-Boer wars, Anglo-Zulu wars and Voortrekker periods as well as showing guests the Sani Pass, bushman art sites and leading multi-day trips around this amazingly diverse region. He loves KZN and he'll show you why.

Prices: *R650 - R750 daily rate for up to 6 people, separate quotes for multi-day tours and if transport is required.*

Tel: *033-263-2632*

ron.gold@iafrica.com

Nicki von der Heyde, Campaign Trails

Nicki runs fully-guided trails through KZN's many battlefields, from the Boer camp at Colenso to the gun emplacement on Doornkop and the Isandhlwana wagon track. Choose whether to be in a minibus, a Landrover, on foot or, to really get into the spirit of it, on horse-back, riding the Tugela line and following in the cavalry's hoof prints.

Prices: *From around R1,600 pp per day depending on trail, including all transfers and transport out of Durban.*

Tel: *031-767-4166*

Cell: *082-653-4166*

nicki@campaigntrails.co.za

www.campaigntrails.co.za

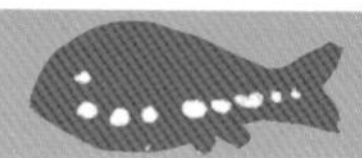

Raymond Heron, Spion Kop Lodge

Raymond is a superb raconteur and an incredibly knowledgeable historian who will bring to life the tragic Anglo-Boer war battle of Spion Kop as well as leading tours to Colenso and Ladysmith (and the Anglo-Zulu battlefields too). Once you've had enough of war, he's also a birding guide and will take you out on the massive Spion Kop Dam bird- and game-watching at sunset and sunrise. A fascinating combination.

Prices: *Spion Kop Battle Experience R395, Colenso, Ladysmith and Churchill capture site R500, bird and game-viewing boat cruises R200. Raymond and Lynette can also organise all sorts of other trips and transfers.*

Contact: *On R600, near Winterton, 20 mins off N3, mid-way between Jo'burg and Durban.*

Tel: *036-488-1404*

spionkop@futurenet.co.za

www.spionkop.co.za

Natal

The name Natal dates back to Portuguese explorer Vasco da Gama who named modern-day Durban "Rio de Natal" or "Christmas River" when he reached it on Christmas Day 1497. It was renamed Durban in 1835 after the then Cape Colony Governor Sir Benjamin Durban.

Digs Pascoe, Mountain Lake Adventures

Digs - sociologist, geologist and historian - is utterly passionate about Zululand. He knows the people and their culture, he speaks the languages fluently and he's keen to share it. Head deep (deep) into the bush with him, visit the people, see rhino and elephant, canoe with crocs, cast for tiger fish, meet the sangoma doctors, listen to fireside stories... and learn about Africa.

Prices: *Tours R50 - R500 per adult.*

Tel: *035-474-5181*

Cell in the bush: 082-926-2571

digspascoe@zulukingdom.co.za

NATURE GUIDES

Elsa Pooley Botanical Tours

Elsa is based on the south coast but zips about all over KZN, and in fact all over the country. She's a "practical botanist", and as well as growing plants, writing and painting she offers talks, walks and tours covering wild flowers, trees, grasses and ferns. She'll take you from mist-belt forests and bushveld to snowy peaks and mountainous dunes - just make sure you book her up well in advance.

Prices: *R250 per hour plus all expenses. Tours can be up to 2 - 3 weeks, also arranges a yearly botanical art course.*

Tel: *039-973-0486*

Cell: *082-487-5385*

pooleywildlife@sco.eastcoast.co.za

DURBAN
EATING and DRINKING

Butcher Boys

You'll struggle to find anything but good steak in S.A. But there's good, and there's really good. This is a serious steak house serving the best grain-fed beef this country has to offer, cut and cooked exactly as you want it. Choose your bottle from a temperature-controlled wine cellar and buy meat and biltong from the butcher to take home. Plenty of line-fishy/seafoody/chickeny options for the non-carnivorous.

Prices: *Starters R25 - R35, mains R45 - R90, desserts R20 - R30.*
Contact: *170 Florida Rd, Morningside, Durban.*
Tel: *031-312-8248*
www.butcherboysgrill.co.za

Havana Grill and Wine Bar

A huge, sizzling grill house specialising in aged beef and seafood. It's set right on the upper level of the casino and has great views of the whole city beach from South Beach all the way to Umhlanga. Dive into a leather-upholstered booth with your pals and treat yourself to Cuban cigars and S.A. wines. Seared tuna, grilled prime rib-eye and juniper berry ostrich steaks are the local favourites.

Prices: *Starters R30 -R50, mains R49 (hand-minced burger) - R230 (seafood platter), desserts around R30.*
Contact: *Shop U2, Suncoast Casino, Suncoast Boulevard, North Beach, Durban.*
Tel: *031-337-1305*
info@havanagrill.co.za or martin or andre@havanagrill.co.za
www.havanagrill.co.za

Manna

Central Durban can, like any city, be exhaustingly hectic, so escape to Morningside for lunch at Manna in its sun-dappled courtyard, a haven of tranquillity. Sandwiches, salads and "exceedingly good" cakes are freshly-baked here every day. If you feel spoilt for choice opt for the fishcakes served on a salad bed and topped with lemon mayo.

Prices: *Sarnies and salads R35, pasta R40, cakes R22, coffees R10.*
Contact: *40 Marriott Rd, Morningside, Durban (in courtyard behind Nauhaus).*
Tel: *031-309-8581*

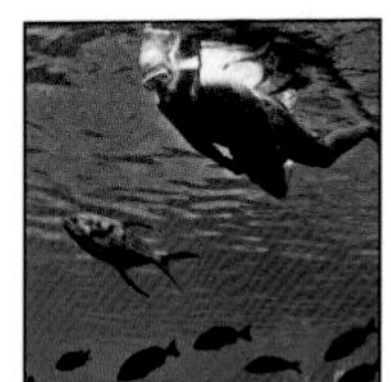

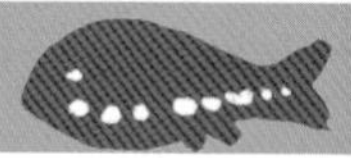

Mo Better Noodles

After too much holiday indulgence treat yourself to a healthy, low-fat meal. Joanne's fast and friendly team serve a light fusion menu of Thai and Japanese cuisine, one of the first of its kind in Durban and very popular with the locals. A typical dish mght be chicken rolled in sesame seeds with chilli and peanut.

Prices: *Starters about R32, mains R55, desserts R16. Lunch 12pm - 2.30pm Mon - Fri, dinner 6pm - 10pm Mon - Sat. Also do take-away.*
Contact: *Shop 5a, 275 Florida Rd, Durban.*
Tel: *031-312-4193*

Roma Revolving Restaurant

On the 32nd floor of John Ross House this restaurant has, without a doubt, one of the best views in the city you can get. Come at sunset and devour the enormous and authentic Italian spread as the Durban lights come on and you gawp over your wine glass at the sparkly, constantly-changing view. It's not called the revolving restaurant for nothing.

Prices: *Average meal R70.*
Contact: *32nd Floor, John Ross House, 22 Victoria Embankment, Durban.*
Tel: *031-337-6707*

The Grillroom Café

A fiizzing café by day that bubbles with the hustle and bustle of city life and a relaxed and romantic restaurant by night that matches calming views with a lip-smacking fusion menu. Hotly recommended come the lentil, Danish feta and mint salad and the smoked chicken with coconut tamarind.

Prices: *Starters R22 - R34, mains R59 - R79, desserts R22 - R28. Closed Mon.*
Contact: *465 Innes Rd, Morningside, Durban.*
Tel: *031-312-3456*
lee@grillroom.co.za
www.grillroom.co.za

Sprigs

"Breakfasts and lunches here are relaxed, healthy and delicious," a regular tells me. Morning omelettes are the way to start the day while at lunch, light deli-style food includes butternut, feta and roasted onion tart or beetroot, balsamic and rocket salad. And if you really enjoyed the food, you can buy Clare and Fiona's cookbook and make it for yourself - or at least try.

Prices: *Lunch dishes R20 - R40. Closed Sun.*
Contact: *Fields Shopping Centre, 15 Old Main Rd, Kloof, Durban.*
Tel: *031-764-6031*
sprigs@telkomsa.net

TransAfrica Express Jazz Café

The African food in this café comes from all over the continent, Congo crocodile, Ethiopian kitfo, Karoo lamb chops with maize meal to name but a few. Wash that down with some jazz from local bands who come to give of their best on the deck overlooking the harbour.

Prices: *Dishes cost R30 - R65.*
Contact: *Bat Centre, 45 Maritime Place, Small Craft Harbour, Durban.*
Tel: *031-332-0804*
Cell: *084-701-4566*
admin@transafricaexpress.co.za

DURBAN
NATURE and ACTIVITIES

Durban Country Club, Beachwood

While many may stick to Durban Country Club's main golf course, the Beachwood course (once a club in its own right) is a fantastically challenging alternative. Redesigned by Gary Player in 1995 it was originally built in indigenous woodland and lies next to a mangrove swamp that's home to a mass of bird life - a pleasant distraction if you're having a terrible round.

Prices: *Unaccompanied visitor's green fee R230, booking essential.*
Contact: *Beachwood Place, off Fairway Drive, about 2km north of Durban Country Club in Durban North.*
Tel: *031-313-1777*
sandera@dcclub.co.za
www.dcclub.co.za

Royal Durban Golf Course

Royal Durban is ringed by a race-track, although still bang in the centre of town. It might look easy being fairly flat and without too many tree-shaped obstacles - but did you account for the wind? Plenty of birds on a newly-constructed dam, but with the club motto "Play to Conquer" you'd better focus on birdies instead. Make time for a drink in the bar before leaving.

Prices: *Visitors very welcome. Green fees about R200, cart hire R150, club hire R100, caddies R120, meals R40 - R70.*
Contact: *16 Mitchell Crescent, Greyville, Durban.*
Tel: *031-309-1373*
rdgc@global.co.za

Indian spice

Most Asians in South Africa are descendants of Indian labourers brought in by the British to work on the sugar cane plantations and today Durban is home to the largest Asian population in sub-Saharan Africa. India's independence leader Mahatma Ghandi was once among that population, working here as a lawyer in the early 1900s.

uShaka Marine World

Africa's newest and largest marine park has been a massive hit since day one. The central attraction is the enormous aquarium built around a mock-up 1920's cargo shipwreck. It's great fun for the kids and there are rock pools and dive tanks to get that bit closer to the sea life. If they've energy left after all that there are water slides galore to hurl them down and then restaurants to fill them up.

Prices: *Sea World: adults R90, pensioners R80, kids R58. Wet 'n' Wild: R64, R48, R48. Combined ticket R128, R100, R80.*
Contact: *1 Bell St, Durban.*
Tel: *031-328-8000*
mkt@ushakamarineworld.co.za
www.ushakamarineworld.co.za

Durban Botanic Gardens

If you'll be visiting gardens in South Africa, start with the oldest. The 16ha Durban botanic gardens were established in 1849 to develop potentially useful commercial crops. Today they're home to a huge variety of plant collections (cycads, African orchids, palms...) and some of the oldest trees in the area. Stay for some tea and scones too. 300,000 visitors a year can't be wrong.

Prices: *Free entry. Open from 7.30am.*
Contact: *70 St Thomas Rd, Durban.*
Tel: *031-309-1170*
www.durbanbotgardens.org.za

The Bat Centre

This is the spot for arts and crafts in Durban, a waterfront arts centre featuring retail outlets, galleries, a drum café, a South African music shop.... There are also eateries, music rooms and an auditorium where you can see a number of artists and bands practising during the week.

Prices: *Prices specific to individual retailers. Open 9am - 2pm weekends, 8.30am - 5pm week days.*
Contact: *34 Maritime Place, Small Craft Harbour, Victoria Embankment, Durban.*
Tel: *031-332-0451*
events@batcentre.co.za
www.batcentre.co.za

The Catalina Theatre

Durban's coolest little brand-new (well almost) theatre, bang on the waterfront and surrounded by restaurants. There are kids' matinées on a regular basis during the school holidays; otherwise it's evening drama, musicals, and comedy for a 166 capacity audience.

Prices: *Average ticket price R60 -R70. Shows every night except Mon, usually start at 8pm, kids shows at 11am.*

Contact: *Wilson's Wharf, 8 Boatman's Rd, Victoria Embankment, Durban.*

Tel: *031-305-6889/7612*

www.catalinatheatre.co.za

The Phansi Museum

Pumzile Nkosi will show you this museum which houses a private collection of South African tribal artefacts beautifully displayed in the basement of Roberts House, a Victorian historical monument. You'll see outstanding examples of Zulu, Ndebele and Xhosa beadwork, headrests, carved spoons, fertility dolls and more, as well as a contemporary collection of modern sculpture... for the culture vulture.

Prices: *R35 entry fee. Open Mon - Fri, 8am - 5pm, weekend viewing by appointment.*

Contact: *41 Cedar Rd, Glenwood, Durban.*

Tel: *031-206-1591*

phezulu1@mailbox.zo.za

SCOTTBURGH
NATURE and ACTIVITIES

Crocworld

Meet Henry, a 100-year-old, 4.8m-long, 750kg crocodile and the big daddy of more than 10,000 crocs, alligators and other crocodilian species at Crocworld. Henry has 10 wives and has killed every other male ever put with him. If you're brave enough there's a rope-bridge across his pool. If you're not there are 30ha to explore here and, aside from reptilian dinosaurs, plenty of bird life, a cycad and wetlands area and an eatery and shop.

Prices: *Adults R30, kids R15. Croc feeding every day bar Mon at 11am and 3pm.*

Contact: *Old Main Rd, Scottburgh, 60km from Durban.*

Tel: *039-976-1103*

crocworld@cbl.co.za

www.crocworld.co.za

PORT SHEPSTONE
NATURE and ACTIVITIES

Wild 5

Major adrenalin action in the fabulous Oribi Gorge, 22km inland from the sea. The wild swing sends you hurtling over the edge of the Lehr's falls in a 100m arc reaching 120km/hr. Once the heart rate has slowed, abseil down the gorge or wild slide across it 160m above the valley floor. Then white-water raft down the Umzimkhulu River and mountain bike and horse ride through the magnificent scenery. Easy!

Prices: *Wild swing R300, abseil R190, wild slide R170, rafting R350. Book ahead.*
Contact: *11km off N2, near Port Shepstone.*
Tel: *039-687-0253*
Cell: *082-566-7424*
info@oribigorge.co.za
www.oribigorge.co.za

RAMSGATE
EATING and DRINKING

La Petite Normandie

A small corner of France where Yvonne serves typically delicious French country cuisine with a slice of Switzerland served on the verandah ("The Matterhorn Corner"). Try beef fondu, raclette or some real Swiss cheese. She opens at 10am for relaxed breakfasters and also serves lunch and afternoon teas and coffees with French cakes and tarts.

Prices: *Starters R37 - R75, mains R67 - R235. Open every day.*
Contact: *73 Marine Drive, Ramsgate.*
Tel: *039-317-1818*
Cell: *073-254-1999*

The Bistro

Veryan's bistro fits the bill of relaxed fine dining and the service is great. Rack of lamb, roast duck and beef Wellington are all popular choices as is the seafood. The desserts are works of art quickly destroyed and devoured and watch out for a surprisingly large and quirky collection of cats ("pictures and ornaments - the real ones are at home").

Prices: *Average spend R150 incl drinks.*
Contact: *Marine Drive, Ramsgate. 3km south of waffle house, 3km north of croc farm.*
Tel: *039-314-4128*
thebistro@isat.co.za

RAMSGATE
NATURE and ACTIVITIES

Conservation of Butterflies in South Africa

The Whiteley family have been promoting the conservation of butterflies for four generations in South Africa. They breed them at the Butterfly Sanctuary from ovum to chrysalis and you can see the results flapping casually around their Lepidome in Ramsgate. Wander alone or let a guide show you what's what.

Prices: *R25 adults, R20 pensioners, R15 kids, field guide hire R5.*
Contact: *46a Fascadale Rd, Ramsgate.*
Tel: *039-314-9307*
tours@sabutterflies.co.za
www.sabutterflies.co.za

Mpenjati Reserve

60ha of interlinking wetlands, grasslands and dune forest make for great birding, fishing, swimming and hiking here, 20km south of Margate. And, unlike some of the vast reserves you'll visit, it's very do-able in a day. Short walking trails follow the banks of the Mpenjati river with various antelope and a breeding pair of fish eagles to be seen. There are observation platforms looking out over the lagoon and picnic sites on either side armed with the ever-present braai areas and also a kids' playground.

Prices: *R10 per adult, R5 per child collected by a roving ranger.*
Contact: *On N2, 20km south of Margate, 12km from Port Edward.*
Tel: *039-313-0531*
www.kznwildlife.com

Pure Venom

The kids will love this one. The largest reptile farm in Africa, Terence Whittle's farm is slipping, sliding and slithering with snakes, crocs, frogs, lizards, alligators and generally anything that might send a shiver down your spine. A great place to really learn about these creatures. They cater for birthday parties and school groups and have gardens, the Viper Pub and Grill for grub and a shop on site.

Prices: *Adults R20, kids R10 (free if under 3).*
Tel: *039-685-0704*
info@purevenom.com
www.purevenom.com

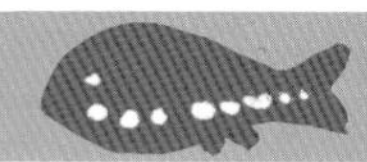

SOUTHBROOM
EATING and DRINKING

Trattoria La Terrazza

Buried behind the South Coast banana plantations this is quite a find. A covered loggia with an open lower deck looking onto the Umkobi Lagoon and the Indian Ocean. The surf beats rhythmically on the rocks and washes up the beach, setting the scene perfectly for Massimo and Niki Negra's innovatively varied but Italian-at-heart menu.

Prices: *Starters R35 - R45, mains R55 - R85, desserts R40 - R45, wines R50 - R210. Booking advisable, open for lunch and dinner, closed Mon.*
Contact: *Bottom of Outlook Rd, Southbroom, Southbroom South exit off N2.*
Tel: *039-316-6162*
masniki@venturenet.co.za

PORT EDWARD
NATURE and ACTIVITIES

Umtamvuna Nature Reserve 

The most southerly nature reserve in KZN, Umtavuna's 3,247 hectares lie alongside its name-sake river and mark the border with the Eastern Cape. The coastal strip becomes evermore lush the further south you travel and Umtamvuna is testament to that. A haven of botanical diversity with a rich display of spring flowers along a stretch of riverine forest and steep rocky cliffs. Come for the flora and the walking trails that can last from an hour to a whole day. Eyes peeled for breeding Cape vulture and fish eagle as well as bushbuck, baboon, duiker and samango monkeys.

Prices: *R10 per adult, R5 per child entry fee payable at the gate.*
Contact: *Outside Port Edward on Eastern Cape border.*
Tel: *039-313-2383*
www.kznwildlife.com

The Battle of Blood River

The British were by no means the only ones to clash with the Zulus - the Boers had been at it for ages. During the Great Trek of the mid-1800s, while many headed north west, thousands of Boer farmers came east of the Drakensberg to present-day KZN. The struggle for land once again led to war and in December 1838, on the banks of the Blood River, 10 - 20,000 Zulu impi attacked some 470 Voortrekkers led by Andries Pretorius (hence the capital Pretoria). Remarkably, thanks to their rifles and strong laager or wagon-ring defensive position, not a single Boer lost his life, while some 3,000 Zulus were killed.

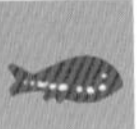

IXOPO
CULTURE and HISTORY

The Buddhist Retreat Centre

Perhaps an unlikely find in the hills around Ixopo, this is a retreat centre offering workshops in philosophy and meditation, bird-watching, yoga, chi kung, creative writing, Japanese brush painting and even kite flying! A fascinating experience and stunning spot to come and simply be.

Prices: *R200 - R300 per day incl all meals, lectures etc.*
Contact: *Exit 61 [Umlaas Road/R56 off ramp] from N3, follow R56 signs towards Richmond/Ixopo. 5km before Ixopo turn R onto D64. BRC on R after 7 km.*
Tel: *039-834-1863*
Cell: *082-579-3037*
brcixopo@futurenet.co.za
www.brcixopo.co.za

UNDERBERG
NATURE and ACTIVITIES

Pennygum Rafting

Liz and Tony are open to guests 24 hours a day and ready to get your blood pumping with rafting on some of the cleanest Drakensberg water in some of the most spectacular Drakensberg scenery. All abilities welcome and if there isn't enough water, they'll organise other activities that are just as exciting, including quad biking, Sani Pass trips into Lesotho and rock art walks.

Prices: *R100 - R280 pp for rafting.*
Contact: *Drakensberg Garden Resort Rd, Underberg.*
Tel: *033-701-1023*
info@pennygum.co.za
www.pennygum.com

Rob Guy Expeditions

Rob Guy and Steven Piper lead adventurous birding trips up the tortuous Sani Pass into the mountain kingdom of Lesotho in search of the rare and endemic bearded vulture (or lammergeier), Cape griffon vulture, Drakensberg orange-breasted rock-jumper and other birds with equally great names. Prepare for rough roads, cold winds, bright skies, great chat, picnics and also trips to mist-belt forest and grasslands.

Prices: *About R2,500 for up to 8 people for a day's birding incl picnic lunch. Starts from and returns to Underberg..*
Tel: *033-701-1020*
Cell: *072-599-7490*
rguysani@webmail.co.za

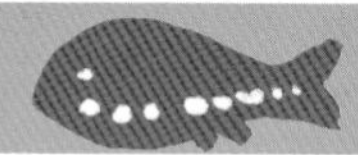

Underberg Open Gardens

This tends to happen in early summer, towards the end of October each year and garden lovers should stop in for a look on the way past - a suitable nerve calmer after negotiating the Sani Pass. Dates are very much dependant on winter and spring weather so call or email to find out when it might be on.

Contact: *For details call Sylvia Shephard on 033-701-2629*
farhorizonbb@mweb.co.za

HIMEVILLE

EATING and DRINKING

Sani Top Pub

Not many pubs can lay claim to being the highest in Africa, well, only one in fact... and it's here, dividing KZN from the Kingdom of Lesotho at the top of the hair-raising Sani Pass 2,874m (9,429ft). 4x4/quad-bike or (if you're really mad) run and cycle your way up here for some of the most dramatic and rugged scenery you'll see in S.A. And also for pub lunches, fine draught ales, glüwein and hot mountain toddies.

Prices: *Lunch R25 - R60, transport R250 - R300 including tour of local Lesotho village.*
Contact: *At the top of the Sani Pass, Himeville.*
Tel: *033-702-1069*
Cell: *082-715-1131*
sanitop@futurenet.co.za
www.sanitopchalet.co.za

Shaka Zulu

Shaka was a Zulu king and Shaka's Rock, so the story goes, is a rock from which he made his warriors jump to show bravery... or threw prisoners to the sharks (depending on what you read). Whatever he did there, he was certainly central to fomenting a still-thriving Zulu culture.

Born the illegitimate son of the clan's chief in 1787, he developed into a formidable warrior and became ruler when his father died in 1816. Honing his military skills, Shaka expanded the Zulu kingdom and identity to include more than 100,000 people with almost half of those recruited into the army.

Through wars with neighbouring tribes the Zulu kingdom grew to cover a large area stretching north to the Mozambique border, west to the Drakensberg and south to the Wild Coast (pretty much modern-day KZN). Shaka welcomed British farmers and sent emissaries to Britain, but was assassinated at the height of his power in 1828 and succeeded by his half-brother. Tensions between the British and Zulus led to the Zulu wars of the 1870s.

HIMEVILLE
NATURE and ACTIVITIES

Off-Road Adventures

Bar doing it on foot, quad bikes and 4x4 are basically the only way up the Sani Pass and, spurred on by 250cc bikes, Chris Corbett will take you right to the top, up the pass and over into the astonishing lunar landscape of Lesotho. Don't worry if you've never ridden a motorbike before. Quads are stable and easy to manage and you'll be trained up before you go. Shorter and longer trips also available.

Prices: *To Dec 1st, 2006: 1hr trail R200, 1.5hr trail R300, 4hr Sani Pass tour R450. To Dec 1st, 2007: 1hr trail R250, 1.5hr trail R300, 4hr Sani Pass tour R550. Don't forget your camera!*

Contact: *Short trails leave from the Sani Pass Hotel, outside Himeville on the Sani Pass road.*

Cell: *083-404-4422*

info@offroadadventures.co.za

www.offroadadventures.co.za

Sani Stagger

Madness, utter madness - so definitely worth seeing. For some reason, someone decided it would be a good idea to hold a race up the Sani Pass - the third highest road pass in the world. You can do the half-marathon up it (terrible), the half-marathon down it (bad... but better) or the whole thing, up and down (insane). Usually takes place in the last weekend of Nov.

Tel: *033-701-1577*

info@sanistagger.com

www.sanistagger.com

BOTHA'S HILL
NATURE and ACTIVITIES

On Air Raptor Display

Free-flying raptor demonstrations where the kids are encouraged to participate. There's also a vulture enclosure where unreleasable birds are kept. Watch the frenzy at feeding time or wander off and enjoy the 60ha of natural bush and great views over the rolling hills and wide horizons.

Prices: *R30 adults, R15 kids, discount for pensioners. Raptor shows Tues - Sun at 10.30am and 3pm.*

Contact: *168 Old Main Rd, Botha's Hill (exit 65 off N3 between Durban and Pietermaritzburg).*

Tel: *031-785-2000*

Cell: *082-925-3023*

onair@africanraptor.co.za

www.africanraptor.co.za

PIETERMARITZBURG
EATING and DRINKING

Artist's Palate Coffee Shop

Penny runs an arty and cross-cultural café here with an eclectic and hectic atmosphere. It's an ever-changing gallery where chairs, walls and even mugs are painted and made by local artists and craftsmen with the focus on traditional fabrics and national art. Scoff down the mild chicken and prawn curry and if you're lucky you may be able to combine your visit with one of Chris Duigan's Music Revival events.

Prices: *Average meal R40. Open 10am - 4pm, Tues - Sat.*
Contact: *45 Miller St, Pietermaritzburg.*
Tel: *033-342-8327*

PIETERMARITZBURG
NATURE and ACTIVITIES

Butterflies of Africa

Hundreds of "flutterbys", as my dad used to call them, from across the globe here... but also iguanas, finches and quails to watch out for. It's pretty educational stuff too with an audio-visual presentation, butterfly museum and a garden planted with butterfly foodstuffs to show you what to plant if you want to attract them to your own garden. Look carefully and you may see one emerging from its pupa.

Prices: *R22 adults, R15 kids and pensioners. Admission to forthcoming monkey house will cost extra.*
Contact: *37 Willowton Rd, Pietermaritzburg.*
Tel: *033-387-1356*
info@butterflies.co.za
www.butterflies.co.za

Pietermaritzburg and Midlands Open Gardens

Admire southern hemisphere green-fingery. The Witness (local paper) Open Gardens has been running for over 15 years and features some of the most beautiful and diverse private gardens in this region of KZN. Some 40 are open to the public (including some industrial green spaces too). The majority are open for the last two weekends of Sept and the first weekend of Oct, depending on the weather.

Prices: *Entry usually free, donations welcomed. Gardens open 9am - 4.30pm. Check opening days and venues.*
Contact: *Gail Cornhill*
Tel: *031-785-1874*
Cell: *082-445-2577*
gail@spottedowl.co.za

PIETERMARITZBURG
CULTURE and HISTORY

Music Revival

If you're lucky enough to be about when Chris Duigan is organising a concert do not miss it. He's a professional musician and presents classical music evenings in wonderful locations across the Midlands from his home in Pietermaritzburg to art galleries and private country houses.
Performances range from informal dinner or picnic concerts to recitals and chamber music by national and international musicians. Performers are encouraged to discuss the music with their audience (usually 50 - 150 people). A truly great way to spend an evening.
Watch out for the music festival Chris organises in Hilton in Sept as well as two in Franschhoek - end of April and end of October.

Prices: *Tickets range from R40 - R180 depending on food and wine included. Franschhoek tickets cost R50 - R500 depending on food and wine - top restaurants included.*
Tel: *033-342-3051*
Cell: *083-742-7497*
chris@musicrevival.co.za
www.musicrevival.co.za

The Midlands Meander

The KZN Midlands is rich in arts and crafts and this route winds its way through the best of them. Ask about it at any tourist office in the area and they will load you down with info and maps that can point you in the direction of potters and painters, brewers and book-binders, as well as a good few eateries too.

HOWICK
EATING AND DRINKING

Caversham Mill Restaurant

Bang on the Lions river in the KZN Midlands Terry and Diana Acres' team serves up piles of deliciously modern comfort food in their restaurant overlooking the tumbling falls and the old wheel of the water mill.

Prices: *Starters R30 - R40, mains R70 - R80, desserts R20 - R30. Open lunch only Sun - Mon, lunch and dinner Tues - Sat.*
Contact: *On D103 between Howick and Mooi River.*
Tel: *033-234-4524*
cavershammill@mweb.co.za
www.cavershammill.co.za

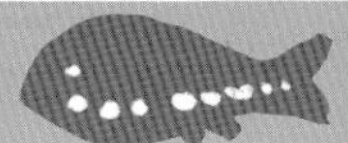

The Afton

Framed by an English garden and named after a Scottish river, this historic stone house was built in 1886 as a family home and 220-odd years later it still has a homely feel. Inter-leading rooms offer a variety of eating spaces and a menu laden with KZN seafood and hearty pies and meat dishes caters for every tummy and every pocket.

Prices: *Starters around R30, mains R45 - R75, desserts R25. Lunch and dinner Weds - Fri, dinner Sat, lunch Sun.*
Contact: *Cnr Bell and Somme St, Howick.*
Tel: *033-330-5256*
afton@satweb.co.za
www.satweb.co.za/afton

Yellowwood Café

Inside: a 135-year-old, wooden-floored stone house with hefty fireplaces, swallow-you-whole sofas and piles of books to read in them. Outside: a park-like garden of tall yellowwoods. Let the kids loose on the jungle gym then sit beneath the trees or on the verandah and gaze at the Howick Falls and the farm animals. This is classic Midlands stuff and alongside the great restaurant there's a café, a bar, an antique furniture shop and an indigenous nursery.

Prices: *Light coffee shop menu (open sandwiches etc) R12 - R15. Restaurant à la carte menu updated every 3 months, starters R15 - R30, mains R30 - R90, desserts R15 - R35, wine R30 - R160.*
Contact: *1 Shafton Rd, Howick.*
Tel: *033-330-2461*
Cell: *082-575-0602*
scm1728@mweb.co.za
www.yellowwood.co.za

HOWICK
NATURE and ACTIVITIES

Karkloof Canopy Tour

If you visit Howick you must make the detour to Karkloof. A 1km zip line (or "foefie slide" in S.A.) makes for an astonishing guided inspection of flora and fauna. The three-hour trip takes you on an adventure through the treetops, zigzagging down a valley of pristine forest via seven platforms - one of few places in the world where you can do this. Oh, and there's a small 54m waterfall abseil available too!

Prices: *Zip line R395, pensioners 10% discount. Abseil R250.*
Contact: *Off the Karkloof/Rietvlei Rd out of Howick, 17 km from town on L.*
Tel: *033-330-3415*
Cell: *083-228-8092*
info@karkloofcanopytour.co.za
www.karkloofcanopytour.co.za

The Midlands (along with the Garden Route around Plettenberg Bay) is popular polo country and if you fancy finding out all about "chukkas", "safety 60s" and "ride-offs" call Tom and Lucinda Bate at **Inversanda** on 033-234-4321 for information on the next game for the local Lions River Polo Club.

NOTTINGHAM ROAD
EATING and DRINKING

Nottingham Road Brewery

I drank rather a lot of Nottingham Road beer when I was in the Midlands (all in the name of research you understand) and can assure you that it's as close to a pint of real English ale as you'll find in South Africa - fantastic stuff. Deon et al are happy to show you around for five minutes or half an hour depending on how interested you are and of course you'll need to do your own research in the bar afterwards. Try the Pickled Pig Porter and the Whistling Weasel!

Prices: *Tours are free, booking advisable though you can just drop in.*
Contact: *Rawdons Hotel, Nottingham Road.*
Tel: *033-266-6044/6728*
brewery@rawdons.co.za
www.brewery.co.za

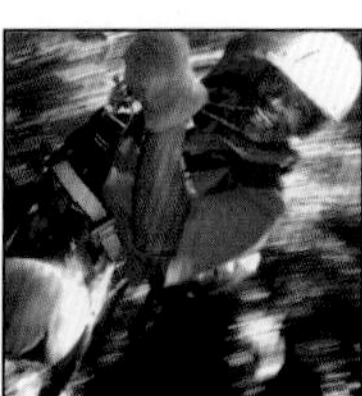

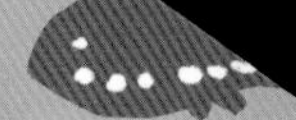

NOTTINGHAM ROAD
NATURE and ACTIVITIES

Airborne Adventures Africa

No need to try and take snaps from the air as you take off in a jumbo jet. Do it from a hot-air balloon and see the Midlands the leisurely way (or Gauteng and Mpumalanga - they do flights there too). Gary will take you up at the crack of dawn (literally) when the weather is good, giving you the most incredible views from the basket.

Prices: *R2,100 pp. You will be told the launch venue when you book.*
Tel: *033-266-6620*
Cell: *084-504-2171*
theoffice@airborneadventuresafrica.com
www.airborneadventuresafrica.com

BALGOWAN
EATING and DRINKING

Cleopatra Mountain Farmhouse

One of the finest and most famous restaurants in South Africa, where dining is reserved to guests only so you'll just have to stay the night. Ordered herb gardens supply many of the ingredients and the restaurant sits on a trout-stocked dam wedged into fantastic Drakensberg walking country. So treat yourself with Mozambique tiger prawns steamed in lemon grass or griddled springbok fillet on fondant potato.

Prices: *R1,000 - R1,400 pp gets you a massive dinner, a massive bed and a massive breakfast too - no-one has ever asked for lunch.*
Contact: *Take R103 to Rosetta from N3, then Kamberg Valley Road opposite the Ugly Duckling for 30km.*
Tel: *033-267-7015*
cleopatramountain@telkomsa.net
www.cleomountain.com

Granny Mouse Country House

This is a family-owned and managed country house (no mice as far as I'm aware) with a great home-from-home atmosphere. Breakfast and lunch are best savoured on the terrace soaking up the Midlands scenery while the dining room comes equipped with an underground cellar of some 4,000 wines to accompany cosmopolitan South African dinners.

Prices: *Starters R18 - R48, mains R50 - R86, desserts R18 - R39.*
Contact: *R103, Old Main Rd, Balgown.*
Tel: *033-234-4071*
info@grannymouse.co.za
www.grannymouse.co.za

Swissland Cheese

A chunk of Switzerland in Africa where Fran Vermaak makes goats' cheese from her small herd in a Swiss chalet. Come and watch the milking (from 3.30pm) and choose from a selection of nine cheeses from Brie to Pecorino, then gobble them on the lawn.

Prices: *From R90 - R160 per kg. Shop open 9.30am - 4.30pm, closed Thurs.*
Contact: *Swissland, Old Main Rd R103, Balgowan.*
Tel: *033-234-4042*
cheez@telkomsa.net

DRAKENSBERG
WALKING

Drakensberg walking trails

This mountain range forms the backbone of eastern South Africa, running from the Eastern Cape all the way up through Lesotho, KZN, Swaziland, Mpumalanga and Limpopo. There are literally thousands of kilometres of walking trails and some of the best are to be found towering over the KZN Midlands. Everything from half-hour strolls to hard-core multi-day hikes are available and the four main reserve camps sell detailed maps. Keen hikers should order a map before you travel to South Africa to really see what's on offer and to plan your expedition.

Prices: *Laminated maps (go on - spoil yourself!) cost around R50 and you will have to pay if you wish to join longer, guided walks.*
Contact: *Royal Natal National Park, off R74 at Bergville, 036-438-6310*
Cathedral Peak, off R600 at Winterton, 036-488-8012/4
Giants Castle, off R103 at Rosetta, 036-353-3718
Cobham Nature Reserve, off R617 at Himeville, 033-702-0831
To order maps call central reservations on 033-845-1000
For specific enquiries contact juliewex@kznwildlife.com
www.kznwildlife.com

WINTERTON
NATURE and ACTIVITIES

Four Rivers Rafting and Adventures

The Fouries family have an effervescent zest for adventure and had been into canoeing and rafting for years before finally turning a hobby into a business. Aside from the river-based activities, they organise go-karts (my favourite), quad bikes, archery, zip lines (not at the same time!) and abseiling.

Prices: *30-min quad out-rides from R165 adults, R110 kids, go-karting from R200 per hour, rafting R300, abseiling R100. Booking essential, prices may rise.*
Contact: *On R600 near Winterton, between Thokozisa and Bell Park/Cayley Lodge turn-off.*
Tel: *036-468-1693*
Cell: *083-785-1693*
info@fourriversadventures.co.za
www.fourriversadventures.co.za

Monk's Cowl Country Club

A real family country golf club where if your handicap isn't up to scratch you can play tennis, swim or eat in the restaurant instead. No-one stomping about telling you off for wearing the wrong socks here. The course is a friendly nine-holer with wide fairways surrounded by pine trees and looking onto the (often snowy) peaks of the Drakensberg. Ask about the night golf.

Prices: *Green fee R85 for 18 holes, discounts for golf union members, students, pensioners.*
Contact: *On D19 off R600, Champagne Valley, nr Winterton.*
Tel: *036-468-1300*
monkscowl@futurenet.co.za
www.monkscowl.co.za

Rolling M Ranch

Lorna Harris and Mike Bentley cherish a reputation for exciting horse trails on this Drakensberg ranch. The terrain of the Uthukela biosphere is rugged stuff and with horses known for their amiable natures and sure-footedness you can lope along in your genuine western cowboy saddle and focus on the surroundings along trails to the Anglo-Boer battlefields, Voortrekker monuments and the ruined healer's kraal.

Prices: *R200 for half-day ride, R500 for full day ride incl champagne picnic in the bush. Novices welcome, tuition given. Many other activities also available.*
Contact: *Near Winterton, off R600 to Spion Kop.*
Cell: *082-773-9914*
rollingmranch@saol.com
www.rollingmranch.co.za

WINTERTON
CULTURE and HISTORY

Drakensberg Boys' Choir

The Drakensberg Boys' Choir are rated one of the best boys' choirs in the world for their repertoire of African music. They perform every Wednesday afternoon during term times in the auditorium on the school's estate as well as at locations around the country during their frequent tours.

Prices: *Weds performances are at 3.30pm and tickets cost R70 - R80 for adults and R30 - R40 for kids. R60 - R70 for adult groups of 10 or more.*

Contact: *About 30km from Winterton towards the mountains, beyond Monk's Cowl and Champagne Sports.*

Tel: *036-468-1012*

info@dbchoir.co.za

www.dbchoir.co.za

KwaZulu Weavers

Of all the trinkets and souvenirs you could buy, a high-quality rug (unlike a bow and arrow) is something you will actually use... and this is the place to find them, designed with just the pattern you want. You can watch the whole process from the glass-panelled show room and you don't need to worry about lugging your rug around as they can easily ship it home for you.

Prices: *Rugs cost R550 - R5,500.*

Contact: *On R600, Winterton, Central Drakensberg.*

Tel: *036-488-1098*

sales@kwazuluweavers.com

www.kwazuluweavers.com

BERGVILLE
NATURE and ACTIVITIES

All Out Adventures

The enormous flying trapeze (with safety net, you'll be glad to hear) that you spot as you arrive at All Out Adventures gives you an immediate idea of what you'll be up to. From bungy bounces to the gorge swing and circus arts workshops, Chris and Loretta are full of surprises. Local staff are talented and enthusiastic and it all makes for great family fun in the most dramatic Drakensberg setting.

Prices: *R30 - R150 per activity.*

Contact: *Montusi Farm, off D119, Bergville.*

Tel: *036-438-6242*

Cell: *072-386-1344*

info@alloutadventures.co.za

www.alloutadventures.co.za

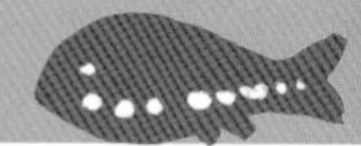

Montusi Horse Safaris

The great thing about riding is that you can let the horse do the work while you drink in the views - and nowhere is that more important than here alongside the wall of Drakensberg rock known as the "amphitheatre". This is a ride that can only be done in a two-day stint and you'll overnight in tents at Sungubala Mountain Camp. Enjoy dinner under the stars and around the camp fire, before riding back the next day. Routes can be varied to suit the saddle-hardened and the saddle-soft alike.

Prices: *Around R1,200 pp all inclusive.*
Contact: *Montusi Farm, off D119, Bergville.*
Tel: *036-438-6243*
montusi@iafrica.com
www.montusi.za.net

HARRISMITH
CULTURE and HISTORY

I know I know, Harrismith isn't in KZN it's in the Free State - but only just, and these three items make more geographical sense when slipped in here.

Intibazwe Township Tours

Let Joyce show you the township of Harrismith. She works in the tourist office and is a friendly and dedicated guide who will introduce you to the people, show you their homes and way of life and teach you about a side of South Africa you are unlikely to see without someone who knows the lie of the land.

Prices: *R50 pp, tour lasts three hours.*
Contact: *Joyce Mthembu*
Tel: *058-622-3525*
Cell: *082-509-2545*
easternfreestate@isat.co.za

HARRISMITH
NATURE and ACTIVITIES

Eagle Safaris

Simon Leach does just about everything from his Free State farm. He's an expert on birds and will take you tramping over the hills on hiking trails or fly-fishing for some lunch. In the evening there's star-gazing on offer before (and/or after) a slap-up meal. Motorbike trails are available too for longer distance travel and Simon is also a professional hunter.

Prices: *R450 for a day's birding, hiking or fly-fishing or for supper and star-gazing. Off-road motorbike trails 5 - 7 days about R1,900 a day all-inclusive (except spirits). Wing-shooting safari 7 - 10 days about R1,700 per day all-inclusive.*
Contact: *Kenroy Farm, Harrismith.*
Tel: *058-622-3225*
Cell: *082-572-7725*
eagle-safaris@isat.co.za
www.eagle-safaris.co.za

Platberg Nursery

This is a beautiful cold-climate garden (down to minus 11°C in fact) where Pietré runs a retail nursery specialising in some 700 cold-climate plants (perfect for us Brits to bring home). She's knowledgeable and friendly and can also point you in the direction of other interesting things to get up to around Harrismith.

Prices: *Free entry. All sorts of plants on sale from R5 - R650. Open Mon - Fri 7.30am -5pm, Sat 7.30am - 1pm.*
Contact: *Pietré Enslin, 101 Biddulph St, Harrismith (Durban side of town in the residential area).*
Tel: *058-622-2254*
pietre@internext.co.za

VAN REENEN
NATURE and ACTIVITIES

Oaklands Country Manor

Twenty years after putting it to one side, former British army officer Jamie Bruce has taken up polo again with a vengeance and he's built a dedicated polo arena at the magnificent Oaklands, a country hotel that he and wife Anna run deep in the Drakensberg. Polo packages are available from introductory courses to itineraries for teams and individuals. For non-polophiles there are tennis courts, the pool, hiking fishing, kids' activities galore and, of course, the pub.

Prices: *So many things on offer it's best to call and ask but a day's instruction costs R1,200.*
Contact: *Off N3 at Van Reenen, turn R at Caltex garage, 7km down dirt track.*
Tel: *058-671-0067/77*
info@oaklands.co.za
www.oaklands.co.za

DUNDEE

CULTURE and HISTORY

Talana Museum

This land once reverberated with the crash of canon fire at the beginning of the Angle-Boer war. Now that the dust has settled, displays of weapons, uniforms and artefacts as well as yearly re-enactments (August) bring the history flooding back. War is not the only subject though. Mining, agriculture and domestic life are also covered in the 17 separate buildings.

Prices: *R15 - R25. Open 8am - 4.30pm.*
Contact: *Vryheid Rd, Dundee.*
Tel: *034-212-2654*
info@talana.co.za
www.talana.co.za

VRYHEID

NATURE and ACTIVITIES

Ithala Game Reserve  

Ithala came recommended time and again as a favourite among game reserves. It's one of those more off-the-beaten track areas that offer a real back-to-nature feel. The terrain is steep and rugged, sliced open by waterways that run into the Pongola River. Waterfalls, pools and gorges are flanked by dense bush and riverine forest. Big game include white and black rhino, elephant and buffalo as well as giraffe, plenty of zebra, wildebeest and antelope. The absence of lion makes for a relaxed air among the animals, though there are the predators that you seldom see like leopard, cheetah and hyena. Keep your eyes on the skies for black eagle and lappet-faced vultures and for ostriches and secretary birds striding across the veld. Self-guided and (twice-daily) guided walks as always are the best way to get to grips with the landscape and flora and fauna, though driving trails and game drives are also an option. Picnic spots and camping aplenty.

Prices: *Entry R35 for adults, R18 kids plus R30 per vehicle. Gates open sunrise to sunset, park office open 7am - 7.30pm*
Contact: *Outside Louwsberg, off R69, 69km from Vryheid.*
Tel: *033-845-1002 or for camp 034-983-2540*
ntshondwe@kznwildlife.com
www.kznwildlife.com

ISANDHLWANA
CULTURE and HISTORY

Isandlwana Lodge

Join lodge guests and historian Rob Gerrard to trace the astonishing story of the Battle of Isandhlwana, when some 25,000 Zulu warriors attacked a British encampment on the peak's eastern slope in January 1879. Zulu village trips are also on offer and call in to see homesteads, the church, school and the sangoma. Part of the income from these is donated to the community.

Prices: *Battlefield tours R300 - R350, Zulu village trip R50. Book ahead.*
Tel: *034-271-8301/4/5*
pat@isandlwana.co.za
www.isandlwana.co.za

The Battle of Isandhlwana and the Zulu Wars

Tension between the British and Zulu kingdoms and an unmet ultimatum sparked the Zulu Wars of 1879. On January 22 some 25,000 Zulu warriors attacked and slaughtered 1,300 British troops encamped at Isandhlwana, killing fleeing survivors at nearby Fugitive's Drift. On the same day another Zulu force attacked a British magazine and field hospital at Rorke's Drift where the "heroic hundred" fought off 4,000 Zulu warriors for 12 hours, losing 17 men and earning 11 Victoria Crosses.

A tour of the battlefields is a must and most years there is a re-enactment at Isandhlwana on the Saturday nearest to January 22nd with a major event every five years. Check details with Isandlwana Lodge.

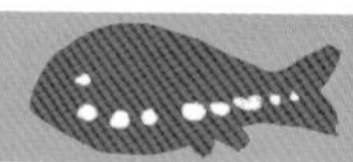

KOSI BAY
NATURE and ACTIVITIES

Kosi Bay Hike

Kosi Bay Nature Reserve drips with greenery and hums with bird- and wildlife. Surrounding the Kosi lake system in northern KwaZulu Natal, it's hemmed in to the north by Mozambique and to the east by the Indian Ocean and the four-day hike on offer circumnavigates almost the entire Kosi system. It'll take some planning as it has to be booked and you need to take all of your own food and kit.

- The first night, your arrival date, is spent at the Nhlange base camp where there are rustic ablutions and a kitchenette with a two-plate gas cooker, frying pan, two pots and a kettle. Day One heads 8km north to a camp overlooking the First Lake, which you reach (in true explorer fashion) by wading thigh-deep across the estuary channel - a great place to come and snorkel later.
- Day Two heads back south for 14km to the Bhanga Nek camp near the beach. Reward yourself here with an afternoon's swimming, snorkelling or fishing off the beach. During the turtle survey season you can take a fabulous turtle-spotting walk in the evening to watch the females lay their eggs on the beach.
- Potter around on the morning of Day Three enjoying the beach and rock pools before hiking 7km on to the riverside Sihadla Trail camp where you'll sleep in small thatch and reed huts.
- Cross the river on a punt to start the longer final day, 15km through stunning raffia palm forest to the Nhlange base camp where you can stay the night again or leave the same day.

See our accommodation guide for places to stay near Kosi Bay that offer a little luxury to reward your travails.

Prices: *R3,500 per group for up to 10 people with a deposit of R1,500 to confirm the booking with the balance to be paid a month before the start. R20 pp and R15 per vehicle entry fee to reserve not included. You will need to take all your own food. Porters are available at extra cost. Accommodation in log cabins and campsites.*
The reserve gates open at sunrise and close at sunset.
It takes about 7 hours to drive to the reserve from Pretoria and 5 hours from Durban. Ask for directions when you book.
Contact: *Kosi Nature Reserve, off N2 at Jozini.*
Tel: *031-783-4610 to book trails.*
Cell: *082-829-8281*
www.kznwildlife.com

SODWANA BAY
NATURE and ACTIVITIES

Coral Divers

Sodwana Bay's Seven Mile Reef is considered one of the best dive sites in the world. There are 1,200 fish species, not to mention the whale sharks and turtles and Coral Divers will show you the lot - well, they'll try. They cater for all levels of scuba diver and snorkeller with gear to hire and every level of PADI dive course on offer. Drier activities include micro-lighting, fishing, riding and quad biking.

Prices: *Course costs: discover scuba R650, open water diver R1,850, dive master R3,800.*
Contact: *Sodwana Bay National Park, Mbazwana.*
Tel: *033-345-6531*
coraldivers@mweb.co.za
www.coraldivers.co.za

HLUHLUWE
NATURE and ACTIVITIES

Emdoneni Lodge Cheetah and Serval Project

Louis and Cecillie Nel are welcoming and friendly and run this rehab centre for orphaned and injured cheetah, serval cats, caracal and African wild cats and so a great place to learn about these animals and see them really close up. There are daily feeding sessions as well as an educational talk and tour.

Prices: *Tour R60 - R80, kids under 12 half price.*
Contact: *Take Bushlands turn, 14km south of Hluhluwe.*
Tel: *035-562-7000*
info@emdonenilodge.com
www.emdonenilodge.com

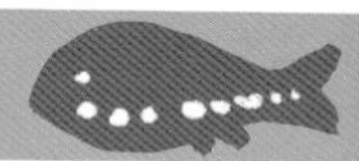

Cape Vidal and St. Lucia Estuary

KZN's Indian Ocean northern coastline is wild and beautiful and one of the best places to appreciate this is in the Cape Vidal Reserve, the long spit of land that encloses the game and lake of the Greater St Lucia Wetlands. It's renowned for its sport fishing and low-tide snorkelling and a series of self-guided walking trails make a great way to see the surrounding wetlands. You won't see southern right whales here but you may spot humpback whales as they migrate north to calve off the Mozambique coast and in December loggerhead and leatherback turtles come onto the beach to lay their eggs (see Kian Barker's tours above for info on this).
On the inland side Lake St. Lucia is home to all sorts of game (crocs, hippos, buffalo, antelope). A great way to see all this is from a launch that heads up the estuary from St. Lucia. Find about the crocs by visiting the St. Lucia Crocodile Centre - not by swimming in the estuary, which could lead to a very sticky end.

Prices: *Day visitors entry fee R20 for adults, R10 for kids, R35 for vehicles.*
Contact: *Take R618 off N2 at Mtubatuba and follow signs through town and on for 25km to St. Lucia.*
Tel: *033-845-1002 or 035-590-1340*
www.kznwildlife.com

Hluhluwe Umfolozi Game Auction

Hluhluwe Umfolozi is one of my favourite reserves in South Africa and it's also the oldest. Established in 1895 in the heart of Zululand it was once the hunting ground of King Shaka. These days the focus is on conservation and surplus game are sold off in an annual auction open to game industry professionals and interested visitors. Species such as hippo, nyala, kudu, zebra, rhino and giraffe are all up for sale. Even rare black rhino are available too, with prospective buyers required to have their properties assessed before they can make a purchase.

Prices: *Visitors must pay entry to the park of R70, R35 per child. The auction usually takes place over a weekend in mid May.*
Contact: *Come off N2 at Hluhluwe exit and follow tarred road to Memorial Gate.*
Tel: *033-845-1000*
www.kznwildlife.com

Ilala Weavers

Established 30 years ago to revitalise the ancient tradition of Zulu handcrafts Ilala has the largest collection of Zulu baskets in the world, co-ordinating the skills of almost 2,000 Zulu weavers and beaders. A great place to support local crafts and pick up goodies like lamps, baskets, pots and bowls. Eat at next door Savannah restaurant and visit the gallery and Zulu historical artefacts museum.

Prices: *8am - 5pm Mon - Fri Sat ad Sun 9am - 4pm. Items R5 - R10,000.*
Contact: *Off N2, in Hluhluwe village, signposted from there.*
Tel: *035-562-0630/1*
ilala@iafrica.com
www.ilala.co.za

ESHOWE
EATING and DRINKING

Adam's Outpost Restaurant and Tea Garden

Popular for being out of the way and also for the lamb curry, home-made health breads, daily-changing soups, Black Forest cheesecake, fresh fish... and, well, everything on a menu that ranges from toasted open sandwiches to great steaks and seafood. It's set in an old settler's house in the grounds of the Zululand museum, so stop in there for a look after lunch. Come for the Sunday buffet (must book).

Prices: *From R15 for a toasted sandwich to R60 for a fillet steak incl choice of sauce, veg or chips and salad, R60 for Sunday buffet. Open Sun - Fri daytime.*

Contact: *Fort Nongqayi, Nongqayi Rd, Eshowe*

Tel: *035-474-1787*

nutriflo@cybertrade.co.za

ESHOWE
NATURE and ACTIVITIES

Ongoye Forest

In the Ngoye Hills south of Empangeni, the Ongoye Forest is fed with numerous fast-flowing streams. It was previously protected by the Zulu royal household for the medicinal value of its plants and is famous for its extremely rare scarp forest. The journey is bumpy and long, but if you're a hard-core nature enthusiast this one is a must - as is a 4x4.

Prices: *Pay R20 entry fee at the entry office. There is no office phone due to the remoteness of the area. Bring all your own food and kit.*

Contact: *15km from the coast due west of Mtunzini. The Amanzimnyama Road to the east of the reserve is steep, crosses three streams and is impassable after heavy rain... so best take the KwaGugugushe road which provides better access from the south-east but is less scenic.*

Tel: *033-845-1999 (KZN Tourist Office)*

www.kznwildlife.com

STANGER
NATURE and ACTIVITIES

Prince's Grant Golf and Country Estate

"It feels like home." Perhaps not my home, but it shows how friendly people find this cracking golf course. The greens here are large and the fairways undulating, giving it a true links feel to go with the seaside setting, surrounded by natural bush. If you really love it, you can buy a house here too!

Prices: *R150 - R200 for affiliated players, R200 - R300 of non-affiliated, R150 golf cart hire.*

Contact: *Off N2 and R74, just north of Blythdale Beach, Stanger.*

Tel: *032-482-0041*

www.princesgrantlodge.co.za

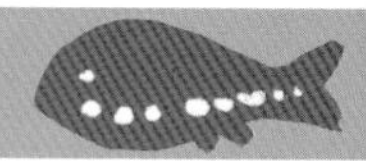

SALT ROCK
EATING and DRINKING

La Casa Nostra

I couldn't get a table at Casa Nostra when I tried. It was heaving with happily munching punters fresh from the beach or off to play golf. Everyone says it's great though and that Emanuele and Vanessa Cantatore serve the best home-made pasta on the north coast. "A warm, relaxed atmosphere and really family-friendly."

Prices: *Starters R30 - R50, mains R50 - R90, shellfish grills R120 - R495 for huge shared seafood platter. No bookings taken. To book try their other family restaurant Bel Punto.*

Contact: *Shop 4, Whitesands Centre, 1 Main Road, Umdloti, Durban.*

Tel: *031-568-1996*

famiglia@mweb.co.za

Bel Punto tel: 031-568-2407

BALLITO
NATURE and ACTIVITIES

Ballito Microlight School

Inspect the sand and surf from the air. Dave and Rona Jackson run daily scenic microlight flights up and down the white north coast beaches and, if you've got the time, you can make the most of the highly-qualified instructors on hand and learn to fly the thing yourself!

Prices: *Roughly R200 for 10min flight, R250 for 15mins and R400 for 30mins.*

Contact: *Ballito exit 210 west off N2, past Umhlali golf club, left at T-junction, follow signs.*

Cell: *082-659-5550*

microlight@yebo.co.za

www.microlights.co.za

UMDLOTI
NATURE and ACTIVITIES

Come Fly! Air Services

An owner-run airfield 30km from Durban and tucked between the sugar cane fields - a honey-pot of aviation enthusiasts. There are cracking coastal flights (a great way to inspect the sea life) and the airfield is littered with microlights, hang-gliders, experimental aircraft, gyrocopters and more. You're welcome to keep your feet on the ground, watch the occasional jet display and let the kids loose on the jungle gym.

Prices: *12min flights R200 - R250, 20mins R300 - R350, 30mins (the most popular) R400 - R450, 45mins R600 - R650.*
Contact: *Umdloti Beach, Umdloti.*
Cell: *084-266-3359 or 083-597-4222*
comefly@mweb.co.za

UMHLALI
NATURE and ACTIVITIES

Croc Valley

There are more than 200 crocs to see at the Croc Valley Reserve, but there's so much else too. As well as ostrich, duiker, tortoise and monkeys, Mark Oldacre is very proud of his latest arrivals, a gang of boa constrictors, anacondas and pythons. Swimming in the swamp is therefore not advisable. Stick instead to a ramble along the forest and wilderness trail. Eyes open for fish eagles and indigenous duck, mouths open for tea and home-baked cakes.

Prices: *Adults R30, kids under 16 R15. Open daily 9am - 5pm, feeding on Sun at 3pm.*
Contact: *Sheffield Beach Rd, Umhlali.*
Tel: *032-525-5374*
crocv@saol.com

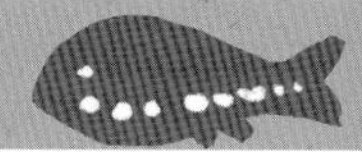

UMHLANGA
CULTURE and HISTORY

Barnyard Theatre at Gateway

Here the 470 capacity audience definitely becomes the final member of the cast. The floor is carpeted in wood chippings and while tables and seating are provided it's up to you to bring your own picnic basket, take-away or even a 3-course meal. Shows are generally musical revues with a full live band and suitable for the whole family.

Prices: *Tickets cost about R90, performances Tues - Sat nights and matinée on Sun.*
Contact: *Shop F222, Gateway Theatre of Shopping, Palm Boulevard, Umhlanga Ridge.*
Tel: *031-566-3045*
gateway@barnyardtheatre.co.za
www.barnyardtheatre.co.za

UMHLANGA
NATURE and ACTIVITIES

Natal Sharks Board

Sharks get a pretty bad press and the NSB work hard to dispel that. Come here and learn all about these awesome fish. There are regular shark dissections here to so you can find out how they work (and smell!) inside too. Alternatively join the Sharks Board team in the early morning boat trips along Durban's waterfront, checking the shark nets that line the beaches and protect swimmers.

Prices: *Adults R25, kids R15. Boat trips cost R150.*
Contact: *1a Herrwood Drive, Umhlanga.*
Tel: *031-566-0400/0435*
Cell: *082-403-9206 for boat trips*
www.shark.co.za

BIRDING BITS

You will see: Red-capped Robin Chat, Lesser-striped Swallow

You'll be very lucky to see: Pink-throated Twinspot, Neergaard's Sunbird

You might see: Palm-nut Vulture, Yellow-rumped Tinkerbird

Eyes peeled around the Mkuzi Game Reserve, north of Hluhluwe.

Northern Cape

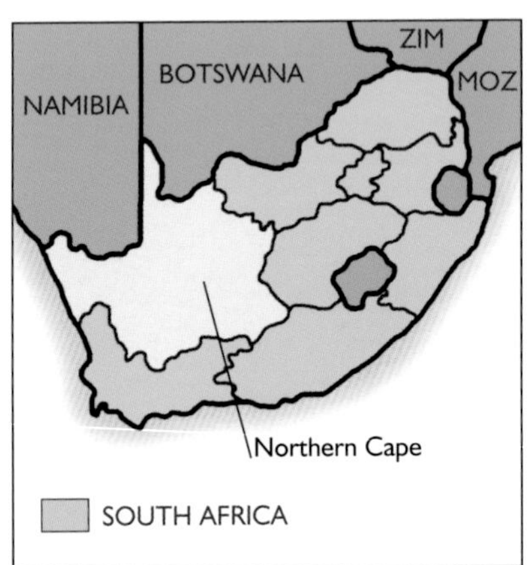

The Northern Cape is by far and away the largest province in South Africa, covering almost a third of its land mass - that's ten times larger than Gauteng and 30% bigger than the entire United Kingdom.

Travelling through this area is really very simple as there are generally very few roads that connect very few towns - just 850,000 or so of the 44 million people in South Africa live here.

But this is what makes it fantastic to visit and a loop around the Northern Cape is perhaps the most thrilling drive in the country. Of course it is long (some 900km from Cape Town to Upington alone) but it is truly epic.

Kicking off through the lush farms of the Cederberg you'll head north through Namaqualand to Springbok, a mining town that grew up around copper, coal and diamonds. A sharp right before the Namibian border and you strike out east, across the desert to the Orange River oasis of Upington before completing the triangle by returning south-west to Nieuwoudtville.

The scenery is truly lunar, the spring flowers are one of the world's great botanical wonders and as long as you have air-conditioning, a passion for huge open spaces and the following itinerary hints - we reckon you'll love it.

The **West Coast and Cederberg** have both already been covered and there are plenty of places to stay around there listed in our accommodation guide - so no extra help needed on that.

northern cape

Our journey starts from **Citrusdal** with a hefty drive (just to warm you up) north to **Springbok**. This will take a good four or five hours, but the road is good and there's no hurry. Springbok springs up sooner than you expect and you can quickly cover the 25km or so west on the Kleinzee road to **Naries Guest Farm** where we suggest you stay. A tractor ride from the farm will take you to the nearest hilltop for a sundowner. From this remote corner of the country the view is spectacular, with rows of peaks marching away 70km to the sea and the Kleinzee diamond mine.

Trips can be arranged to the mine or to head out hiking while back in town is locals' eatery Carne Casa. Take the opportunity while you are there to mug up on a little local history at neighbouring Nababeep.

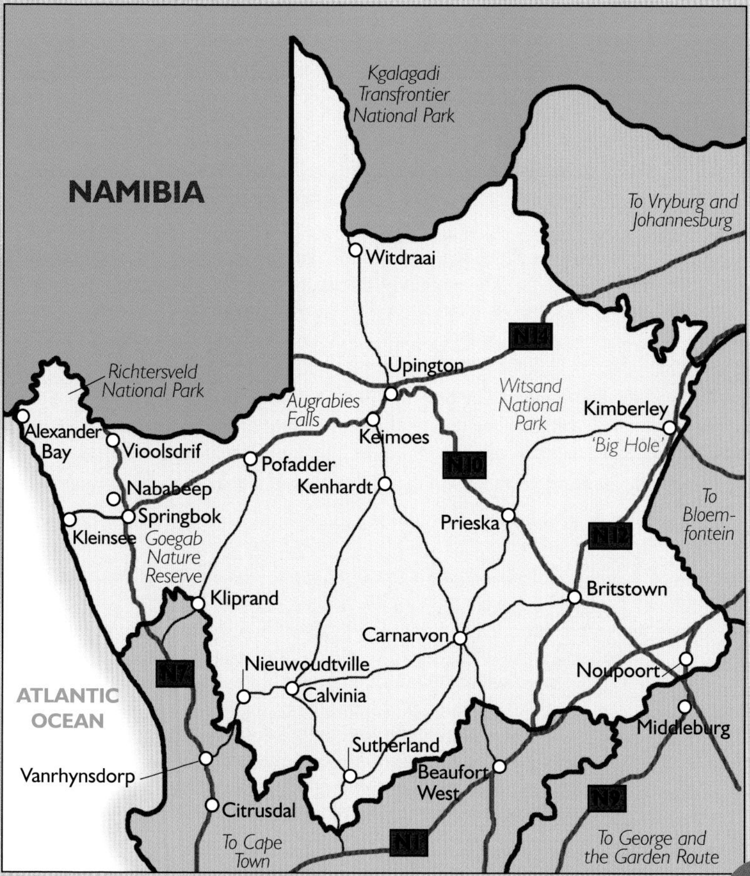

Kgalagadi Transfrontier National Park
NAMIBIA
To Vryburg and Johannesburg
Witdraai
N14
Upington
Richtersveld National Park
Augrabies Falls
Witsand National Park
Kimberley
'Big Hole'
Alexander Bay
Vioolsdrif
Keimoes
Pofadder
N10
Nababeep
Kenhardt
To Bloem-fontein
Springbok
Kleinsee
Goegab Nature Reserve
Prieska
N12
Britstown
Kliprand
Carnarvon
Nieuwoudtville
Noupoort
N7
ATLANTIC OCEAN
Calvinia
Middleburg
Sutherland
Vanrhynsdorp
Beaufort West
N9
Citrusdal
To Cape Town
N1
To George and the Garden Route

Carne Casa

Linguists (and Italians) will guess from the name that Wilma does a great line in meat and indeed the grills are great (beef and lamb lovers unite). But there's all sorts on offer here including fish and it's very affordable - meaning you could easily come for lunch and supper!

Prices: *Average meal R60.*
Contact: *39 Voortrekker St, Springbok.*
Tel: *027-718-1475*

Nababeep Museum and Springbok Lodge

Pop in to these two venues to mug up on your local history. The Nababeep Museum traces the history of copper mining in this region while at Springbok Lodge there's an extensive collection of books on Namaqualand's flora, fauna and history as well as geological, art and photographic exhibitions. You can eat there too!

Prices: *Free entry to museum (open 9am - 1pm, all day during Aug, Sept flower season). Springbok Lodge breakfast R20 - R45, light meals R25 - R50, dinner R40 - R80 excluding drinks.*
Contact: *Springbok Lodge, 37 Voortrekker St, Springbok.*
Tel: *027-712-1321*
sbklodge@intekom.co.za
Nababeep Museum, Main St, Nababeeb village off N7 just north of Springbok.

Visit the **Goegab Nature Reserve** 15km east of Springbok for the low-down on the amazing array of succulents found in the area.

From here the N14 calls you east but before you go you can continue north on the N7 to the Namibian border town of **Vioolsdrif** for watery fun on the Orange River, camping and expeditions into the distant Richtersveld National Park.

Hot tip

Only 2.4% of the Northern Cape population speak English as a first language, so try and pick up some Afrikaans pleasantries before you go.

Afrikaans emerged originally from the Dutch spoken by the Cape's first settlers. From the late 17th century their Netherlands Dutch began to change in pronunciation and vocabulary adopting new words from indigenous African languages as well as Portuguese and Malay from imported slave labourers. New French Huguenot and German settlers soon spoke the creolised Cape Dutch and it became recognised as its own language by the 19th century, though Afrikaans and Dutch are still - more or less - mutually intelligible today.

Bushwhacked Outdoor Adventures

Teetering on the Namibian border these guys specialise in half-day to multi-day Orange River canoe trips. The guides are very knowledgeable and will point out the array of bird- and wildlife as you head downstream. Plenty of time too for swimming, picnicking and napping in the sunshine. Very relaxed and great fun. Richtersveld 4x4 trips also available.

Prices: *Half-day trip from R120, full-day trip from R200, 4-day 5 night trip R1,865 pp. No under 6s. Call ahead.*

Contact: *Fiddlers Creek, 10km west of Vioolsdrif/Noordoewer border post between South Africa and Namibia, turn west off N7 onto dirt road and follow river.*

Tel: *027-761-8953*

info@bushwhacked.co.za

www.bushwhacked.co.za

Gravity Adventures

Also run great Orange River trips.
See Cape Town Activities Guides for details.

The Springbok to Upington drive was my favourite stretch of road in the whole country. I found the desert scenery and utter silence mesmerising. It's worth setting out in good time on this leg as it is a long way, which was made longer by my constant stops to take landscape photographs. I recommend making at least part of the journey early in the morning as the surrounding terrain turns to striking reds, oranges and purples when the sun is low.

Pofadder provides a convenient, if uninspiring, half-time rest. Watch out for cursory police checks here. Being a swarthy lone traveller I had my licence and passport inspected, though was fairly confident of getting away with it when the officer wrote my name and number down incorrectly on the back of his hand.

Shortly before Upington you will reach the banks of the Orange River and a sudden swathe of greenery - the Northern Cape's wine-growing country. Grapes are grown for wine, table grapes and raisins and there is also a large amount of date farming in the area. Here are two contrasting wineries to visit to get a feel for the industry in this part of the world.

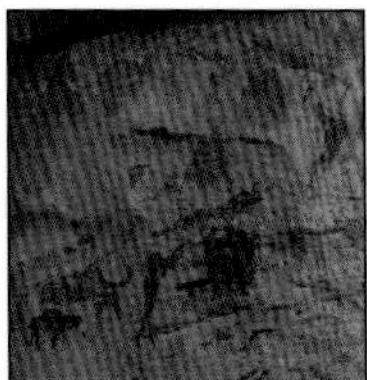

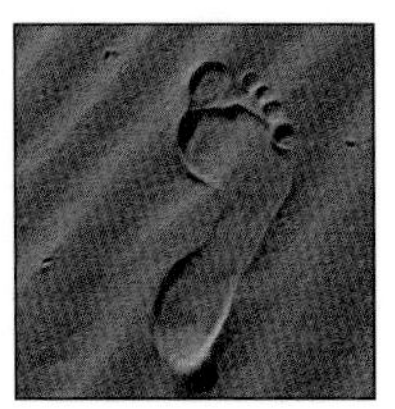

Bezalel Dyasonsklip Wine Cellar

This winery and distillery is wedged into the beautiful scenery between Upington and Keimos. You can do tours and tastings with very friendly hosts Inus and Mieke and prepare yourself for fiery liqueurs! Alternatively phone ahead and book in for lunch or dinner.

Prices: *Tours and tastings are free*
Contact: *On N14 between Upington and Keimos.*
Tel: *054-491-1325*
Cell: *083-310-4763*
bezalel@dyasonsklip.za.net or inus@dyasonsklip.za.net
www.dyasonsklip.za.net

Orange River Wine Cellars

The Orange River Wine Cellars is a co-operative of some 750 vine growers strung along the fertile riverbanks. Their grapes combine to make easy drinking, fruity and affordable wines and visitors are welcome to taste them on a tour of the cellar between Jan and March. They make grape juice too for non-drinkers.

Prices: *Tours are free. Dry white R13, semi-sweet and rosé R13.40, red R19.67, dessert wines and sherry R19.38, grape juice R9.80. Cellar tours at 9am, 11am and 3pm, shop open and tastings available all year round.*
Contact: *Orange River Wine Cellar, 32 Industria Rd, Upington.*
Tel: *054-337-8800*
www.owk.co.za

Get to know the Orange River

- *South Africa's longest river, rising in the distant Drakensberg in Lesotho and flowing westwards some 2,200km before it finally hits the Atlantic Ocean at Alexander Bay.*
- *First discovered by the Europeans in 1760.*
- *A huge catchment area extending over 973,000km2 reaching deep into Namibia, Botswana and Lesotho.*
- *The generous provider of Namibian and South African coastal diamonds, washing them downstream from the volcanic pipes of Kimberley and depositing them in the coastal dune fields.*

At this point congratulate yourself - you made it to Upington.

A bed will most likely be the first thing on your mind, so try Anneke Malan at **Riviera Garden B&B** . After an hour or so dozing on the river bank at the foot of her garden you'll feel as right as rain. Alternatively for great dinners as well as a great host call Evelyne Meier at **La Boheme** . A professional translator, she is a superb cook and dinner overlooking the Orange River flood plain is hard to beat.

Basing yourself in Upington there are a number of day trips you can do from the town to the fruit farms and wineries or back to the Augrabies Falls National Park (of which the falls is the best bit). This is a place to really relax before a Kalahari expedition and Francisca Bolweg will help you do just that.

The Healing Hands

Francisca is a masseuse and after driving all the way to this part of the world you'll need some help loosening up. She does therapeutic massage and also specialises in herbal teas and medicines for most ailments. She's incredibly friendly and while slabbed out enjoying your massage you can look out over the fantastic river view.

Prices: *Full body massage R300 for about an hour, half-body massage R180 for about 30mins.*
Contact: *3 River St Studios, River St, Upington.*
Tel: *054-332-7290*
Cell: *082-670-4140*

To make the most of the Kgalagadi Transfrontier National Park (part of the enormous Kalahari system) you really need to spend a few days there and to go with a guide. And so:

Pieter Hanekom, Kalahari Safaris

Pieter was born and bred in this area and learnt much of his incredible bush knowledge from the legendary bushmen. He'll take you on tours of the Kgalagadi and Augrabies Falls parks and show you just how much plant and animal life lives in this harsh desert climate. Tours range from one to seven days and accommodation is in camps or lodges depending on your preferences.

Prices: *Three-day tour from R2,550 - R3,750. Tours tailor-made to your plans.*
Contact: *3 Orange St, Upington*
Tel: *054-332-5653*
Cell: *082-435-0007*
pieter@kalaharisafaris.co.za
www.kalaharisafaris.co.za

Namaqualand - blooming marvelous

Named after the Nama nomadic herders who occupied these lands Namaqualand stretches from the Orange River in the north to Garies in the south (about half way between Springbok and Vanrhynsdorp on the N7) and from Pofadder in the east to the Atlantic coast.

Every year, for a few weeks, the usually dry and apparently lifeless scrubland of this part of the world is transformed into a sea of colour for an incredible display of spring blooming. The land is literally carpeted in flowers for only a few weeks between mid-August and mid-September. It is very dependent on the weather and some years can be disappointing. The spring bloom is truly one of the wonders of the natural world and travellers come from across the globe just for this. So if you are planning to go, book your accommodation VERY early.

The spring display is led by a phenomenal variety of daisies as well as violets, gladioli, pelargoniums and many more that I can't name. Although the flowers are at their best in the Northern Cape, you need drive only as far north as Darling for a flavour of what it's like (but I'd advise seeing the real McCoy further north).

Kalahari Tours and Travel

Dantes leads tours in some of the wildest landscapes in Southern Africa, covering the Northern Cape, Namibia and Botswana. There are some 3.7 million hectares under conservation here, home to 58 mammal, 55 reptile, countless insect and plant species and 298 bird species. Follow in the footsteps of the black-maned Kalahari lion and immerse yourself in true wilderness.

Prices: *Guided tours from R900 pp per day (camping accommodation) or R1,250 (chalet accommodation).*
Contact: *Mazurka Waters, 12 Mazurkadraai, Upington.*
Tel: *054-338-0375*
Cell: *082-493-5041*
dantes@kalahari-tours.co.za
www.kalahari-tours.co.za

Those looking for a more manageable Kalahari experience, which they can do for themselves, should head east to the **Witsand Nature Reserve** G. The 3,500ha park is dominated by a 65 million-year-old dune system of sky-scraping, multi-coloured sand ridges. There are a series of 6-man chalets to stay in and plenty of other activities to keep you and the kids busy (birding, game viewing, biking, sand-boarding etc). The reserve is off the R64 between Upington and Kimberley.

Speaking from experience I can say that, after the enormous trek to Upington, driving the extra 411km east to Kimberley (on R64) makes the Northern Cape route excessively long.

If you do want to go though, the Big Hole is certainly worth visiting. This is part of the De Beers diamond mine, which reached a remarkable depth of 1,097m before it was closed in 1914. There's a good museum here that traces the entire history of the diamond industry and principal players like Cecil Rhodes and Barney Barnato. It was under reconstruction at the time of writing but set to re-open in April 2006 (Tucker St, Kimberley, Tel: 053-839-4902).

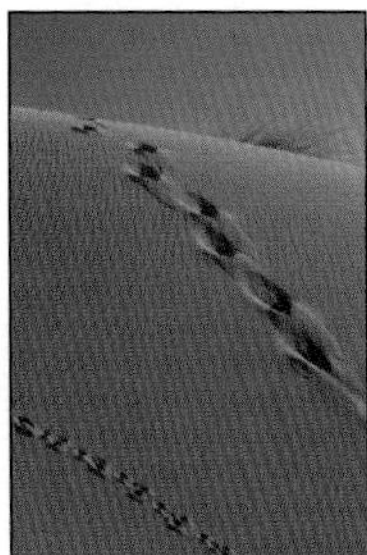

Those not doing the Kimberley leg should prepare for an epic journey south instead. Set off very early on the R27 from Upington all the way back to Nieuwoudtville. This will take you most of a day (it's about 500km) including pee and picnic stops, but it is an exciting drive for those who enjoy being out on the open road with giant vistas all around. You will see very few other cars for miles and hours. And at the end of it all **Papkuilsfontein** G awaits. Consistently rated Simon's favourite place to stay in S.A. this farm oozes warmth and hospitality. The van Wyks are truly wonderful hosts and this is THE place to come for the spring flower season - though you will need to book a year in advance (no joke).

Spend a couple of days in the Nieuwoudtville area, adventuring on the farm and in the surrounding countryside, visiting the local community and star-gazing:

Ex Libris

Philipp Buchsenstein is a sculptor and qualified field guide and he'll take you out on field trips around this fascinating area, especially when it's thick with flowers during spring. The emphasis is not on searching out lion and elephant (which is lucky as there aren't any here) but instead focuses on the little things. You're encouraged to touch, smell, eat and open yourself to the rich intricacy of the region's flora and fauna.

Prices: *R300 per day, meals and drinks excluded but can be arranged.*
Tel: *027-218-1135*
Cell: *082-538-5290*
nix3@telkomsa.net

Telescope S.A.

One of the few nocturnal guides you'll come across. Paul Dogon, as you might well imagine, is a super keen astronomer and, as well as importing and exporting equipment, he'll guide you around the Northern Cape's famously clear night skies using a selection of telescopes at his base in Nieuwoudtville. Learn to identify your Southern Cross from Orion's belt and much more besides.

Prices: *R400 per party for up to five people at a time.*
Contact: *Paul Dogon, Kerk St, Nieuwoudtville*
Tel: *027-218-1613*
Cell: *082-823-7384*
paul@telescopesa.za.org

Melkkraal Women's Group

These women offer an insight into local life on a tranquil farm south of town on the beautiful Bokkeveld Plateau. Guided walks around the farm will give you the low-down on medicinal plants and their uses, local architecture, rock art and rooibos tea. And after all that learning you can head back to the farm for great traditional food.

Prices: *Tours average R60, about R35 for lunch, R60 for dinner. Book in advance.*
Contact: *About 35km south of Nieuwoudtville, direction Clanwilliam.*
Tel: *027-218-1029*
info@indigo-dc.org

And finally...

After a massive journey, complete the loop back down the N7 stretch you started on, through the Cederberg (you'll no doubt want another night there) to Cape Town - your memory banks stuffed with visions of distant landscapes and your car stuffed with empty water bottles.

BIRDING BITS

You will see: Sociable Weaver, Red-headed Finch

You'll be very lucky to see: Sclater's Lark, Black-eared Finch-lark

You might see: Karoo Korhaan, Pygmy Falcon

Eyes peeled around Pofadder.

Free State

FREE STATE

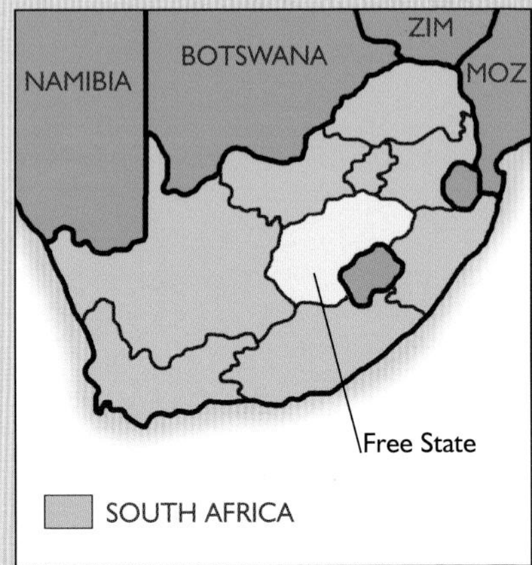

Driving the 1,402km from Cape Town north-east to Johannesburg is not as crazy as it may at first seem. Our Cape Town neighbour regularly used to do it in a day. It is undoubtedly a long way, though, and so, accustomed as we Europeans are to somewhat shorter distances, here is an itinerary of things to do and places to stay en route that will not only break up the drive but make travelling through this part of South Africa really enjoyable. Clearly you can use and abuse our suggested route in whatever way you think best. It generally follows the N1 - so you shouldn't get lost!

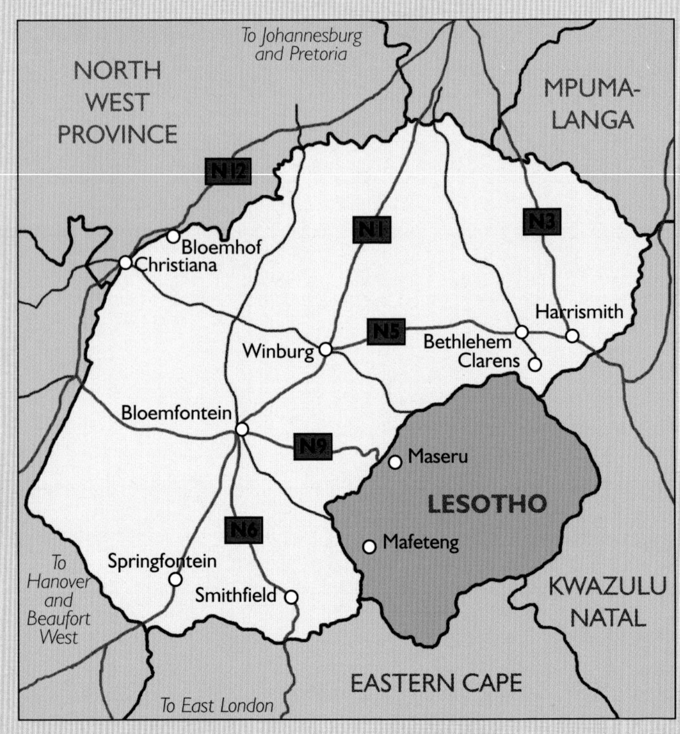

SO HERE GOES:

The first target is **Beaufort West**, at the end of a hefty 460km (286 mile) slog up the N1 from Cape Town - made far more pleasant by a gentle detour and night in the Winelands.

In 1818 Cape Governor Lord Somerset founded Beaufort West (and named it after his father) to keep the peace in the hinterland. It's a pretty little place slap, bang in the middle of the Great Karoo. The Karoo scenery is as wildly romantic and open as you will see anywhere in S.A., its patchwork of earth colours broken by lumpy koppies (small hills rising out of the veld) and the herds of sheep that wander on giant farms.

Aim here for **Lemoenfontein Game Farm** GG where Ingrid Köster will reward your journey with great plains game viewing, cool drinks on a wooden verandah, a superb dinner and a well-earned bed. Two nights here are better than one, giving you time to recharge the batteries fully before moving on. (See Western Cape Karoo for further details). Another Köster, Diana, also runs GG-selected accommodation here, the nearby **Ko-Ka Tsara Bush Camp** GG.

Karoo National Park

Birders should keep an eye out for the 20 pairs of black eagles that live in this park. Springbok thrive in the dry environment too and you'll also see the boldly striped Cape mountain zebra. Compare these to the quagga - a formerly extinct species now thought to be a zebra sub-species and gradually being reintroduced. There are two walking trails for those who need a leg stretch.

Prices: *R60 a day for adults, R30 for kids under 12. Open all day every day.*
Contact: *Off N1, just outside Beaufort West.*
Tel: *023-415-2828*
www.sanparks.org.za

From Beaufort West the road strides onwards to Hanover, the ideal stop for the birding brigade.

New Holme Karoo Birding

P.C. and Marisca Ferreira offer day guides or packaged birding explorations on their farm deep in the grassy Karoo. With a modest 12,000ha of plains, dams and hills to explore you'll see everything from Ludwig's bustard, black and blue korhaan to Burchell's and double-banded courser and many more. Tours take in bushman paintings and (importantly) allow plenty time for evening sundowners. You can stay here too.

Prices: *Day birding at R80 pp, birding specials at R390 pp per night for parties of 6, R360 pp per night for 7 - 10 all-inclusive except for drinks.*
Contact: *New Holme Guest Farm, signed left off N1, 22km north of Hanover.*
Tel: *053-643-0193*
Cell: *082-567-9211*
karoogariep@mjvn.co.za
www.karoogariep.co.za

For those who feel they need to press on and get more miles under the belt (though why rush?), **Springfontein** is the next natural stop. As you would imagine, this town grew up around water and the nearby Gariep Dam Nature Reserve, fed by the Orange River, makes a great place for biking (around it as opposed to in it), hiking (ditto), fishing, sailing and much else besides.

Graeme Wedgwood is the man to ask about the whats, wheres and hows of local activities and he also runs **Springfontein House** GG - our choice for a bed in the area. Here a sense of shade and cool pervade, creepers twist over the stoep, flowerbeds are ordered and well-fed and the pool is just made for leaping into.

From Springfontein our route divides in two (just when you thought we were going to make all the decisions for you). You can either continue on the quick route via Bloemfontein to Jo'burg, or take your time over a large and exciting easterly diversion.

The Quick Route

Bloemfontein, South Africa's judiciary centre, is a (relatively) short hop from Springfontein up the N1.

By now you'll be ready for a proper breather so don't worry about hurtling around trying to do a million and one things. Base yourself for a couple of days at **De Oude Kraal Country Estate** GG Marie and Gerhard are about 35km south of Bloem (yes, just off the N1). Their massive farm was a hive of Boer-War activity and you can ride out for a history tour or to check the sheep and ostriches. Marie's dinners are a stand-alone event.

Alternatively, for overnighting the other side of the city, Ted and Bits Quin at **Bishop's Glen** (20km north of Bloem) are the most giving hosts you'll find. Join them for dinner beneath yellowwood timbers in their 200-year-old house or sit on the stoep looking out for 200+ bird species in the garden.

The city itself is cosmopolitan and lively and well worth a look. Make sure you have time to soak up some culture.

Oliewenhuis Art Museum

Part of Bloem's National Museum, this is set in one of the most magnificent gardens in the city, a large section of which is natural vegetation. The permanent collection has a basis of S.A. artists and the museum is continually expanding on its collection of contemporary works. Don't miss the outdoor sculptures. Walk the walking trail and eat light meals at the Terrace restaurant in the picnic-friendly garden.

Prices: *Free entry, open Mon - Fri 8am - 5pm, Sat 10am - 5pm, Sun 1pm - 5pm. Museum offers guided tours, a reference library and lectures and workshops.*
Contact: *16 Harry Smith St, Bloemfontein.*
Tel: *051-447-9609*
oliewen@nasmus.co.za

And for lunch or dinner (or both) you can't miss Kim Brackenridge's eatery…

7 on Kellner

Our favourite restaurant in Bloemfontein. 7 on Kellner has a distinctly Moroccan feel with a relaxed ethnic atmosphere. The food too is North African with a Mediterranean twist and great pizzas from the wood-fired oven. Sit outside in the walled garden.

Prices: *Average meal R60. Open for lunch and dinner Mon -Fri, dinner only Sat.*
Contact: *7 Kellner St, Westdene, Bloemfontein.*
Tel: *051-447-7928*

With all of this complete you'll feel ready to tackle the last hurdle to Johannesburg. It's a stretch that's best seen, frankly, at speed. So fill up the petrol tank, put on some good music and the A.C. and let the 398km zip past to land you up in the big smoke for tea-time.

MISSION ACCOMPLISHED.

Unless you opted for…

The Large and Exciting Easterly Diversion Route

Natural GG travellers have a chink in their armour when it comes to efficient travel: we don't like main roads. So by the time you've driven the 900km or so to Springfontein, you'll most likely be itching to find a dirt track or even just a minor road. Have no fear.

From Springfontein take the R715 and R701 to **Smithfield** and immediately reward your bravery with dinner, care of Kelvin Young.

The Colony Room

Delicious country cooking in a restaurant where everything is locally sourced from the freshly-picked vegetables to the region's best game, lamb and pork. Home-made breads, butter, creams and (most importantly in my book) ice creams. Eat al fresco on the stoep in the shade of the vines.

Prices: *R85 for 3-course dinner, 3 choices of starters, mains and desserts. R35 for pub lunches, R35 for full English breakfast.*
Contact: *17 Juana Square, Smithfield.*
Tel: *051-683-0021*
colonyroom@telkomsa.net

After a meal like that you will want to turn in pretty quickly, which is where **Pula House** (051-683-0032) comes in. Retired journalists Barbara and John van Ahlefeldt have breathed a new lease of life into a Karoo-style home here and their freshly-made breads and creamy scrambled eggs in the morning will set you up for even the most Livingstonian of adventures.

Smithfield is a fairly easy detour to retrace if you wish and you can hop onto the northbound N6 for a swift journey north to **Bloemfontein**.

Alternatively you could head south on N6 and take the R26 to Zastron where Piet and Zanobia Labuschagné run the welcoming **Die Ou Stal** GG. Piet has an infectious fascination with geology and pre-history and will give you a tour of local rock formations, spiced up with bushmen legends.

The Orange Free State

The Orange Free State (today's Free State) was the result of the Great Trek, an independent country established by the Boers to distinguish themselves from the British in 1854 alongside Natalia (in modern-day KZN) and Transvaal (from Gauteng north). Britain annexed the Boer states following the Boer Wars of 1880 - 1881 and 1899 - 1902.

From here the **Mountain Kingdom of Lesotho** is just a stone's throw away - ish - and it is obligatory that you visit it! Continue north on the R26 to Wepener, where you can enter Lesotho on the A20 to Mafeteng.

Lesotho's harsh terrain helped protect it from the colonial desires of the Europeans and it has always remained a kingdom unto itself, totally separate from - though completely encircled by - South Africa. Interaction with the locals is the best way to really experience it and no-one is better at helping you do that than Mick and Di Jones.

Malealea Lodge and Pony Trek Centre

Mick and Di really are A-grade hosts and they offer one- to six-day guided pony treks and so much more besides at their mountain lodge. Malealea thrives on its relationship with the neighbouring village. The kids act as walking guides and in the evenings you'll listen to the local choir before the band strikes up on their home-made instruments. Rub shoulders with backpackers and ambassadors over canteen-style suppers and spend evenings on the fire-lit stoep or in the pub.

Prices: *Day rides from R100 pp, horse treks R200 pp per day. Lunch R45, dinner R65. Rondavels R220 pp sharing, farmhouse R175 pp sharing. Best to visit Dec - May.*
Contact: *Brandhof, Lesotho, call for directions.*
Tel: *051-436-6766*
Cell: *082-552-4215*
malealea@mweb.co.za
www.malealea.co.ls

Lesotho is a long way off your intended Jo'burg drive, but it is well worth going the extra distance and will make a huge difference to your holiday. From the western border post at Maseru, the N8 whisks you back to Bloemfontein and you'll be heading north again before you know it.

Afrikaners, Boers and Voortrekkers

Afrikaners are white South Africans descended from Dutch and later French Huguenot and German settlers. These ancestors settled in the Cape of Good Hope from 1652 when the Dutch East India Company first established a small supply post on this seemingly available and remote peninsula - a convenient half-way point on the journey to the Indonesian colonies.

Boer is the Afrikaans (and originally Dutch) word for farmer used in English to refer to white Afrikaans-speakers in general, though these days this can be seen as a derogatory term (so don't use it).

Voortrekker Sreet runs through dozens of towns across the country. The word refers to pioneer Boer farmers who lived on the Cape Colony's eastern frontier but, sick of the overcrowding and anglicisation of what is now the Eastern Cape, migrated north into the interior.

Some 12,000 of them made the move to escape British colonial rule during the mid-1800s and became known as the Voortrekkers or forerunners of the Great Trek.

CLARENS AND HARRISMITH

The perceptive will notice a glaring omission of Harrismith for which we boldly make no apology. We have tried to lay this book out using as much geographical nous as possible, basing it on the most commonly travelled routes (you may have noticed that neither Beaufort West nor Hanover are actually in the Free State). Harrismith is therefore included in the KZN chapter as it lies almost exactly half-way along the Durban - Johannesburg route.

The town makes a great launch-pad into KZN and Ryk and Bea Becker at **The View** G will help you plan your attack. Bea's great-grandfather was President of the Free State and Ryk grew up in the area so you couldn't be in better hands.

If you're heading there from Bloemfontein, cut across on the N5 and definitely make the detour south at Bethlehem to Clarens (a comfortable 3 - 4hr drive from Bloem).

It's a fascinating village that has become a haven for artists and, on the doorstep of the magnificent Golden Gate National Park, you can see why. **St Fort Country House** 5km out of town has the most incredible setting and walking trails galore help you make the most of it (as well as Ernestine's breakfast).

BIRDING BITS

Eyes peeled around Mokhotlong, Lesotho.

Gauteng

FNB
First National Bank
IPELEGENG

Gauteng occupies a high and dusty interior plain and is the smallest and most densely populated of South Africa's regions, with some 20% of the country's population living within its boundaries. This is the financial powerhouse of South and Southern Africa from where industrious Gautengers often rib their Capetonian cousins for their relaxed approach to life and consider Cape Town itself a fishing village. Jo'burg and Pretoria are indeed play-hard and work-hard cities that offer endless eateries, museums and other urban pursuits that are well worth investigation.

Many travellers wrongly assume that if they go anywhere near Johannesburg they will at best be mugged, at worst - well, worse. This is simply not true. Yes, security is an issue and Johannesburg, like any major city, can be a dangerous place. But as long as you take the usual precautions you should have no problems. I spent some time visiting Johannesburg and neighbouring Soweto on my own and never had any difficulties.

So, don't just fly in and zip straight out. Take a few days to soak up some culture from the Apartheid and Africa Museums or on a tour to Soweto, eat out, enjoy the botanical gardens and green urban spaces and only then jump back in the hire car and drive the easy few hours out to the game reserves.

gauteng

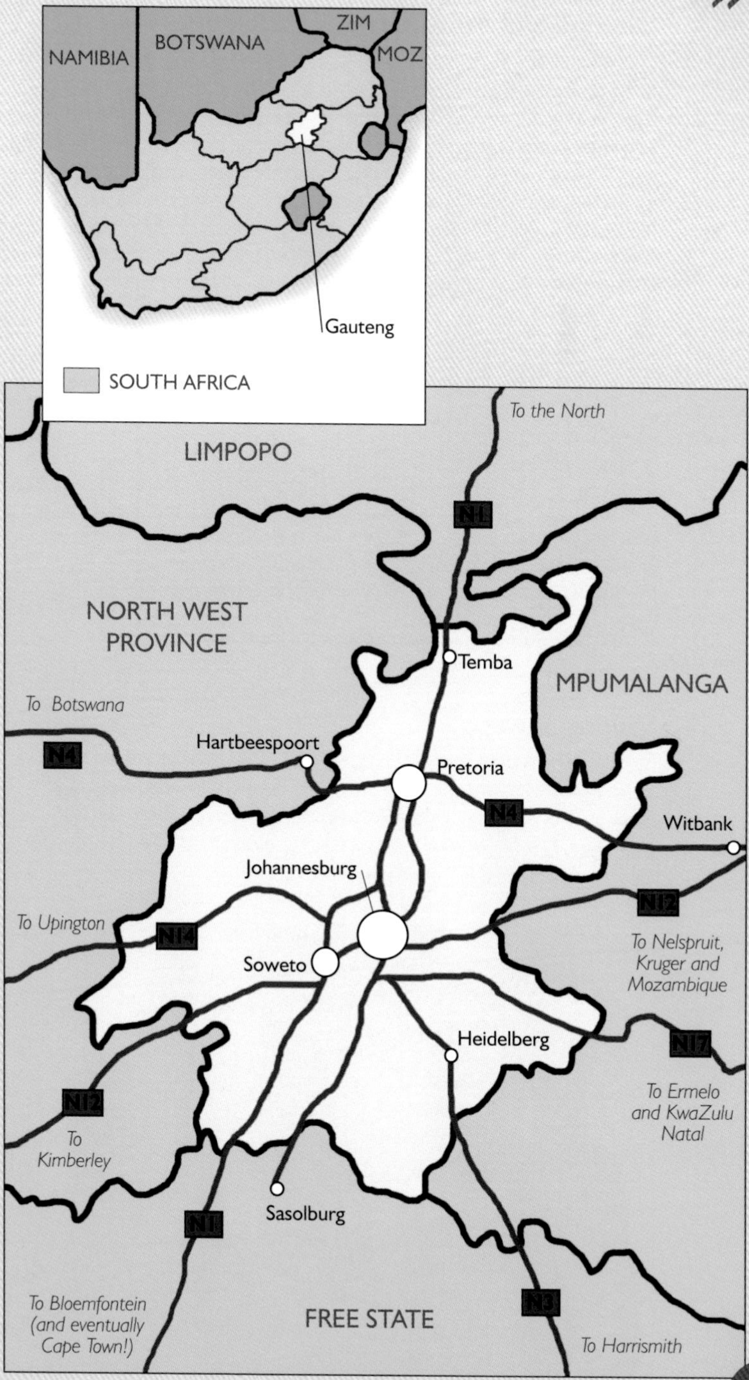

NAMIBIA
BOTSWANA
ZIM
MOZ
Gauteng
SOUTH AFRICA

To the North
LIMPOPO
N1
NORTH WEST PROVINCE
Temba
MPUMALANGA
To Botswana
N4
Hartbeespoort
Pretoria
N4
Witbank
Johannesburg
N12
To Upington
N14
Soweto
To Nelspruit, Kruger and Mozambique
Heidelberg
N17
To Ermelo and KwaZulu Natal
N12
To Kimberley
Sasolburg
N1
N3
To Bloemfontein (and eventually Cape Town!)
FREE STATE
To Harrismith

GUIDES AND EXPERTS

GENERAL

Suzanne and Amos Ordo, Ordo Tours

Spending your entire holiday sorting out logistics? Let someone else do it for you. Suzanne and Amos share our philosophy when it comes to travel and use their local knowledge to take care of as little or as much as you want, from commission-free flight-arranging to car and mobile phone hire. Alternatively they offer guided tours that usher you round the country in air-conditioned micro-buses.

Prices: *Vary according to itinerary. Package tours from R3,875 pp for 3 days in Kruger Park to R12,125 for 9-day South Africa Highlights trip. Other trips include Cape Town and the Winelands, the Garden Route, Johannesburg and Pretoria and Vic Falls.*

Tel: *011-883-0050*

Cell: *083-252-6776*

ordotours@global.co.za

www.ordotours.co.za

> **Soweto**
>
> *Soweto was constructed in 1950 under apartheid as a self-sufficient housing project. The name is a contraction of South Western Townships and today it is a city in its own right, with a population of more than three million people.*

Visiting Soweto

Soweto is central to the turbulent recent history of South Africa and a visit there if you're in Johannesburg is a must. But you do need a guide so book in with Suzanne and Amos who never cease to amaze us with their country-wide connections and will send you on a really informative visit to the world's most famous township.

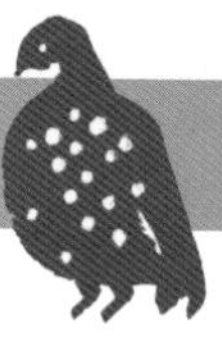

Apartheid

Apartheid literally means "separateness" in Afrikaans and refers to the former government policy of totally segregating minority whites from the other races in South Africa. Introduced in 1948 (although some segregation laws were already in place) this system survived almost half a century, dividing South Africans into racial groups that delineated their economic, social and political rights. The system defined three groups, 'Whites', 'Blacks' and 'Coloureds'. This last group were further sub-divided according to a whole series of complicated regulations, which meant that those of Chinese descent had more rights than those of Indian for example. Determination of which group you were supposed to belong to was often a simple question of which group you looked like you belonged to. A white person was defined as "in appearance obviously a white person or generally accepted as a white person." A person could not be considered white if one of his or her parents were non-white. A black person would be of or accepted as a member of an African tribe or race, and a coloured person is one that is not black or white.

Under the National Party's apartheid system, interracial marriages and even relationships were quickly outlawed. Blacks and whites were appointed separate beaches, schools, ambulances, buses and even drinking fountains and park benches. Blacks had at all times to carry much-hated pass books, their movements strictly controlled.

In 1951, the Bantu Authorities Act established the "homelands" or Bantustans. These were independent states to which each African was assigned by the government according to the record of origin (which was frequently inaccurate). Political rights, including voting, held by an African were restricted to the designated homeland. The idea was that they would be citizens of the homeland, losing their citizenship in South Africa. From 1976 to 1981, four of these independent homelands were created (Bophuthatswana, Transkei, Ciskei and Venda), denationalizing nine million South Africans. Africans living in the homelands needed passports to enter South Africa: aliens in their own country.

Internationally condemned as unjust and racist the apartheid system met instant resistance from within from the ANC or African National Congress (led, for a period by Nelson Mandela) which fought for a non-racist and democratic society. But apartheid survived a remarkably long time, becoming ever more brutal in its suppression of black opposition despite international sanctions designed to force change. The state strictly controlled the press and violently quashed any form of protest.

In 1960 police killed 69 people and wounded 178 when they fired on a black demonstration against the pass laws. Sixteen years later, on June 16th 1976, police opened fire on students in Soweto, protesting against enforced Afrikaans teaching. By the end of the day 566 children were dead.

Eventually, though, the pressure broke through and the system was finally dismantled by President F.W. de Klerk in 1990.

JOHANNESBURG
EATING and DRINKING

There are a million and one places to eat in Johannesburg so here we've tried to choose a selection of our favourite that, like a well-spread buffet, offers you a little of everything.

Café Flo

An innovative menu and an eclectic café with tables lined up on the pavement, just built for sipping cappuccinos at and watching the world go by. Tim has been in the restaurant trade for decades and if the loyal local regulars have packed the place out you can head over to sister set-up, nicely-named Over Flo, instead.

Prices: *Starters around R40, mains R70, desserts R40. Serves breakfast lunch and dinner.*
Contact: *116 Greenway, Greenside.*
Tel: *011-646-6817*
cafeflo@telkomsa.net

Carnivore

Vegetarians sometimes crave a bacon sandwich - but I'm not sure that craving would stretch this far. Carnivore is one for the true meat lover. Adapted Masai spears around an open fire are skewered with dozens of different meat dishes from the usual beef, lamb and chicken to the unusual - ostrich, impala, crocodile, zebra… you get the idea.

Prices: *R125 for lunch, R145 for dinner. Open daily.*
Contact: *16 Drift Boulevard, Muldersdrift.*
Tel: *011- 950-6000*
carnivore@rali.co.za
www.rali.co.za

Giles

Unpretentious eatery with plenty of outdoor dining space. Deep-fried camembert is a popular starter and beef Wellington comes hotly recommended on a French-leaning menu, but there's a constantly shifting menu of specials to go for too. Wine lovers are welcome to bring their own bottles (no corkage charged).

Prices: *About R120 for 3-course meal. Open for lunch and dinner Mon-Sat, plus breakfast on Sat and breakfast and lunch on Sun.*
Contact: *Grafton Ave, Craighall Park.*
Tel: *011-442-4056*
gilesrez@lantic.net

La Cucina di Ciro

Ciro's constantly-changing Italian menu is a real hit with the locals and this small restaurant is always busy (so book ahead). Pastas are obviously great as is the fillet with avocado soufflé. Tables spill out onto the pavement in summer, perfect for balmy evenings. Ciro is also opening a deli nearby on 7th Avenue so you can take all those yummy treats home.

Prices: *Meat dish R75 - R80, starters R22 - R35, desserts R25. Open 8am til late Mon - Fri and till 3.30pm Sat.*
Contact: *17 4th Ave, Parktown North.*
Tel: *011-442-5346*
cirom@worldonline.co.za

Montpellier de Tulbagh

An intimate restaurant serving French provençal dinners and bistro lunches. Call ahead and see if you're around for the Sunday evening opera and dinner. Worth the trip even without the opera as the food is great and complements wines from the Montpellier wine estate in Tulbagh.

Prices: *Starters around R25, mains R55 - R75, desserts R25.*
Contact: *Cnr 7th Ave and 3rd Ave, Parktown North.*
Tel: *011-880-1946*
info@montpellierrestaurant.co.za
www.montpellierrestaurant.co.za

Osteria Tre Nonni

Stelio (yes, his roots are Greek) is utterly passionate about his ingredients and as a result even the simplest dishes are mouth-watering. The food is regional Italian and the lamb-stuffed ravioli particularly good. Veggies almost steal the limelight though. Order a heap of his fried potatoes with salt and rosemary and you'll understand why everyone else is eating them too.

Prices: *About R130 for 3-course meal. Open for lunch and dinner Tues - Sat. Book well in advance.*
Contact: *9 Grafton Ave, Craighall Park.*
Tel: *011-327-0095*

Service Station

"Small but great, the trendy spot where the arty and intellectual set head for brunch/lunch." Perfect description of our discerning readership! Part of Melville's Bamboo Centre (along with Wine+) and a light and airy café with widely spaced tables. Serves excellent breakfasts to a regular stream of early risers and salads, quiches and the like to the loyal lunchtime crowd. Works as a help-yourself buffet so take as much or as little as you want.

Prices: *Breakfasts R30 - R40, breakfast buffet R55/kg, sandwiches R30, lunch buffet R82/kg. Average spend R50 - R60. Open Mon - Fri, 7.30am - 6pm, Sat 8am - 5pm, Sun 8.30am - 3.30pm.*
Contact: *Bamboo Centre, 53 Rustenberg Rd, Melville.*
Tel: *011-726-1701*

Sides Restaurant, Ten Bompas

Fabulous food and a bubbly informal atmosphere in this, one of Jo'burg's chicest, boutiquest hotels. The Sides team modestly call their menu "comfort food" which you can wash down with a choice of 4,000 bottles of wine housed in a glass cellar. Eat in the 40-seater dining room or on the terrace overlooking the pool.

Prices: *Average starters R30, mains R65, desserts R30, corkage R50.*
Contact: *Ten Bompas Hotel, 10 Bompas Rd, Dunkeld West.*
Tel: *011-341-0282*
reservations@mix.co.za
www.tenbompas.co.za

The Bread Basket

A really well-known bakery, deli and café that has three sister branches across the city. Everything is freshly prepared or baked on a daily basis - no mean feat considering there are some 1,800 products on offer. Hot tip: if you're spoilt for choice, I'd recommend going for the cheesecake.

Prices: *So many options it's best to go and see for yourself.*
Contact: *Shop L1, Village Walk, Sandown.*
Tel: *011-883-9886/7*
maria@breadbasket.co.za
www.breadbasket.co.za

Tsunami Seafood Emporium

A stylish and chic spot to suck up great quality seafood. Create your own marine platter from a fresh fish and seafood counter or splash out on delicacies like fresh rock lobster and oysters. Sushi and sashimi is beautifully laid out on a revolving bar and the teppanyaki is to die for. Non-seafood fanciers catered for with plenty of meat, chicken and veggie options. Book a table on the al-fresco balcony.

Prices: *Starters from R25, sushi from R14 per portion, mains from R65, desserts from R25, wines R65 - R395.*
Contact: *Rosebank Mall, Rosebank.*
Tel: *011-442-9109*
info@tsunamisa.co.za
www.tsunamisa.co.za

Westcliff Hotel

For sundowners... an essential part of any holiday timetable!

Contact: *67 Jan Smuts Ave, Westcliff*
Tel: *011-481-6000*

Where's the capital?

Many people incorrectly assume that business centre Johannesburg is the capital of South Africa but it is actually Pretoria, with Cape Town its legislative centre and Bloemfontein the judicial centre.

Wine+

South Africa produces a prodigious amount of great wine and, in Johannesburg, this is the place to buy it. Whether you're a budding vintner, a wine trade professional or simply looking for a dinner party tipple, they'll have a bottle with your name on it. Call ahead and see if you've timed it right for the fortnightly tasting session.

Prices: *Wine+ offers a tasting each fortnight for R100 pp including snacks, limited to 20 people so book early, starts at 6.30pm sharp.*
Contact: *Bamboo Centre, 53 Rustenberg Rd, Melville.*
Tel: *011-482-1020*
wine@wineplus.co.za

JOHANNESBURG NATURE and ACTIVITIES

Delta Park

A 104ha big green lung in the city centre full of jack russells and collies and great for walks. Jo'burg, like any big city, can be a tiring place to visit so come here for a bit of a breather and some fresh air. Visit the environmental centre and snooze in the shade of a huge array of exotic trees, teeming with bird life.

Contact: *Off M7, Victoria Park.*
Tel: *011-888-4161*

Johannesburg Botanical Gardens and the Emmarentia Dam

Another green option. These two meld together in a continual flow of vegetation and water that makes for a gigantic area of parkland. Enjoy a brisk (and long) walk or chill out on shaded benches. Boating on the dam, rose and herb gardens, statues, fountains... and the freedom to wander from dawn till dusk.

Contact: *Off Olifants Rd, Emmarentia.*
Tel: *011-782-7064*

Parkview Golf Club

Founded in 1916 this is one of Jo'burg's oldest clubs but has some modern challenges - its tough new greens and bunkers were completed in 2002. If you manage to avoid the sand you may not be so lucky with the Braamfontein stream that meanders through the length of this parkland course. Visitors are welcome through the week and on Sun afternoons. Booking essential.

Prices: *Green fee for non-affiliated visitors R330 - R363. Lessons, cart/caddie/club hire and meals all available.*
Contact: *Emmarentia Ave, Parkview.*
Tel: *011-646-5400*
bookings@parkviewgolf.co.za
www.parkviewgolf.co.zae

And here, word for word, is another well-kept Jo'burg gem coyly offered by a friend that lives there:

"... a great place to chill out is Zoo Lake, a park near Rosebank and across the road from the zoo where you can play tennis, hire a pedalo and have a game of croquet at the bowling club. It's definitely a locals' place, though, and a good little secret so it's much against my better nature that I tell you this! In fact, why don't you keep it vague... mention the croquet, but not the bar. Intrepid travellers can find it if they search hard enough."

JOHANNESBURG
CULTURE and HISTORY

Apartheid Museum

For almost half a century the South African government purposefully divided whites from other races, splitting its country in two through the apartheid system (an Afrikaans word literally meaning "separateness"). This museum tells the story of that separation - of those who fought to dismantle it, those who sought to justify it and those who lived through it.

Prices: *R25 for adults R12 for kids, open Tues - Sun 10am - 5pm.*
Contact: *Northern Parkway and Gold Reef Rd, Ormonde.*
Tel: *011-309-4700*
info@apartheidmuseum.org
www.apartheidmuseum.org

Museum Africa

Part of the Newtown Cultural Precinct and housed in the Victorian building that was once the fresh goods market. A vivid retelling of Johannesburg's history from the discovery of gold to the present day and an excellent section on Mandela's treason trial of the 1950s that uses old film and radio broadcasts to tell the story. The precinct's rock art and photography museums are also worth a look.

Prices: *Entry free. Open Tues - Sun 9am - 5pm.*
Contact: *121 Bree St.*
Tel: *011-833-5624*

The Anglo-Boer Wars a very potted history

The British and the Boers just never seemed to hit it off, finally settling centuries of strife in two wars. It was the discovery of gold and the explosive growth of Johannesburg that was their final undoing.

British colonial expansion and the annexation of the Transvaal sparked the first Boer War or War of Independence, when the Boers revolted, defeating the British at the Battle of Majuba Hill in February 1881 after three months of confrontation. The Second Boer War or South African War was to be a far more bloody affair.

The Transvaal became autonomous and the strongly pro-Afrikaaner Paul Kruger the leader of this impoverished but strongly independent state. The discovery of a huge gold field in the Witwatersrand (the "Rand") south of Pretoria, changed its fortunes overnight. Hoards of British outsiders or "uitlanders" descended on the Transvaal and Johannesburg was born. To prevent their inevitable insurgence on Transvaal politics the British were denied voting rights. British gold mine owners complained bitterly of unfair taxation and overpriced black labour and tension grew to bursting point after a failed coup attempt backed by Cape Colony premier Cecil Rhodes.

Aware that the British were lining up for war Kruger made the first move and, allied with the Orange Free State, declared war on Britain in 1899. Some 500,000 British soldiers faced 65,000 Boers with black soldiers recruited by both sides in a war that dragged on until 1902 and was fought right across the country.

The Boers adopted a style of guerrilla warfare that made them almost impossible to defeat and it was only through a scorched earth policy and the first concentration camps that the British finally ground them down. Some 24,000 Boer women and children and 14,000 black and coloured people died in appalling conditions in the camps, which decades later would stamp their mark on history during World War Two.

Paul Kruger had it right when he reputedly said his countrymen should cry rather than rejoice at the discovery of gold in the Transvaal, as it would "cause our land to be soaked in blood".

PRETORIA
EATING and DRINKING

Lucit Restaurant

Get ready for something totally unique. Gideon owns and runs this restaurant and is renowned for his pure and healthy cuisine (prepared and served by him). It's a magical setting in a candle-lit water garden complete with night-blooming water lilies, waterfalls and a little brook. The 15 guests are welcome in the kitchen for a chat, a taste of the latest recipes and to suck in the wonderful smell of fresh-baked bread.
Prices: *R150 pp for a 5-course meal, though individual courses can be ordered, menu published on website every Mon.*
Contact: *42 Belrene St, Rietondale, Pretoria.*
Tel: *012-329-4180*
Cell: *083-306-2830*
info@lucit.co.za
www.lucit.co.za

Jacaranda

A jacaranda in blossom is a stunning sight and Pretoria is the place to see them. Almost every avenue is lined with them (some 70,000 apparently). As other spring blossoms fade the jacaranda bursts into an explosion of blue-lilac flower that hangs heavy on the branches and coats the pavements in a carpet of colour.

PRETORIA
NATURE and ACTIVITIES

Cullinan Diamonds

The diamond industry is central to South Africa's history so to find out about it visit Cullinan, a still operational, century-old mine. Tours include tea and scones on arrival (a very civilised start), a 4x4 excursion around the mine plant and then - for those that really want to get the feel for mining - the 763m cage descent underground. Others will be shown around the village instead. Finish off in the shop gazing at sparkling jewels being cut next door and then buy one!
Prices: *R350 pp for 3hr tour, shorter tours for R100, meals around R75 - R90 pp.*
Contact: *The Diamond Hub, De Beers Cullinan Diamond Mine, Cullinan (on R513 east of Pretoria, 16km from N4).*
Tel: *012-734-2625/26*
Cell: *082-482-0819*
virginia@cullinandiamonds.co.za or info@cullinandiamonds.co.za
www.cullinandiamonds.co.za

You'll most likely hear talk of the renowned Big Hole in Kimberley - well the Cullinan diamond mine is four times bigger!

Union Buildings

For one of the best views of Pretoria drive up to the Union Buildings. Fronted by two enormous canon, the seat of the South African government is 275m long and was designed by Sir Herbert Baker (an architect whose name pops up all over the place). It is the official residence of the presidency and the parliament is held here during the winter months, spending the summer in Cape Town. The view over the city is magnificent and the hilltop is usually bustling with other visitors, buskers and a few souvenir stalls for those craving some retail therapy.

Pretoria Botanical Gardens

A pleasant 76ha oasis of greenery packed with everything from succulents to cycads and made even more enjoyable by a tea garden for sitting and sipping in (open Tues - Sun) and winter picnic concerts that feature a range of South African music including pop, jazz and military bands.

Prices: *Gardens open daily R10 entry. Concerts held on Sundays Apr - Sept, usually early afternoon tickets about R15.*
Contact: *2 Cussonia Ave, Brummeria.*
Tel: *012-843-5194*
info@sanbi.org
www.nbi.co.za

BIRDING BITS

You will see: Black-shouldered Kite, Grey Turaco

You'll be very lucky to see: Rufous-breasted Wryneck, Red-billed Wood Hoopoe

You might see: Crested and Black-collared Barbet

Eyes peeled around Johannesburg and Pretoria.

North West Province

NORTH WEST PROVINCE

After seeing the sights of Johannesburg and Pretoria you will be chomping at the bit to get out into the wilderness. Now's your chance. The highlights of the North West Province to my mind are the Magaliesberg close to Pretoria and the Madikwe Game Reserve so we've suggested an itinerary that takes you to both.

You can of course do all of the Magaliesberg suggestions within an easy day trip from Jo'burg or Pretoria and they can make a pleasant change from the hectic city streets.

The **Magaliesberg** is estimated to be one of the oldest mountain ranges on Earth. Almost half the age of the planet itself, it stretches 120km from Pretoria west to Rustenberg. Looking south sheer quartzite cliffs stare down onto a wide valley where tributaries drain into five different rivers, while watercourses down the northern slopes have carved deep kloofs and gullies.

Hartbeestpoort Dam (on the R512 if you're coming from Jo'burg), known as "Sandton-on-Sea" after the smart Johannesburg suburb, is the focal point of most activities in the area though not, itself, a beauty.

Depending on what you fancy, De Wildt Cheetah Project and Paddle Power Adventures are among the best of the area's action activities. For those after slightly more sedate pursuits, we recommend a visit to the Cradle of Humankind and Sterkfontein Caves. If you're in no hurry a couple of days here should give you time for plenty of book-reading in the sun (or shade) wherever you choose to stay.

De Wildt Cheetah and Wildlife Trust

De Wildt is renowned for its breeding of rare and endangered species, namely cheetah, king cheetah and wild dog. This is a chance to get close to animals you will rarely see in the wild. Learn all about their nature and habitat on a three-hour open vehicle tour. Make sure you book (kids under 6 not admitted).

Prices: *R165 for tour, R200 for photo with ambassador cheetah.*
Contact: *On R513 Pretoria North, 10 mins from Hartbeestpoort Dam. See web or call for details.*
Tel: *012-504-1921*
cheetah@dewildt.org.za
www.dewildt.org.za

north west province

The North-West Province (can you guess where it is?) covers about 10% of South Africa's landmass, stretching along the Botswanan border. Much of the region is swallowed up by vast and arid tracts of land crossed by few roads and dotted with even fewer towns that lead you west into the Northern Cape (though it's tricky to tell exactly where one ends and the other begins). Even we have spent little time there and have instead focused our attention on the north-eastern corner of the region - where the action is.

And this is a pretty good place to start, an area populated since the arrival of early man on the scene and nowadays the out-of-town play area for the hard-working city folk of Jo'burg and Pretoria. The 120km-long Magaliesberg range makes for the most obvious geographical feature, standing over the Hartbeestpoort Dam and providing the gateway to easily accessible wilderness - for which, see below!

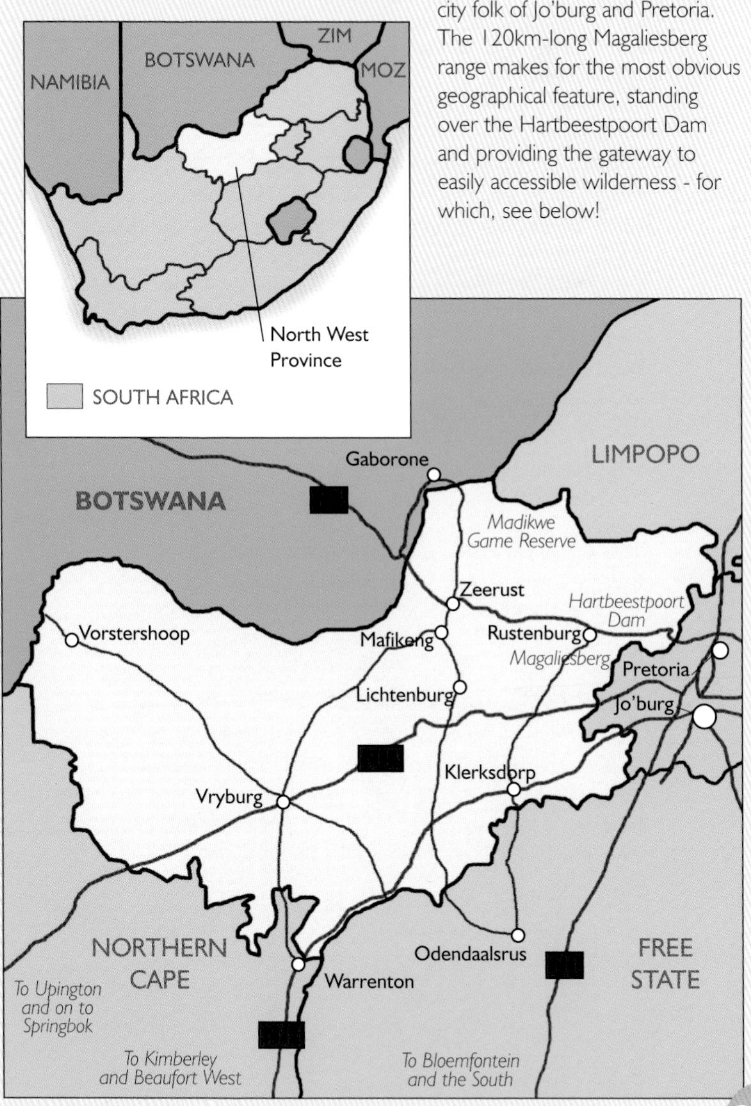

Paddle Power Adventures

Make a beeline for the Crocodile River with Rowan and David for some serious rafting action. Negotiate the narrows, master the rapids and be prepared to get very wet indeed. A full day trip will cover roughly 18km of river with 18 rapids to cross and a huge picnic lunch included. Two day trips will give you time for birding and fishing too.

Prices: *Half-day rafting trip R255, full-day R335, 2-day R800. Dozens of other activities also organised.*
Contact: *37 Broedestroom, on R512, 25mins from Pretoria and 20mins from Lanseria Airport.*
Tel: *011-794-3098*
Cell: *082-742-1922 or 082-956-3597*
padpower@lantic.net
www.paddlepower.co.za

Cradle of Humankind and Sterkfontein Caves

This cave complex is one of the world's richest human and pre-human archaeological sites, where the 2 million-year-old skull of Mrs Ples was found, one of almost 500 skeletal fossil findings dating back to the stone age. Guides take you down 120 steps into the caves to a vast underground lake; once out the other side they'll show you the ongoing digs too.

Prices: *1hr guided tours leave on the half hour every day. R35 for adults, R20 for kids.*
Contact: *Off R512 10 mins from Lanseria Airport.*
Tel: *011-668-3200*
info@discoveryourself.co.za
www.discoveryourself.co.za

Once you've exhausted your body with action and your mind with history you'll be in need of a seriously good feed. De Hoek and the Mount Grace are the best venues for those looking for a real gourmet treat.

De Hoek Country House

A real five-star dining treat in this elegant country house set on the banks of the Magalies River in the foothills of the Magaliesberg. Sumptuous five-course French-leaning dinners are served up in the grand dining room by Swiss chef and co-owner Michael Holenstein and his team and there are beautiful gardens to walk it off in afterwards.

Prices: *4-course lunch R175 - R185, 5-course dinner R200 - R225. Subject to availability, reservations are essential.*
Contact: *7 Seekoehoek, Magaliesberg.*
Tel: *014-577-1198*
reservations@dehoek.com
www.dehoek.com

Mount Grace

If you need some pampering before or after a tough bush expedition then this is the place to come. On the food front it's buffet or à la carte and The Stoep's menu says it all: fillet beef carpaccio, ricotta-stuffed trout and braised shoulder of lamb, pavlova and crème brûlée and many more mouth-watering treats. This country hotel is set in 10 acres of beautiful Magaliesberg gardens and the GG bush telegraph tells me the spa is great too.

Prices: *Breakfast R97, lunch R100, dinner R150 and renowned Sunday lunch R173. 30min massage R195, facials from R250. Definitely book in advance.*
Contact: *Old Rustenberg Rd, Magaliesberg.*
Tel: *014-577-1350 or 011-215-3900*
restaurants@grace.co.za or spa@grace.co.za
www.mount.grace.co.za

The Name Game

One problem with a country of so many different languages is that different places have different names. This can become quite a navigational challenge, particularly as road sign-makers are struggling to keep up with the law-makers who since the first democratic elections in 1994 have been reclaiming their heritage and busily giving towns new African names. Generally, road maps will have both names on but here are a few to get you started:

Firstly the old pre-election provinces themselves:

- Transvaal = *North-West Province, Mpumalanga, Limpopo (was Northern Province for a while too) and Gauteng (a Sesotho word meaning "at the gold")*
- Cape Province = *Western Cape, Eastern Cape and Northern Cape.*
- Orange Free State = *Free State.*
- Natal = *KwaZulu Natal.*

Renamed towns are generally concentrated in the north and particularly include those named after Afrikaner historical figures, so:

- Pietersburg = *Polokwane*
- Louis Trichardt = *Makhado*
- Potgietersrust = *Mokopane*
- Warmbaths = *Bela-Bela*
- Nylstroom = *Modimolle*

You may also hear new references and African colloquial names for major cities like:

- Nelson Mandela Metropole = *Port Elizabeth and East London*
- eKapa = *Cape Town*
- eGoli = *Johannesburg (meaning "place of gold")*
- eThekwini = *Durban (meaning "in the bay", although there was notable controversy when respected Zulu linguists insisted it meant "the one-testicled one" referring to the shape of the bay).*

Travellers on a more meagre budget will enjoy the super-relaxed African Swiss restaurant at **Hideaway at the Farm** guest house, which, conveniently, makes a great place to spend the night too, as does nearby **Dodona**.

African Swiss and Hideaway at the Farm

Both great food and great beds are available at Mike's hillside spot overlooking the Hartbeestpoort Dam. He's Swiss of origin but has adopted - and adapted to - his new home with real enthusiasm. Chef George turns out fantastic grub at the African Swiss restaurant and the atmosphere is wonderfully relaxed and welcoming. Beds here are in a comfortable farmhouse or slate-floored, thatched rondavels.

Prices: *R250 - R300 pp sharing.*
Contact: *Take R512 from Lanseria Airport towards Hartbeespoort Dam. At the T-junction turn L and the farm is on the L.*
Tel: *012-205-1309*
info@hideawayatthefarm.com
www.hideawayatthefarm.com

Dodona is the home of Beres, an illuminating art historian, a vellophile (or cycling enthusiast) and a direct descendant of Andries Pretorius, the Boer commander who led the massacre of the Zulus at Blood River, and who originally settled on this farm. A night or two spent with him is fascinating and Dodona is wonderfully cathartic for those on a long voyage. The Boathouse has two old-fashioned apartments looking onto the lake, a great place to sit and ponder the birds and the mysteries of the universe.

Tortoises are dangerous because...

... you spend a remarkable amount of time on the road swerving to avoid them. Despite the tide of advice put forward for their benefit, tortoises are forever crossing busy roads. This is not totally surprising as they do move very slowly and there are a lot of them. South Africa is home to 13 species in fact, giving it the richest tortoise diversity on earth. These includes the leopard, the hinge-back, the speckled padloper (which sounds more like a suspiciously cloudy English ale), the geometric and the tent.

Fed, watered and sufficiently activated by the Magaliesberg you're ready to move on to Madikwe. It's about a three- or four-hour drive to head straight there in one go, but so very worth it. The N4 is by far and away the quickest route to Madikwe, taking you west to Zeerust (a convenient and advisable place to fill-up). There you turn north (R) onto the R49 to Madikwe. Taking the cross-country route is long, hot and not advisable.

The 70,000ha **Madikwe Game Reserve** is precisely one of those off-the-beaten track reserves that we keep banging on about. Here there are just a handful of lodges and so minimal game vehicle traffic, but all the wildlife you'd see in the Kruger. Right on the border of Botswana it's wild country but on the accommodation front there are all the creature comforts. For those on more of a budget and looking for a real down-to-earth bush experience **Mosethla Bush Camp** GO is a must. Families wanting to meet other families or those looking for some serious luxury will prefer **Jaci's Tree Lodge and Safari Lodge** GO. Stay at least two nights here.

From Madikwe it's a short hop into Botswana or, as I did, you can head east. Those with a passion for dirt roads can take the back route to Thabazimbi, a mining town on the fringe of the stunning Waterberg range in Limpopo. This takes a good few hours and requires plenty of lefts and rights that would be unrecognisable without a very good set of instructions. To avoid leaving a criss-cross of dust trails that would lose even the best Bushman tracker, make sure you ask one of the lodges for a well-drawn map before you set out.

Alternatively, after an enjoyable bush extravaganza, Gauteng is an easy zip back east down the N4, the same way you came.

BIRDING BITS

You will see: White-browed Sparrow-weaver, Scaly-feathered Finch

You'll be very lucky to see: Orange River Francolin

You might see: Northern Black korhaan, Capped Wheatear

Eyes peeled around Ventersdorp.

Limpopo

The great, grey-green, greasy waterway, after which this most northerly of South African provinces is named, curls 1,600km in a wide arc around the top of the Drakensberg, separating South Africa from neighbouring Botswana, Zimbabwe and Mozambique.

The fact is, in thousands of dusty miles, I never actually made it to the river's banks to see how greasy the water really was. It's an enormous journey generally only made by those looking to cross the border. But I did see pretty much everywhere else. Limpopo is an area, which, for the visitor, roughly breaks down into four zones.

The Waterberg, between Thabazimbi and Vaalwater, sits plum in the middle of the region. Its well-watered and lumpy peaks conceal some of the best-kept private reserves in the country, less plagued by both mosquitoes and tourists than their Kruger contemporaries.

Push east from there and you reach Tzaneen, a town surrounded by unexpectedly lush forest and fruit farms and well kitted-out for walkers and adrenalin junkies. To the south lies Hoedspruit and the heart of South Africa's wildlife industry.

Head north though to Louis Trichardt (or Makhado as it is now known) and you'll be rewarded with off-the-beaten-track adventure in the midst of the Venda culture and the fabulous Soutpansberg range.

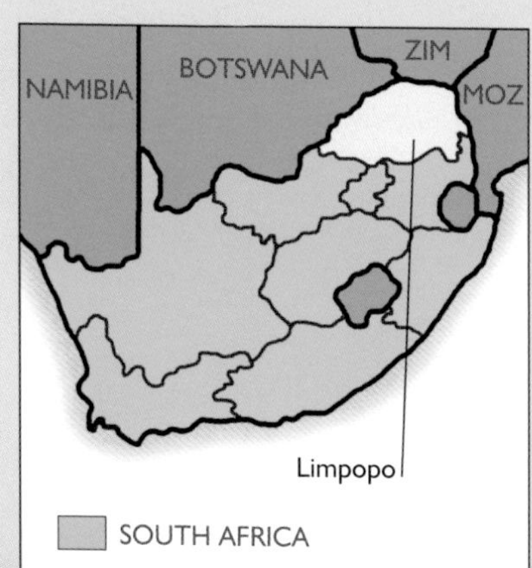

Limpopo has enough variety to warrant a substantial trip to just this one province. One of my favourite regions of the country.

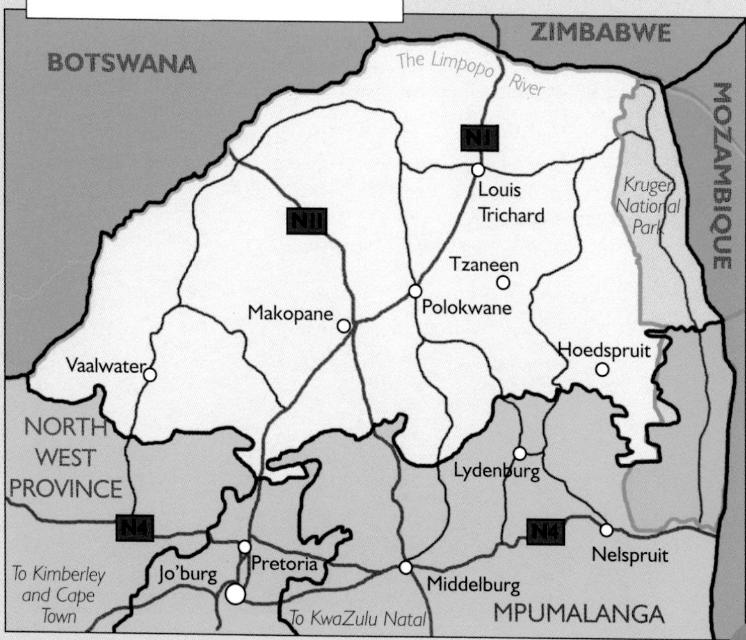

GUIDES AND EXPERTS
ACTIVITIES

Willie Botha, Travel Africa Trails

Willie runs tours all through Limpopo and Mpumalanga, including the enormous Kruger Park. She's a multi-talented birding/walking/hiking/riding guide who's as happy organising indigenous forest picnics and trails as history, culture and art tours, including visits to the Venda people near her base in Louis Trichardt. Trips are as short or long as you want to make them.

Prices: *Willie says ring her and ask as it varies so much depending on what you do.*
Tel: *015-516-5779*
Cell: *082-957-0102*
retreat@lantic.net

The Big 5 is not the be-all and end-all

The Big 5 was originally a hunting term, referring to the five most sought-after game prizes. These are the animals considered the most dangerous to hunt, which would come after you like the wrath of God if you failed to kill them outright, namely:

Elephant
Lion
Leopard
Rhino (strictly speaking the black rhino - though white rhino can get pretty angry too)
Buffalo - often considered the most dangerous of all.

Please don't let Big 5 sightings make or break your safari. These days it really is just an annoying and slightly ludicrous marketing term. If it were a Big 5 of animals to see rather than to kill, would the cheetah not be in there, and the buffalo out?

Every animal is individually amazing but it's the whole mosaic of bush life which (I think) is really fascinating, from enormous elephants all the way down to the beetles that deal with their dung. Open your eyes to this and you will get much more out of your safari. Here endeth the lesson!

Townsends Adventure Lifestyles

The best way to make the most of the indigenous forest, mountains, rivers, cliffs and waterfalls of Limpopo. With Garry in charge you couldn't be in better company. You'll see it all on foot, on horse-back, on a bike, with a fishing rod in hand, on a rope (going up or down), in a canoe, in a 4x4, in the sunshine, in the dark of a cave, from behind your binoculars, from the pub, from underwater... and more!

Prices: *Day trips R300 - R800 pp (excluding meals), discounts for groups. Weekend packages R1,250 - R3,000+, pp (excluding accommodation and meals).*
Cell: *082-446-7672 or 082-321-5430*
info@adventurelifestyles.co.za
www. adventurelifestyles.co.za

NATURE GUIDES

Hamish Rogers, Tula Mati Field Guide Training and Safaris

Spend just a day on safari and you'll realise how totally fascinating the bush really is. And for those who want to learn more (like me), Hamish is your man. He offers teaching courses that will deepen your knowledge on everything from bush flora to animal spoor. If you're seriously keen, he can even train you to be a qualified field guide. He also offers guided birding, nature and game tours and - most importantly - is a hugely friendly and enthusiastic chap.

Prices: *Full-day birding from R750 pp (max 8). Big 5 day-trip from R850 pp (min 4, max 10). 12-day field training course around R6,200 all inclusive. Speciality trips such as bushman art also available.*
Contact: *Cell: 082-857-0985*
info@fgtraining.info or info@tulamatisafaris.com
www.fgtraining.info or www.tulamatisafaris.com

HOEDSPRUIT
NATURE and ACTIVITIES

Airborne African Adventures

Microlighting is one of the best ways to see the bush and its wildlife. Bruce and Theresa McDonald will take you on flights or flight training over the fantastic scenery of the big five country adjoining Kruger Park. "Our guests love it every time," Motswari's Steve and Kathy Bergs told me.

Prices: *R300 for a 20 min flight, R600 for an hour. Training costs on request.*
Contact: *Xanatseni Safari Camp, Klaserie Game Reserve, Hoedspruit.*
Tel: *015-795-5803*
Cell: *083-601-3229*
mondzweni@hotmail.com

Trackers

After many years as a national park warden Dave started his own reserve with wife Julienne below a 5,000ft escarpment overlooking the Lowveld that adjoins the Kruger Park. He's a highly experienced field guide and will take you on birding and 'botanising' walks to the best local spots from mountains and cliffs to bush, riverine and grassland habitats. Give them some warning and they'll cook for you too.

Prices: *Guide bushwalks R50 pp (min 2, max 8) lasts 3 - 4hrs. Accompanied birding (max 6) R300 per group for a half a day, R600 for full day. Breakfast R50, dinner R90.*
Tel: *015-795-5033*
Cell: *082-494-4266*
trackers@lantic.net
www.trackers.truepath.com

Tropical Tzaneen

When I first visited I expected Limpopo to be big, empty and dry all over. I couldn't have been more wrong. In fact, it has rich agricultural zones, growing massive volumes of fruit and vegetables, including 75% of the country's mangoes, 65% of its papaya, 36% of its tea, 25% of its citrus, bananas, and litchis, 60% of its avocados, two thirds of its tomatoes. The Tzaneen area is particularly lush, with mountain lakes and streams feeding thick forest and terraced plantations. Take some time after your game drives for some fantastic walks in this area.

TZANEEN
EATING and DRINKING

Coach House Hotel

"We do everything we can, as well as we can," says Guy and that pretty much sums up the Coach House. From casual breakfasts to three-course, set-menu dinners everything is immaculately presented and utterly delicious. Walk off a huge meal in the 560ha of lush, forest-fringed grounds - much of it set aside for nut plantations - and then stay the night just so you can indulge again the next day.

Prices: *Dishes from R25 - R150.*
Contact: *Old Coach Rd, Agatha, nr Tzaneen.*
Tel: *015-306-8000/27*
info@coachhouse.co.za or reservations@coachhouse.co.za
www.coachhouse.co.za

Ashley's

A healthy eatery serving a wide selection of food for all appetites inside or out in the garden. Devour furnace-stoking breakfasts, snack on gourmet sandwiches and (Thai beef, Greek, pasta…) salads, share marinated kebabs and polish it all off with cheesecakes, pancakes and waffles and ice cream. Come with a very empty stomach.

Prices: *Salads R32 - R38, mains R34 - R52, light meals and gourmet sandwiches R14 - R34, desserts R10 - R22, wines R45 - R160. Open 8am - 4pm Mon - Fri, 9am - 2pm Sat.*
Contact: *30 Agatha Rd (main road), cnr Herman St, Tzaneen.*
Tel: *015-307-7270*
pamspeedy@telkomsa.net

TZANEEN
NATURE and ACTIVITIES

Kings Walden

Without a doubt one of the most beautiful private gardens I saw in South Africa. David and Tana's enormous creation was designed like a ship, its numerous decks hiding ponds, herb gardens and beds, its sides falling away steeply to the waves of hills that slide off into the Drakensberg. This is a place to get lost in daydreams before hauling yourself back to the edible reality of an enormous picnic.

Prices: *R10 entry, R65 pp for picnics.*
Contact: *Old Coach Rd, Agatha, nr Tzaneen.*
Tel: *015-307-3262*
info@kingswalden.co.za
www.kingswalden.co.za

Lesodi Trail

This short trail should take about two hours and is great for birding. Starting opposite Sanford Heights Tea Room (near the Magoebaskloof Hotel) it carves down the gorge through magnificent protected indigenous forest where the birding is at its best. There's a particularly good view-point en route too. Look out for amazing strangler figs and the cathedral tree as well as a troop of samango monkeys near the hotel and the narina trogon and Cape parrot.

Prices: *Nominal entry fee at the start.*
Contact: *Tzaneen Info, Old Gravelot Rd, Tzaneen.*
Tel: *015-307-2680 /1933*
Cell: *083-309-6901*
reservations@tzaneeninfo.co.za
www.tzaneeninfo.co.za

Louis Changuion Trail

This is a 11km circular trail established by local volunteers to show you the beauty of their 240ha stretch of afro-montane grassland on this northern fringe of the Drakensberg. Starting from Haenertsburg it meanders up to the cemetery crossing grassland and indigenous forest with wild flowers and endemic plants to look out for en route. The views are great, there's a little brook to dangle hot feet in and conveniently constructed picnic spots to sit at and watch for the Wolkberg Zulu butterfly and the blue swallow (Sept - Apr).

Prices: *Free entry, buy the map for R5 from the Atholl Arms or Haenertsburg Tourist Office, or Magoebaskloof Hotel.*
Contact: *Tzaneen Info, Old Gravelot Rd, Tzaneen.*
Tel: *015-307-2680 /1933*
Cell: *083-309-6901*
reservations@tzaneeninfo.co.za
www.tzaneeninfo.co.za

Rooikat Trail

You're unlikely to actually see a rooikat (the Afrikaans name for caracal) on this trail as they are nocturnal, but you may well see bushbuck, duiker, baboon and vervet and samango monkeys. A good walk for hot days, much of the 11km circular trail heads through indigenous pine forest and trees like forest cabbage, Natal mahogany and matumi. Be ready for some seriously steep inclines and declines. Allow five hours in total (to make time for that picnic and a dip in the Bobs River).

Prices: *Nominal entry fee to be obtained at entrance to the New Agatha State Forest station. Map available on request.*
Contact: *Tzaneen Info, Old Gravelot Rd, Tzaneen.*
Tel: *015-307-2680 /1933*
Cell: *083-309-6901*
reservations@tzaneeninfo.co.za
www.tzaneeninfo.co.za

Plenty of other walks in the area too so ask at the tourist office for more info.

LOUIS TRICHARDT
EATING and DRINKING

Inn Tea Gardens and Gallery

An unexpectedly English country tea garden awaits you if you're on the road north to Zimbabwe or pootling around the Louis Trichardt area. Rae serves breakfasts, light (baguette/lasagne etc) lunches and tea and cakes here in a wonderfully tranquil spot looking onto the mountains. She also exhibits local artists and has an interior design shop stuffed with goodies for the gift hunters.

Prices: *R50 - R60 for a meal. Open Tues -Sun, 9am - 5pm.*
Contact: *11km north of Louis Trichardt on N1.*
Cell: *083-772-4978*
innteagarden@telkomsa.net

Textures

Utter tranquillity at the end of a dirt road (always good news). Meals on the verandah (or by the fire) looking onto an indigenous garden fluttering with bird life. Friendly Venda staff, South African jazz in the background and art on the walls, a shop stuffed with collectables and a rich menu of simple foods. Bobotie, ploughmans, smoked chicken salads, all day breakfast, bottomless tea and coffee, cheesecakes and muffins....

Prices: *Café meals up to R40. Shop prices from R20 for hand-painted beaded pickle sticks to R4,500 for hand-carved ceremonial chair from Congo. Open every day 9am - 5pm.*
Contact: *In Louis Trichardt take R524 to Thohoyandou and Punda Maria Gate (Kruger), Textures signed L 15km along this road.*
Tel: *015-516-6872 or 015-517-7249*
Cell: *084-400-4595*
maythamg@cybertrade.co.za

LOUIS TRICHARDT
NATURE and ACTIVITIES

Hanglip

Adventuring into the stunning Soutpansberg around Louis Trichardt is something you can't miss and Hanglip is a great way to do just that - an afro-temperate mist-belt forest with a picnic site and short hiking trails in easy reach of town. The birding here is great and you should watch and listen out for the scaly-throated honeyguide and the rare blue-spotted dove. Two short circular walks and one four-hour one all start at the picnic site.

Prices: *R10 per vehicle, R5 pp entry fee.*

Contact: *Take Krogh St due north through Louis Trichardt all the way to the Hanglip plantation gate. Continue 8km to picnic site.*

Tel: *015-516-0040 for tourist office.*

LOUIS TRICHARDT
CULTURE and HISTORY

Shiluvari Lakeside Lodge

Shiluvari offers a number of cultural tours in this part of the world. Join them to find out all about the Venda people, their traditions and spiritual awareness; or take the Ribolla Arts Route to see the best of the region's artists and craftsmen, visiting them at work in their studios. Then return to the lodge for home-cooked afro-fusion food (butternut and wild ginger soup, seared chilli beef fillet).

Prices: *Half-day with a guide R300, full day R400. Light meals from R35 open to visitors during the day, 3-course set-menu dinner R120 pp, booking essential.*

Contact: *On Elim/Levubu Rd, turn off N1 outside Louis Trichardt on to R578. After 18km turn L at crossroads.*

Tel: *015-556-3406*

shiluvar@lantic.net

www.shiluvari.com

Purple-crested lourie

A quick mention for one of my favourite birds. There are a number of lourie species in South Africa but this is, for me, the most beautiful one, found in northern and eastern S.A. They're very distinctive and you'll tend to see them in coastal or riverine forest, often in pairs "furtively clambering through dense foliage" as one book eloquently puts it. The crest on these magnificent birds is indeed purple, its wings and tail a blueish colour and you'll catch flashes of red in the wings when it flies. The purple-crested lourie is a noisy character and before you see it you may well hear its call - a loud kok-kok-kok-kok increasing steadily in volume. So keep your ears and eyes open.

VAALWATER
EATING and DRINKING

Bush Stop Café

Jean was in the middle of a crispy bacon, avocado and sweet chilli ciabatta roll when I called - a good sign. A British import, her breakfast and lunch eatery is extremely popular. Early mornings centre around waffles, bacon, scrambled egg and fry-ups, while lunch-time favourites include a huge range of fresh salads. Try steamed chicken breast, local halloumi goat's cheese, or pepperdew and greens.

Prices: *Breakfast R15 - R28, lunch R20 - R30. Open 7.30pm - 5pm in summer, 8am - 5pm in winter.*

Contact: *Spar Centre, Voortrekker St, Vaalwater, 1.5km out of town after the one and only stop sign.*

Tel: *014-755-3508*

Cell: *083-326-5098*

rodnjean@mweb.co.za

VAALWATER
NATURE and ACTIVITIES

Charles Baber's Farm Tours

Charles Baber offers more of a detailed introduction to the Waterberg and its history than a simple farm tour. His family have been here for generations and on a visit you'll see the oldest dwelling in the area, stop in at St.John's Herbert Baker-designed church, and inspect his herd of Bonsmara cattle. Expect family accounts of the Boer War, sightings of a lively herd of hippo and tea and scones to end it all.

Prices: *Roughly R400 per group (max 4).*

Contact: *Boschdraai Farm, Vaalwater.*

Tel: *014-755-4000*

Cell: *083-276-0518*

thecalcotts@yahoo.co.uk

Equus Horse Safaris

For those who'd rather see game from the saddle than the car seat horse-lovers John and Wendy have traversing rights of some 5,000ha of wild valleys, stream beds and mountains where you'll spot zebra, wildebeest, eland and other plains game. Learn about the area's flora and fauna on a morning ride or stay for a full day and lunch. There are also multi-day trips available to those looking for an entire riding holiday.

Prices: *2 - 3hrs of riding R250 pp plus R100 optional lunch. R600 for full day incl lunch at bush camp or carried in saddle-bags. R1,750 pp per night for all-inclusive horse safaris. No beginners, booking essential.*

Contact: *Travel 24km on Bakkers Pass Rd from where it starts at the tar road 6km west of the four-way stop in Vaalwater. Equus sign at Bakkers Pass Road.*

Tel: *014-721-0063*

reservations@equus.co.za

www.equus.co.za

Geluksfontein Goat Cheese Farm

Possibly the only goat farm where the herd is looked after by a baboon. This alone is reason enough to visit Christo and Aubrey's 400-acre farm where three different cheeses are made daily. They are open to visitors every day and Aubrey will show you around and demonstrate the cheese-making process and give you a taster. Breakfast and lunch available.

Prices: *R15 adults, R10 for kids. Open 9am - 5pm, closed Tues.*

Contact: *Take Melkrivier road from Vaalwater, 32km then L to Dorset and immediately R on farm road signed to cheese farm.*

Tel: *014-755-4331*

Cell: *083-704-4229*

christov@goatmilk.co.za

www.goatmilk.co.za

Dirt roads and flat tyres

Drive anywhere in South Africa and at some stage you will hit dirt roads. Limpopo is no exception. The one thing to remember is to take it carefully. These roads often become furrowed and it's easy to lose control if you hit a deep patch of gravel. Flat tyres are not unknown. Make sure you check the spare tyre on your hire car before you leave in case you need it (as I did) when, inevitably, you're in the middle of nowhere. Get the flat tyre repaired at a tyre centre in the nearest town (even the smallest towns seem to have them). It takes just a few minutes and will cost you much less than having the hire company do it when you return the car.

Horizon Horseback Adventures and Safaris

Laura and Shane have more than 60 horses and offer almost as many options for riding them. Anyone from novice to accomplished expert is welcome for lessons, polo-crosse, cattle mustering and exciting horseback safaris. On a game ride you'll see antelope, zebra, rhino, giraffe and hippo and even canter alongside them - well, perhaps not the hippo. Big five safaris can also be arranged.

Prices: *Riding for day visitors R180 pp per hour. Safaris from R2,350 pp per night. Book ahead.*
Contact: *Triple B Ranch, Klipfontein Farm, Vaalwater, Waterberg.*
Tel: *014-755-4003/4418*
horizonranch@telkomsa.net
www.ridinginafrica.com

Xtreme Attraction

The first devoted adventure camp in the Waterberg. Xan is a great guy who gave up running private game lodges to set up his new project. Come here to abseil and climb, bike and hike, raft and swim and really get to grips with one of the most exciting parts of the country.

Prices: *From R180 pp per day.*
Contact: *Farm Taaibos, Vaalwater, 28km from town on Bulgerivier Rd.*
Tel: *014-754-4463*
Cell: *082-698-2994*
x@xtremeattraction.co.za
www.xtremeattraction.co.za

BIRDING BITS

Eyes peeled around Pont Drift.

Mpumalanga

Mpumalanga, formerly the Eastern Transvaal, means "the place where the sun rises", which should give you a pretty good indication of where it is: smack on South Africa's eastern border, wedged in between the Drakensberg and Mozambique.

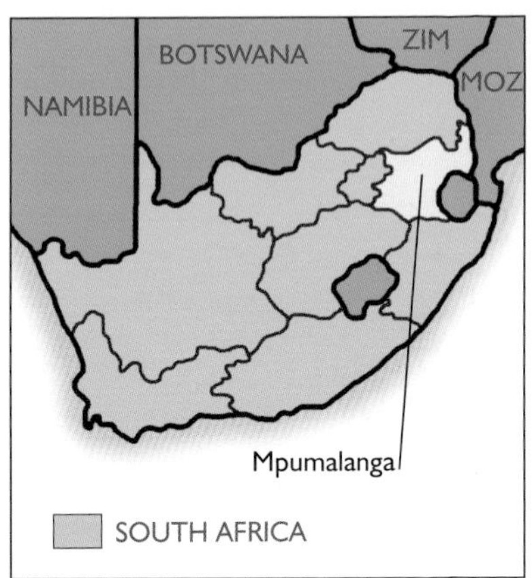

Geographically it's divisible into the drier highveld and the low-lying and humid lowveld, which combine to cater for a huge range of agriculture. In fact, while many may associate the region purely with the big cats of the Kruger National Park, 68% of it is set aside for agriculture and the farming of everything from wheat and barley to sugar cane, tobacco and citrus.

But, while you'll see it whizz by in the car, it's unlikely you'll want to focus your holiday on crop rotation. Or perhaps you do? Come here instead for Boer War battlefields, bungy-jumping, birding and big game, most of which is conveniently condensed within the north of the province.

The town of Nelspruit provides the most natural springboard into the region (or across to Maputo and Mozambique) while many of the guest-houses lie around the towns of Hazyview and White River.

I would urge you to plan for more than just a single game park visit. Lions and elephants are, of course, a must-see on anyone's list but there is so much else to do too. Take time out to drive via the so-called Panorama Route through the mountainous Highveld with its escarpments, passes and gorges (most dramatic of these being the Blyde River Canyon).

mpumalanga

Far below you lie the Lowveld and the Kruger National Park that sweep away towards Mozambique. Play some golf (!), try out our dining suggestions, investigate the history and find out about Long Tom Pass. And then you can go and get your animal fix. See our accommodation guide for the best places to stay in the private reserves attached to the Kruger Park

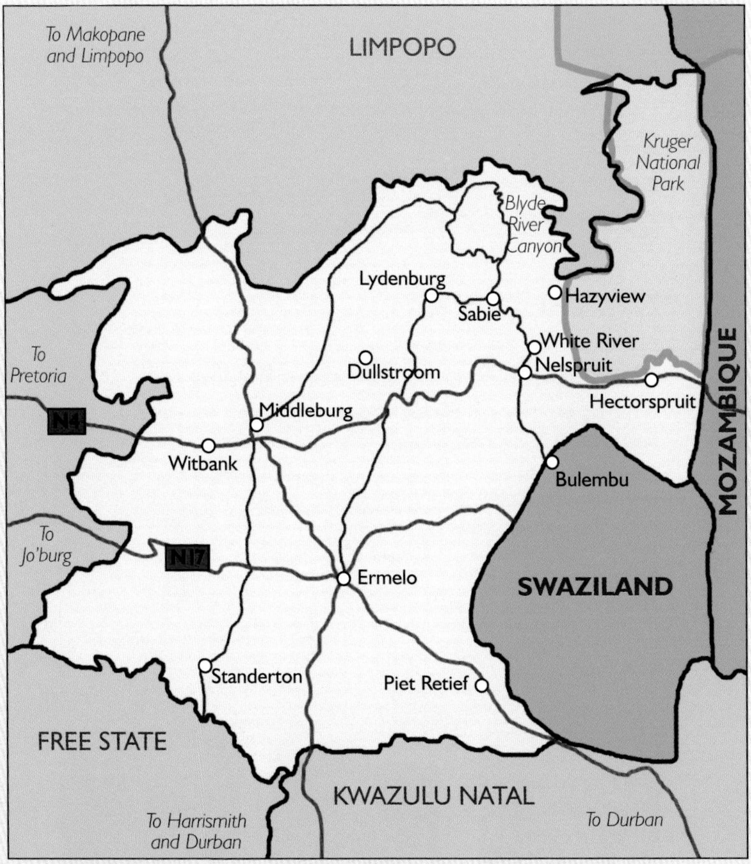

GUIDES AND EXPERTS

CULTURE and HISTORY

Tony and Ansi Erasmus, Earth Africa Tours

Tony and Ansi will take you anywhere you want to go in Mpumalanga. From the game experiences of the Kruger Park and surrounding big five private reserves to the incredible viewpoints of the Panoramic Route and the Blyde River Canyon (the third deepest canyon in the world) they cover the lot.

Prices: *Kruger Park R995 - R1,210 pp, Blyde River Canyon and Panoramic Route R950 - R1,150, two-day, one-night Kruger package R2,100 - R2,550.*
Tel: *013-744-0781*
Cell: *084-472-1231 or 072-229-9350*
earthafrica@iafrica.com
www.earth-africa.com

Marion Moir, Cottonwood Tours

The Ango-Boer battlefields of the Mpumalanga highlands are far less well-known than their KZN or Free State cousins, but Marion weaves together an intriguing story with a tour of Bergendal (the last set-piece battle of the Second Anglo-Boer War), the garrison town of Lydenburg and other historically weighty sites.

Prices: *R600 - R900 per day travelling in client's car with up to 6 people. Rates exclude tolls, picnic lunch or vehicle provision.*
Tel: *013-235-3771*
Cell: *082-448-6546*
enquiries@cottonwood.co.za
www.cottonwood.co.za

NATURE GUIDES

Mavourneen Pearce, Lawson's Birding

A hugely experienced birding tour company who cover the whole of South Africa and its neighbours. One-day to two-week trips are run for a maximum of 12 (or 15 at a push) and trippers love the unhurried and leisurely programme. Mammals, insects, reptiles and botany and butterflies are also covered.

Prices : *Tours average R1,100 pp per day all-inclusive.*
Tel: *013-741-2458*
mavourneen@lawsons.co.za
www.lawsons.co.za

DULLSTROOM
NATURE

Dullstroom Bird of Prey and Rehabilitation Centre

The largest bird of prey rehab centre of its kind in the country, Mark Holder and his team look after sick or orphaned birds, releasing as many as possible back into the wild. There are two educational demonstrations daily lasting about an hour with about 100 birds in aviaries, a petting zoo, tea garden and fly-fishing - plenty to keep the family out of mischief.

Prices: *R30 adults, R10 kids, under 3s free.*
Tel: *013-254-0777*
Cell: *072-378-8562*
falconer@dullstroom.net
www.birdsofprey.co.za

NELSPRUIT
EATING and DRINKING

Chez Vincent

Chez Vincent is the perfect spot to stoke the furnace before (or after) a trip to Mozambique or the Kruger. Heralding from Toulouse (and wife Sara from Liverpool) Vincent's S.A.-influenced menu has French roots. The restaurant is a casual affair with local art hanging on the walls and a regular crowd of Nelspruit locals and Maputo expats.

Prices: *Starters R30 - R40, mains R60 - R75, desserts R22 - R27.*
Contact: *56 Ferreira St, Nelspruit.*
Tel: *013-744-1146*
bookings@chezvincent.co.za
www.chezvincent.co.za

The quick way to Kruger

Thanks to GGer Peter Winhall for pointing out that cheap South Africa flight company Kulula (S.A.'s Easy Jet and Ryan Air equivalent) has recently introduced flights from Johannesburg to Nelspruit taking you right to the Kruger Park's doorstep. We flew with them a number of times around the country and found it a very affordable and hassle-free way to travel. See www.kulula.com for details.

NELSPRUIT

ACTIVITIES

Pierre's Mountain Inn, Sudwala Caves

These guys offer great tours of the stunning Sudwala Caves, the oldest known dolomite caves in the world. The trips last about an hour and are suitable for young and old, while the more adventurous (adults only) may want to take the adventure tour of the Crystal Chamber, lasting about four hours. And after all that excitement, head back to Pierre's for some food.

Prices: *1hr tour R36 for adults, kids R18, Crystal Tour R130.*
Contact: *36km from Nelspruit on R539 Sudwala/Sabie road.*
Tel: *013-733-4152*
info@pierres.co.za
www.pierres.co.za

HECTORSPRUIT

NATURE

Kwa Madwala

At 4,000ha this is a small reserve by South African standards but the big five are all present and you can see them on the usual 4x4 game drives or get even closer on guided bush walks. For the more adventurous of spirit there are microlight and elephant back safaris too (an experience not to be missed).

Prices: *30min game viewing microlight flight R700, 1hr flight R1,200, 3hr night game drive and dinner R350, 3hr bush game walk R200*
Contact: *Off N4 at Jeppes Reef turning, Hectorspruit, beyond Nelspuit.*
Reservations tel: *013-792-4526/4219*
gazebog@mweb.co.za
www.kwamadwalasafaris.co.za

WHITE RIVER
EATING and DRINKING

Jatinga Country Lodge

The most fantastic Med/traditional dining offering the lot from venison to chicken curry and superb home-made ice cream. Bang on the banks of the White River we'd advise coming for gourmet picnics by the water or on a Sunday for the weekly roast. Staying guests can go also on Kruger and Panorama Route tours as well as day trips to Maputo for a city tour and excellent seafood lunch. John and Lyn really do know how to look after you. Fabulous garden too!

Prices: *R120 - R150 for 3-course meal excluding wine. R60 for Sunday roast.*
Contact: *Jatinga Rd, Plaston, White River.*
Tel: *013-751-5059/5108*
Cell: *082-456-1676*
info@jatinga.co.za
www.jatinga.co.za

Impress your ranger

The trouble with game rangers is that they know so much. Here's a list of 10 animal facts that you can slip into conversation to try and impress them when bumping up and down in a game vehicle.

1- Hippos produce their own sun-block, a sticky pink liquid secreted from the skin that protects them from the sun and stops them drying out. They also kill more people than any of the other game that you will see on safari.
2- Lions spend some 20 hrs a day resting.
3- Black rhinos are actually grey... as are white rhinos, the white comes from Afrikaans widje, meaning wide and referring to the wide lower lip they use for grazing.
4- Of all the big cats cheetahs are the only ones that cannot retract their claws, which they use for grip when they are running.
5- Dung beetles don't actually feed on dung - they feed on the juice, by squeezing the dung between their jaws. It takes all sorts to make a world.
6- The word giraffe comes from the Arabic zarafah, meaning "the one who walks quickly".
7- It's thought that a leopard can lift three times its own body weight and there have been reports of them even dragging young giraffe kills into trees.
8- A new-born zebra can stand within 15mins of birth.
9- African wild dogs live in packs of up to 20 and cover ranges of hundreds of square miles.
10- An African elephant can drink up to 50 gallons of water a day.

And here are three absurd fabrications to slip in to see if they were listening:

1- The brown hyena regularly eats up to 86 times its own body weight in a day.
2- A full-grown buffalo measures up to 8.5m at the shoulder.
3- Fish eagles don't eat fish, they eat grass.

Salt Restaurant

Constantly recommended as an always buzzing local favourite, Salt is in the Kingdoms of Africa Centre (which may become the Baghdad Centre) and is a great venue for light salads and pastas at lunch or an excellent fusion dinner menu. Try the de-boned duck glazed in apricot jam. Brian is taking over the Baghdad pub here too and will soon be serving breakfasts as well.

Prices: *Average spend R70 on lunch, R150 on dinner. Open for dinner only Mon, Tues, lunch and dinner Weds - Sat, lunch only Sun.*
Contact: *Shop 7, Kingdoms of Africa Centre, on R40 1km from White River.*
Tel: *013-751-1555*
Cell: *082-766-4410*
brian@yum.co.za

WHITE RIVER
ACTIVITIES

White River Country Club

The sub-tropical climate here makes for perfect golfing weather all year round at this attractive championship 18 holer, just half an hour from the Kruger gates. Originally 9 holes designed by Gary Player and Reg Taylor in 1973, extended to 18 holes in 1993 and now very much open to visiting golfers.

Prices: *Visiting golfers R170 18 holes and R115 for 9, cart hire R135.*
Contact: *7Km from White River on the R40 Hazyview road, turn L to White River Country Estate (Pine Lake Drive), entrance of the golf club is 1.5km further on.*
Tel: *013 751 3781*
wrcc@intekom.co.za

SABIE VALLEY
EATING and DRINKING

Tree Tops

Stuart and Cindy Thomas have one of the most fantastic settings in the (already magnificent) Sabie Valley. The restaurant is a renovated wooden house where fireside meals in winter become outdoor deck dining in summer looking from the tree canopy over a small stream. Cindy's à la carte menu includes loads of local produce, home-grown veggies and particularly good game.

Prices: *Starters R20 -R38, mains R50 -R70, desserts R20 - R38, wines R50 -R200.*
Contact: *10km from Hazyview on R536 to Sabie.*
Tel: *013-737-8294*
Cell: *072-341-6117*
treetops@huxnet.co.za

Windmill Wine Shop

A compulsory stop on the Hazyview - Sabie stretch. Thomas and Jacqui converted a dilapidated farmhouse into a great shop/café/bar. Jacqui is a trained chef and her tapas and home-baked breads and ice creams (frozen as opposed to baked) are a real hit with cheese, wine and beer tasters. Eat them from rustic wooden boards al fresco on the deck (great views) or inside by the fire.

Prices: *Wine tasting R30 for five wines, beer tasting R5.50, cheese tasting R25 for five, lunch platters R60 - R95. Open Mon - Sat, 9am - 5pm.*
Contact: *On R536, 18km from Hazyview, 26km from Sabie.*
Tel: *013-737-8175*
Cell: *082-930-6289*
scrumpys@mweb.co.za
www.thewindmill.co.za

HAZYVIEW
EATING and DRINKING

Rissington Inn

Candle-lit tables, edifying conversation, entertaining hosts (in the form of owner/mover/shaker Chris), a great view over Hazyview's hazy valley and excellent grub - just a few ingredients to ensure you have a top evening at the excellent value and super-relaxed Rissington Inn.

Prices: *Average R100 for 3 courses.*
Contact: *2km south of Hazyview on R40 White River Numbi Gate Rd.*
Tel: *013-737-7700*
info@rissington.co.za
www.rissington.co.za

Game viewing and the Kruger National Park

It will quickly become clear that we have included little information about game viewing in the Mpumalanga and Limpopo chapters. This might seem strange given that safari is what people mainly come here for, but there is method in our madness.

To really make the most of the safari experience we would advise not zipping around a reserve in your hire car, ticking off as many animals as you can before the gates close. Instead, take a few days to visit lesser-known or private game reserves. These can be expensive, but it's an experience worth paying for. Stay in an all-inclusive lodge or camp for two to three nights to allow for plenty of game drives and walks. In-house rangers are the key to a great bush experience and the more questions you ask them, the more you'll get from the experience.

The GG accommodation guide is full of ideas on this - hence their absence here. We have instead tried to provide a range of interesting things to do (and places to eat) outside the game parks, to fill those days either side of your safari experience.

You can also, of course, visit the massive Kruger National Park. Perhaps Africa's most famous game reserve, it covers nearly two million hectares of land stretching along South Africa's north-eastern border with Mozambique.

Established in 1898 it was later named after the then president of the South African Republic Paul Kruger and is today home to a fantastic array of flora and fauna: 336 trees, 49 fish, 34 amphibians, 114 reptiles, 507 birds and 147 mammals.

This is a public park and, unlike the many private game reserves, you are free to drive around it in your own car, as motorists have been doing since 1927. This can clearly be a great experience. But the Kruger is massively popular and in high season can feel like more of a zoo, with traffic jams of visitors queuing to see this sleeping lion or that grazing rhino, leaning out of their cars to get a better look.

If you are going to go to Kruger, don't just turn up at the gates. Plan your trip in advance. The park's website has all the details you could possibly want for this, so take a look at it on www.sanparks.org (particularly the code of conduct page which informs us that the use of roller skates and skateboards is strictly prohibited!).

BLYDE RIVER CANYON
NATURE and ACTIVITIES

Panorama Route

This is one of the great drives of the country that heads north (or indeed south) through Mpumalanga, linking the towns along the Drakensberg's northern escarpment. It's best done in the dry winter months as summer brings rain clouds that have a tendency, when forced over the mountains, to burst on top of you - as they did with me. En-route sights like "God's Window" and "The Pinnacle" are worth some snaps but save plenty of film for views over the Blyde River Canyon, a vast 33km stretch of water fed by waterfalls and bubbling with wildlife.

Blyde River Adventures

The Blyde River Canyon is also a nature reserve and the best way to see its inhabitants is on the water. Karel's team organise boat trips on the dam. (They operate out of Hoedspruit, Limpopo, but the dam's just in Mpumalanga.) Trips last an hour and a half and take you to the thundering waterfall via crocs, hippos and lots of birdlife. Alternatively, for the more adventurous, there's a selection of thrilling rafting trips available.

Prices: *R55 for adults, R35 for kids under 8. Lower Blyde rafting R135pp (min 4) or R480 pp for Olifants River rafting trip incl lunch and transport.*
Contact: *Aventura Swadini, Hoedspruit, Limpopo.*
Tel: *015-795-5961*
Cell: *082-562-6379*
blydeadventure@lantic.net
www.blydeadventure.co.za

BIRDING BITS

You will see:
Bald Ibis, Cape Glossy Starling

You'll be very lucky to see:
Gorgeous Bush Shrike, Rudd's Lark

You might see:
Orange-throated Longclaw, Bush Blackcap

Eyes peeled heading into Swaziland and Wakkerstroom

index

ANIMALS:

ARCHERY:

ART:

ASTRONOMY:

BIRD-WATCHING:

BOAT CHARTERS:

BOAT CRUISES and FERRIES :

BREWERIES:

BUNGY JUMPS:

COOKING:

DANCE AND PERFORMANCE:

DOLPHINS:

DRAGON BOAT RACING:

FESTIVALS:

FISHING:

index

GARDENS:

GEO-CACHING:

GOLF:

HELICOPTER TOURS:

HORSE-RIDING:

HOT-AIR BALLOONING:

JAZZ:

KARTING:

KAYAKING and CANOEING:

KID'S ACTIVITIES:

KLOOFING (CANYONING) :

MASSAGE:

MICROLIGHTING:

MOUNTAIN BIKING and CYCLING:

MUSEUMS and HISTORY:

KwaZulu Natal:	Tour guides pp.176-177, Durban p.182 (The Phansi Museum), Dundee p.199 (Talana Museum), Isandhlwana p.200 (Isandlwana Lodge)
Nothern Cape:	Itinerary p.212 (Nababeep Museum), p.217 (De Beers Diamond mine)
Free State:	p.225 (Oliewenhuis Art Museum)
Gauteng:	Johannesburg pp.240 - 241 (Apartheid Museum and Museum Africa)
North West Province:	p.248 (Cradle of Humankind and Sterkfontein Caves), p.250 (Dodona - Art Historian)
Limpopo:	Louis Trichardt p.262 (Shiluvari Lakeside Lodge), Vaalwater p.263 (Charles Baber's Farm Tours)
Mpumalanga:	Tour guides p.270

NATURE RESERVES, GAME PARKS and NATIONAL PARKS:

Cape Town:	Noordhoek p.24 (Solole Game Reserve), Cape Point p.28
West Coast & Cederberg:	Langebaan p.52 (West Coast National Park)
Cape Winelands:	Franschhoek p.78 (Mont Rochelle Nature Reserve), Paarl p.80 (Paarl Mountain Nature Reserve), Tulbagh p.84 (Kleinfontein)
Overberg:	Betty's Bay and Kleinmond pp.96-97 (Harold Porter Nature Reserve), Bredasdorp p.105 (De Hoop Nature Reserve and the Whale Trail)
Garden Route:	Heidelberg p.115 (Grootvadersbosch Nature Reserve), Knysna p.122 (The Phantom Forest Eco Reserve), Plettenberg Bay pp.127-128 (Robberg Nature Reserve)
Karoo:	Beaufort West p.149 (Lemoenfontein Game Reserve)
Eastern Cape:	Paterson p.162 (Amakhala Game Reserve), Addo Elephant Park p.163
KwaZulu Natal:	Port Edward p.185 (Umtamvuna Nature Reserve), Vryheid p.199 (Ithala Game Reserve), Hluhluwe p.203 (Hluhluwe Umfolozi Game Auction), Eshowe p204 (Ongoye Forest), Umhlali p.206 (Croc Valley Nature Reserve)
Northern Cape:	Itinerary p212 (Goegab Nature Reserve), p.215 (Augrabies Falls National Park), p.216 (Kgalagadi Transfrontier National Park), p.217 (Witsand Nature Reserve)
Free State:	p.222 (Karoo National Park), p.224 (Gariep Dam Nature Reserve), p.229 (Golden Gate National Park)
Gauteng:	Johannesburg p.139 (Delta Park)
North West Province:	p.246 (De Wildt Cheetah and Wildlife Trust),

SAND-BOARDING:

SCUBA DIVING:

SHARK EXPEDITIONS:

SHOPPING:

SKYDIVING:

SNORKELLING:

SURFING:

TENNIS:

THEATRE, OPERA and CONCERTS:

WHITE-WATER RAFTING:

WINDSURFING and KITE-SURFING:

WINERIES:

YACHTING and SAILING:

THE GREENWOOD GUIDE TO

SOUTH AFRICA

WITH MOZAMBIQUE

Hand-picked Accommodation

Now in 4th edition. Annual editions published in June each year.

This guide-book contains some 300 B&Bs, guest houses, game lodges, self-catering places and farms spread across the whole country. Each place has been personally visited by the authors and chosen for its great charm, character and friendliness. The current edition of the guide also includes a section on Mozambique, while the upcoming 5th edition will also include a section on Namibia.

This book is designed for holiday-makers, both South African and from overseas, who want to travel independently, avoid mass tourism and meet friendly, humorous and hospitable people at every turn.

The two books, Greenwood Guides to South African Highlights (i.e. this book) and the accommodation guide are designed to be used in tandem.

Here again is a round-up of our prejudices:

Things we like: natural, unstuffy, humorous hosts, gardens, good food, untouristy places, dirt roads, the lived-in look, the artistic, the unusual, big baths, open fires, real coffee, freshly-squeezed orange juice. We like places where the hosts are doing their own thing and treat their guests like friends.

Things we don't like: swirly, frilly, lacy décor, conference centres, identikit bedrooms, chain hotels; hosts who disappear irretrievably after your arrivals... or never leave you alone; the smelly, the over-priced, the sickeningly cutesy; fake smiles, hatchet faces and steely eyes!

We also have guides to accommodation in New Zealand, Australia and Canada. To order Greenwood Guides books please fill in the order form on the opposite page.

www.greenwoodguides.com

Order form

	copy(ies)	price (each)	subtotal
GREENWOOD GUIDES: SOUTH AFRICA HIGHLIGHTS **Hand-picked things to do and places to eat**		£13.95	
THE GREENWOOD GUIDE TO SOUTH AFRICA **Hand-picked accommodation** (ANNUAL EDITION)		£13.95	
THE GREENWOOD GUIDE TO AUSTRALIA **Hand-picked accommodation**		£9.95	
THE GREENWOOD GUIDE TO NEW ZEALAND **Hand-picked accommodation** (ANNUAL EDITION)		£9.95	
THE GREENWOOD GUIDE TO CANADA **Hand-picked accommodation**		£9.95	
post and packing costs £2 per order in the UK or South Africa £3 per order within Europe £4 per order elsewhere		**Total**	

Name ....

Address to send the book to ....

....

....

Payment is by UK sterling cheque made out to 'Greenwood Guides Ltd' or by VISA/Mastercard (only)

Card number

Expiry date

CCV number

Please send this coupon to:

46 Lillie Road, Fulham, London, SW6 1TN, UK

simon@greenwoodguides.com

picture credits

Greenwood Guides would like to thank the following for their kind permission to reproduce the photographs (t = top, b = bottom, c = centre, l = left, r = right). All other images copyright of Jamie Crawford.

CAPE TOWN: 0932 Restaurant, p20 bl & p34 bc; The Afton, p10 bc; Apex Shark Expeditions, p29 bc; Aubergine, p11 bc; Bascule Bar, p11 br & bl; Beluga, p20 br; Cape Town Holocaust Centre, p16 bl; Cape Town Pelagics, p10 bl; Comida Bar, p22 br; Constantia Uitsig, p18 bc, p19 bc, p31 b & p33 bc; Dragon Boat Racing, p16 bc, br & p17 b; Gavin Hau, p10 br; Hout Bay Yacht Club, p22 bl & bc; Kalk Bay Theatre, p29 bl; La Colombe, p33 bl & p34 br; Dance For All, p8 bl; Pastis, p33 br; River Café, p35 bl; Savoy Cabbage, p19 bl & p21 b; Sea Kayak Simon's Town, p20 bc; Scratch Patch, p29 br; Solole Game Reserve, p8 c; The Nose Bar, p19 bc. **WEST COAST and CEDERBERG:** Evita Se Peron, p52 bc; Groote Post Winery and Restaurant, p52 bl; Matroosberg Reserve, p56 bc; Muisbosskerm Open-air Restaurant, p58 bc. **CAPE WINELANDS:** Diemersfontein Wine and Country Estate, p69 br & p79 bc; Fairview Wine and Cheese Estate, p68 bl; Kleinplasie Living Open-air Museum, p69 bl & p79 bl; La Motte, p79 br; Moreson Wine Farm, p65 tc, p66 b, p73 bl, p82 bl. p89 tl & tr; Nini Bairnsfather Cloete, p68 bc; Paarl Golf Club, p80 bc; Résidence Klein Oliphants Hoek, 68 br; Stellenbosch University Botanical Garden, p72 bl & br; Stony Brook, p82 br; Thelema Mountain Vineyards, p73 bc, p82 bc & p89 tc; Twee Jonge Gezellen, p80 br; Waterford Estate, p80 bl; Warwick Wine Estate, p73 br. **OVERBERG:** African Horse Company, p98 bc; Bukkenburg Pottery Studios, p108 bc; Drostdy Museum, p108 bl; Dyer Island Cruises, p100 cl & p100 cr; Jan Harmsgat Country Restaurant, p106 b; The Cuckoo Tree, p98 bl; The New Junk Shop, p100 c; The Post House, p108 br. **GARDEN ROUTE:** 34 Degrees South, p124 br; Eden Adventures, p122 br & p129; Garden Route Botanical Gardens, p118 bc & p124 bc; Face Adrenalin, p127 bl; Forest Horse Rides, p122 bl; Ile de Pain, p122 bc & p124 bl; Ocean Blue Adventures, p127 br & p131 br; The Old House Shop, p131 bl. **KLEIN KAROO:** Joubert-Tradauw Private Cellar and Deli, p140 bc; Balloon Drifters, p136-137 & p144 b. **EASTERN CAPE:** Addo Elephant Park, p159 br, p162 b, p165 bc, p168 br & p170 bl; Albany Museum, p161 tl; Alexandria Hiking Trail, p164 bc, p165 bl; Cape St. Francis Lighthouse, p156 b; Dolphin Trail, p157 br, bc,& bl, & p161 tr; Fish River Sun Golf, p155 b; Great Fish Point Lighthouse, p168 bl & bc; Seaview Game and Lion Park, p161 bc; Valley of Ancient Voices, p161 tc. **KWAZULU NATAL:** Barnyard Theatre, p206 b; Come Fly! Air Services, p205 c; Isandlwana Lodge, p200 b &p201 br; Karkloof Canopy Tour, p192 bl & br; Music Revival, p190 bl; Natal Sharks Board, p197 br, p199 bc & p202 b; Campaign Trails, p178 bc; Off-Road Adventures, p191 b; Pure Venom, p184 b; Rolling M Ranch, p194 b; Shakabarker Tours, p182 bl; The Buddhist Retreat Centre, p190 bc; uShaka Marine World, p178 br; Zululand Eco-Adventures, p182 br, p192 bc & p197 bc. **NORTHERN CAPE:** Orange River Wine Cellars, p214 b. **FREE STATE:** Oliewenhuis Art Museum, p225 bl &bc. **GAUTENG:** Wine+, 236 bl; Lucit Restaurant, p236 br; Sides Restaurant, p240 b. **LIMPOPO:** Kings Walden, p260 b. **MPUMALANGA:** Mavourneen Pearce, Lawson's Birding, p270 bl & bc; Dullstroom Bird of Prey and Rehabilitation Centre, p270 br.

Cover image hot-air balloon courtesy of Balloon Drifters. Cover image landscape courtesy of Jamie Crawford. Small photos from left courtesy of the following: front 1, 2 & 5 Jamie Crawford, 3 Dance For All, 4 Restaurant 0932; back 1 Jamie Crawford, 2 Dragon Boat Racing Cape Town, 3 The Savoy Cabbage.